THE INNOCENT ASSASSINS

THE INNOCENT ASSASSINS

BY FRED A. SALAZAR WITH *Jack Herschlag*

E. P. DUTTON & CO., INC.   *New York*
1967

To my mother, in gratitude for her unswerving faith, and to Gerard Falls and Arnold Dietrich for their help in making this expedition possible

This is the true story of an expedition led by Fred Salazar into an unexplored part of Brazil. It is an adventure shared by the explorer, who followed his restless curiosity far up the Rio Negro to an isolated corner of the Amazon jungle, and a Waica Indian named Kamboe, whose life was changed profoundly and permanently by his first contact with the twentieth century.

CONTENTS

LIST OF ILLUSTRATIONS

Following page 128

one

MANAUS, CITY BETWEEN TWO WORLDS

I awoke with the midday sun bright against my eyelids. My head felt as if it were supporting a heavy stone, and for a few moments all I could do was sit still to keep it from falling off.

Suddenly I was fully awake and irritable. Half the day was gone and I was still in bed. So was Arnie. I could hear him sneeze in the next room. I forced myself out of bed and pounded on his door. Someone had left the window open, and warm air was creeping in. As I shut it, I looked out at Manaus.

The city was beginning to get to me. In the street below, donkey carts and trucks were jostling one another and creating a din. At first I saw only a few pedestrians, but when my eyes became adjusted to the sharp contrasts of light and shadow I discovered them strolling along at their normal, unhurried pace in the shade of the trees. The stray dogs, which were wild and vicious at night, also ambled along at a desultory daytime trot.

In the distance I could see smoke rising from the stacks of a liner headed up the Amazon to Iquitos, Peru, fifteen hundred miles away. Off in the same direction a Catalina flying boat was gliding down for a landing on the river. I wondered whether it was a commercial plane coming back from the mines and planta- tions or an Air Force plane returning from its weekly rounds of the missions.

Suzy, my pet ocelot, came out of her hiding place and rubbed against my leg to let me know she was hungry. My reverie disturbed, I pulled myself away from the window. I loved to look at Manaus, but I preferred to get out into it.

Our breakfast was the standard morning fare of the Hotel Amazonas: fresh orange juice, strong coffee, powdered milk, lumpy cane sugar, and coarse bread.

Arnie was harder to take than the food. That morning was a morning after, and it showed in his forlorn eyes that looked like two red moons sinking over the horizon of his stubbly cheeks.

"I feel rotten," he croaked. "Just coffee, black." He rested his elbows on the table and supported his head with both hands. He was six feet and two inches of bad smell and misery. But I knew it was just a matter of time—not too much time—until he rebounded to his normal state of exuberance. The coffee began to bring him around.

"Maybe just one slice of bread. Isn't there any butter?"

Arnie was that way. Not erratic, just buoyant, and it showed in everything he did, whether it was working, loving, playing basketball, or highballing it halfway across the United States in other people's cars. He had done them all and he had done them well.

"Are you ready to talk business?" I asked.

"Yes, *Chefe* (he gave it the Portuguese pronunciation: *shéh-feh*), I am at your command." He threw me a cock-eyed salute.

"First of all, we've got a lot of buying to do. We're still short on medical supplies. Some of our luggage is still at customs. We haven't even looked at boats yet. I want to—"

"Stop counting. You've only got twenty fingers."

"I see only ten."

"I see twenty. I think I'll just rest today. Maybe we ought to wait until Jerry gets here. Then we can do it all together."

"You're singing a different tune, now. When we decided that one of us had to stay behind at the beginning to save money, you voted to go. Now that you're here you want to goof off and leave the work for Jerry."

"I was only kidding. You're too serious for so early in the morning."

"It's nearly one o'clock."

"You're kidding!" Arnie turned toward the window and blinked. "Look at that. It *is* late! Man, that rum is potent! I've got to learn enough Portuguese to order something else. How do you say 'Pink Lady' in Portuguese? Ech! Don't tell me. I'm sick." He took another swallow of coffee and went back to staring into space. Suzy settled down on the table and stared back into his filmy eyes. I couldn't stay put any longer. I got up and went into the john to shower.

I didn't shave, however. Arnie and I were starting to grow beards so that by the time we got into the jungle we would have a full growth and not have to bother with shaving at all.

There was another reason. The idea of looking like Hollywood-style explorers—boots, beards, and safari hats—appealed to us, and everyone else went along with the gag. But I knew, even if Arnie didn't, that we would not look that way for long in the jungle. As soon as the biting bugs came out the wide-brimmed hats would be replaced by turban-style towels, netting, and greasy insect repellents. As for the boots, they were needed for overland travel; but they would become nothing but anchors whenever we had to swim or wade. Low sneakers were a must for this expedition.

When I got out of the shower Arnie had gone to get ready. Suzy was alone, licking milk out of a saucer on the table. My room was in its normal state—clothes hanging everywhere, boxes against the wall and under the bed, cameras, books, and personal belongings piled high on every level surface. I felt closed in. I really had to get out.

Before leaving the hotel we stopped at the bar, not to drink, but as a matter of custom, for the bar of the Hotel Amazonas was the meeting place for all foreigners passing through Manaus, and for many who had stopped there and had never quite got around to leaving. There were businessmen, miners, travel agents, jungle guides—some genuine, some fake—newspapermen, dealers in legal and illegal merchandise, government officials, and an occasional tourist.

For them the bar served as a rumor market and a black market, a bank, an overseas press club, and a clearinghouse for all sorts of business ventures and social adventures. There was nothing mysterious about the popularity of the bar; it was simply the most comfortable place in town. The city had no public electricity, and the hotel was one of the few buildings with its own generator. This meant air conditioning, electric lights, a constant supply of ice cubes, and a thousand other rare luxuries.

We received a lukewarm greeting, quite the opposite of the cheery welcome we had received a week earlier upon our arrival. At that time they knew nothing about us. There was the tantalizing possibility then of a quick profit, somewhere, somehow.

When it became known that I planned to lead the expedition myself, the guides lost interest in us. When it was learned that we had no map of gold or buried treasure, no smuggled goods and no get-rich-quick schemes, the miners, dealers, and other assorted opportunists lost interest. The news of our limited budget laid all other tantalizing possibilities finally to rest.

Now they knew us as we were: two young men, both twenty-one, filled with the excitement of exploring some untouched part of the jungle and making contact with remote Indian tribes. The "professionals" thought us naïve at best.

On the other hand, we were absolutely determined to go through with the expedition. This evoked a small measure of grudging admiration, the kind usually reserved for circus daredevils.

A reporter for *O Jornal* who spoke English interviewed us:

"Senhor, I understand you intend to make an expedition into the jungle."

"Yes, along the Rio Negro. There are Indians there who have never been contacted by outsiders. We want to give it a try."

"Those are the Waica Indios. They are very dangerous."

"Only the ones who have had dealings with white men. I believe that the untouched groups will be less hostile. That has been my experience in the past."

"Then this is not your first expedition?" He showed real interest. "How many others have you made?"

"Three major expeditions, in the Guianas and Venezuela. This is the first for the others—my friend who is here and another who is coming."

"Three expeditions! And you are how old?" He suddenly sounded very dubious.

"Twenty-one. I made my first expedition at sixteen."

After that the reporter asked a number of routine questions— the names of the others, how long we expected to be in the jungle, our national background, and so on. He noted that my name sounded Portuguese. When I explained that I was a naturalized American citizen born in Venezuela, he gave me a very long look. At that point he seemed to think I was trying to make a fool of him. My opinion is that he decided to complete his notes so that if my story did prove true, he would have them for the obituary. At any rate, I never saw the story in print.

I was somewhat relieved that the interview had been cut short, because the next question was certain to be "Why?"—Why are you making this expedition? Why to this place? Why at this time? Reporters always get to that sooner or later. I suppose it is their way of getting a "complete" story. What they usually get is a neat arrangement of information, with the "why" tacked to the end so that it can be lopped off if space is tight. Apparently the *New York Times* had space to spare on April 23rd. The last two paragraphs of its story about us read:

"All three are going into a jungle region near the border of Venezuela and Brazil. Their object is to reach the Waika, Shiriana, Maia, Araraibo and Shametari tribes, none of whom has had much contact with civilization, according to Mr. Salazar.

"The young explorers hope to trade with the Indians, take motion pictures of them and bring back objects of their culture. Mr. Salazar said that, as a result of previous trips, he has had specimens accepted by the Museum of Natural history."

"Their object is to . . . The young explorers hope to . . ." This was the answer of the *New York Times* to the question

"Why?" but it was a question I was still asking myself after five years and three expeditions. I gave myself many answers: Because I am restless. To make my fortune. Out of curiosity. To do something different. For kicks. These were closer to the core of my reason, but still not the burning heart of it.

The great George Mallory, when asked why he had climbed Everest, answered, "Because it is there." His deep calm suggested to me that the true answer could not be communicated.

Mallory had found his answer at the peak of the mountain. Perhaps I would find mine in the jungles of Amazonia. Perhaps a Waica Indian who had never spoken to a twentieth-century man would tell me the answer.

I knew for certain that the answer could not be found in the bar of the Hotel Amazonas. We took one turn around the room, said a few hellos, and left the barflies to nurse their gin-and-tonics and their plans for taking over the country.

Actually, the events of the time lent an air of probability to many of the schemes being hatched in the bars, barracks, and universities of Brazil. The Goulart regime had come into power just six months earlier, and the turmoil over such matters as Communist influence, the stabilization of the exchange rate, and the nationalization of industry had not abated. Excitement ran high among people directly concerned with the political and economic tides of the country. But there was no apparent concern among the ordinary citizens of Manaus. To them, and especially to the illiterate lower classes, these great events took place in another world, dim and distant. They could work up more emotion over a dogfight in the street.

We were closer in spirit to the street society than to the barflies in their air-conditioned cloister. The typical Brasileiro loves excitement more than money and never worries about tomorrow. We were very much like that.

Stepping out of the hotel, Arnie and I received a noisy reception from several of the local characters who knew us. We stopped to practice our few words of Portuguese on them. They laughed openly at our mistakes, but were anxious to help us correct them. Their indulgent attitude amused me. We might have acted the same way toward them had the meeting taken place in New York. It seems that ignorance is confused with stupidity in every city of the world.

The fact that we were Americans caused the local people to treat us with special indulgence, for a peculiar reason. The cinema and America are so closely linked in their minds that any visitor from the United States can pass as a movie star. In our case many of the less educated individuals we met came to this conclusion by themselves, though we may have helped a little with our tall boots and safari hats. On occasion we allowed the false impression to work to our advantage.

It is difficult to overestimate the influence of motion pictures on Brazilians, particularly in such out-of-the-way places as Manaus and the more isolated communities. I saw people who couldn't understand English or read Portuguese watch American films with Portuguese subtitles. Despite a strong propaganda effort by the United States Information Service and the work of the newly arrived Peace Corps, almost everything they knew, or thought they knew, about Americans seemed to come directly from the screen. Their impression was that Ianques are crazy, violent, generous, wealthy, and funny. One would think that they had come into contact with American tourists of the kind that frequent Rio and São Paulo. This was not the case. Most Americans who came to Manaus were businessmen, employees of shipping and mining companies, government men, missionaries, and scientists. Still the Brasileiros clung to their romantic, mistaken ideas.

Arnie, who towered over the Brazilians, suited the image well enough. His athletic appearance and friendly, casual manner made him very popular among them. I, on the other hand, looked almost like one of the local types. At five-foot-seven I was about the same size as the average adult male, and my Portuguese ancestry showed in my olive complexion. Although I had never spoken Portuguese at home, I was picking up the language quickly, local inflections and all, and could see the day when I might pass as a Brasileiro.

Meanwhile, I was still an American with luggage tied up in

customs. We had tried to liberate our belongings several times, and were turned away each time for reasons that were difficult to fathom and even more difficult to accept. Once, for example, we were told we had to see a certain official who at the moment, it so happened, was a thousand miles away in Brasília.

Another problem was that extravagant values had been placed upon our cameras, scientific equipment, and personal possessions. At each visit the figures were read off to us with great finality, and each time they changed. The duty also fluctuated wildly, ranging from eight hundred to two thousand U.S. dollars.

For a while we planned, like investors, to "buy" our luggage back when the "market" was low. But we lost patience with this game and decided to find someone with experience in these matters. We found him, an Englishman named Baily, at one of the shipping offices. He told us that the sharp edge of a dollar bill would cut through any amount of red tape. The only problem was in getting the right man to represent us.

In Manaus, Baily told us, the right man was a *despachante*. The word literally means "shipping agent" in Portuguese, but these men operated more like lawyers or, strictly speaking, solicitors. The money used to clear our luggage was handled by one of these men. How much went for duty, how much for "tips," how much for the *despachante* and, as a matter of fact, how much for Baily remained a professional secret. But he did deliver, and quickly, and at a reasonable price.

It is possible that without the help of our *despachante*, Ruey Alencar, some of our possessions might have been confiscated. In those confused times, when the new government was scrutinizing the operations of each of its agencies, a customs official could have provided himself with career insurance at our expense by reporting our possessions as contraband.

The charge might have stuck, for the customs regulations seemed to include rules against half the items that entered and left Brazil with every ship and plane. And in this I do not include the gold, shrunken heads, and narcotics that were the province of professional smugglers.

Ruey proved helpful in other ways. When we got our things

out of customs, he offered us storage space in his office, at a price. The fact that he offered no favors but asked a fair price for each of his many services made us decide to trust him. In a place where law and custom and superstition merge and overlap at every turn, the *despachante*, with his connections and influence, is a natural and necessary phenomenon. We took him up on his offer and headed for customs to get our things.

Even this routine chore had its moments. The porter who helped us carry the boxes to the taxi presented us with a fantastic bill, written out in cruzeiros. He apparently mistook us for newly arrived gringos, because the figure came to about fifty dollars in American money. I shoved a dollar into his hand, still a small fortune, and piled into the taxi with Arnie. We left the porter screaming as if we had kidnapped his family, and before we were out of sight a crowd had gathered. We knew by then that when tempers flared it was best to leave the scene. Although the police usually protected the foreigner, you never knew when you were arguing with an armed man.

The trip to the *despachante*'s office was made under the protection of the special angel that looks after Manaus taxis. We made the entire trip on two wheels, with the horn clearing the way, racing through stop signals, the few that there were, and coming within inches of every vehicle, pedestrian, and animal on the road. When we pulled up at our destination in a flourish of squeals and dust, the driver, Miguel, turned to us with a look that said, "See how a man must risk his life in order to make an honest living?"

We checked the contents of the boxes hurriedly, our minds already on the evening's pleasures. We were planning to take in a nightclub. Manaus night life was an exhilarating new experience for us, filled with gaiety, explosive excitement, and possible danger.

The club we went to that night, called the Shangri-La, was not in the center of the city, but on its very fringes where the streets came to a dead end against the jungle. It was an open-air structure enclosed by filigreed ironwork and bathed in multicolored lights. The band played local music that was typically lush, sensual, and sad. There were a few couples dancing on a raised platform about the size of a boxing ring, and many drinkers sitting at the tables. And everywhere there were prostitutes.

Most of the prostitutes were *caboclas*, which is to say, they were part or all Indian. Each could trace her ancestry back to the Indios who lived free in the Guianas or the rain forests of Rio Branco and the upper Amazon, but all accepted the dress, behavior, and laws of Western civilization as it was known in Manaus.

The enticing panorama revealed many other racial strains. We could pick out Caucasian types; there were olive-skinned and fair-skinned girls, some with wavy black hair and some even with blond tresses. I could see the pale skin and almond eyes of the Oriental. And there was evidence of Negro blood having been mixed into this Amerindian fleshpot. The Negro thread is woven deeply into the fabric of Brazilian culture, and can be traced back to the sixteenth century with the coming of the first slaves. I was told that in this land a trace of Negro blood in a girl is thought to add to her sexual attractiveness and enhance her beauty.

Be that as it may, there was beauty enough there to take away the breath of any man, and it came in every shade, from the black of the African elephant hunter to the white of ivory.

Some of the girls were only in their teens. All were gaudily dressed and decorated with cheap costume jewelry. But they did not affect the bored sophistication of their North American sisters. They were openly competitive, and as jealous of one another as if they were vying for men's affections rather than for their money. They were proud, volatile, and ferocious. We learned that on many occasions they forgot the cardinal rule of their trade and fell in love with their clients.

I supposed that this was the result of an entire segment of the population being forced by circumstances into prostitution, the strong with the weak, the self-sufficient with the dependent, the willing with the half willing. Their male counterparts in the economic scheme of things were the laborers who broke rocks in the blazing sun for fifty cents a day.

This, then, was the end of the line for the Indio, perhaps descended in some instances from the Waica, the tribe we hoped to contact. Having been swept out of the jungle at the headwaters of the Rio Negro, he had drifted down to Manaus to mingle with other races, just as the Rio Negro merges its black waters with the yellow flow of the Solimões to become the Amazon. It was there in Manaus that the river and the Indio lost their identities.

In the nightclub, as everywhere else, when we met the caboclo we sensed the presence of the Indio, in the look of defeat that stared mutely at us from across a chasm of centuries.

It was difficult to tell at first whether we were welcome at the Shangri-La. It was our intention to go very slowly with the whiskey and women in order to make a good first impression. But the girls noticed our interest and interpreted our glances as invitations.

One after another they approached our table. We tried to put them off politely in our best Portuguese, but they were proud and vain, and in a short time we had made several fierce, lovely enemies. To their way of thinking, the only explanation for our refusal was that we did not think them pretty enough.

The men also showed signs of hostility. Most of them resented us merely as outsiders. Others had a more personal reason. These were the jealous paramours of girls working in the club. Although they saw nothing wrong with living off their earnings, they resented their girl friends getting romantically involved with other men. Sex was public, they felt, but love was private. To this group we seemed to represent a challenge.

Judging by the looks of the waiters, we were a topic of conversation everywhere in the room. One of a pair of policemen in the doorway raised a glass of beer in our direction and smiled. I smiled back and lifted my shot glass of rum. I wondered what we were toasting. The waiter cleared up the mystery later when he showed us two extra beers on our check. By then we were happy to have paid for the beers. They proved to be a very inexpensive form of insurance.

The police at the door were Guarda Civil, one of three types of

Brazilian law enforcement. They were colorful, casual, a little corrupt, and the least impressive of the three. Those that we saw wore a standard khaki uniform which they embellished according to their individual tastes. Some looked like cowboys, some like pirates, some like desperadoes and some like armed hoboes. They wore any kind of gunbelt that suited their fancy, and any color necktie or none at all.

After a while, when we were beginning to feel more relaxed, a beautiful girl of about nineteen came over to our table and sat down. I almost asked her that universal and universally ridiculous question: "What is a nice girl like you doing in a place like this?" She had that kind of look—innocent, fragile, defenseless. A moment later she dispelled the illusion.

One of the local men made a remark as he passed the table, and she snatched up a bottle and threw it at him. The glass shattered and cut him across the wrist. Since the girl was at our table I felt obliged to offer him my assistance. I had hardly opened my mouth when he swung at me. By this time the girl was shrieking at the injured man and the whole place was in an uproar. It suddenly dawned on me that I had stepped into the middle of a personal quarrel; what was worse, I appeared to be taking sides.

I looked around and saw that all the men were on their feet, including Arnie, who was at my side. Two men approached us. Fortunately, neither was armed, or at least they showed no weapons. A few punches were thrown, but before anything serious could happen the police were pulling the two men away and waving the others back.

I believe it was a point of honor among the Brasileiros to band together against the gringos, though I felt they meant us no real harm. In a few moments the Shangri-La was once again as peaceful as its name, and I had learned a valuable lesson about these people—that when something aroused their interest, nothing else mattered, and when they lost interest in that something, nothing mattered less. The change could take place in the blink of an eye.

We felt compelled to linger at our table even though we were on edge, for we, too, had pride, and did not want it to appear that we were leaving out of fear. We finished our drinks and walked out casually, pausing only to slip the Guarda Civil a fistful of cruzeiros. There was nothing surreptitious about the way they accepted it.

Miguel was waiting outside, his jeep parked in the rim of twilight that surrounded the glittering nightclub. Flying insects filled the multicolored glow like living dust, and the blackness beyond swelled with the shrill discord of a billion tiny creatures.

On the trip back to the hotel we saw only what the headlights revealed—at first a narrow rutted road walled in on both sides by foliage; then a wider road flanked by broken jungle growth and an occasional shack; and finally the flat streets of the city, which were overrun by dogs.

The gaunt animals roamed everywhere, glaring red-eyed into the headlights, skipping clear of the bumper, wheeling in herds out of the path of the jeep and swirling in behind it like snarling backwash. Nothing of waking humanity was evident but the interminable sound of distant *macumba* drums, a slightly disturbing undercurrent of which we were then hardly aware. I understood at that moment why light is the symbol of civilization the world over. Even in the heart of the city, when darkness reigns the animal is master.

Some nocturnal animals, however, come in human shape. A few blocks from the hotel we heard pistol shots, then saw a running figure pursued by two other shadowy forms. We kept our heads down and continued on our way, allowing the mysterious gunfighters to continue on theirs. Violence was part of the night, and no one raised an alarm: not the inhabitants, not the police, not the gringos.

Manaus was in many ways a city between two worlds. The confluence of the forces of jungle and civilization was evident in virtually every sphere of life. We saw it in the marketplace, where products of the region were on display. In addition to the Brazil nut, or *castanha-do-Pará,* which is the most important cash crop of the state of Amazonas, the jungle around Manaus yielded a colorful array of animals and vegetables. There were lush tropical fruits—plantains, which are a large variety of banana; mangoes, grapes, and citrus fruits—along with staple products—rice, cacao, manioc, yams, and beans. There were live animals and birds—macaws, Brazilian parakeets, parrots, marmosets, spider monkeys, capuchin monkeys, and ocelots—all in cages or on leashes made of coarse rope. The commercial animal products were often even more exotic—huge, stiff skins taken from the cayman, Brazil's eight-foot member of the alligator family; the red and green skins of tree boas; turtle meat; an occasional jaguar pelt, and the fried meat of the pirarucú, a freshwater fish weighing as much as two hundred pounds and measuring up to seven feet in length.

Out on the river these creatures could often be seen surfacing for air, their red-tipped scales flashing in the sun. The pirarucú, the manatee, and the porpoise are the three benevolent giants of the Amazon. The manatee, or sea cow, is a mild-mannered vegetarian that provides meat in three flavors—fish, beef, and pork. The porpoise is a playmate of the river dwellers, and is protected by the same kind of superstitions that protect its seagoing cousins. Among the Brazilian species is the fabled pink porpoise of the Amazon.

Though tiny by comparison, the piranha were a chilling sight to see, whether thrashing about in a tin bucket, crazed by the scent of blood, or dried and mounted for display, their fearful teeth exposed as though voracious even in death. These are the famous predators of South American waters that travel in great schools, attack creatures of any size, and strip the bones bare in a matter of minutes.

The hunters, fishermen, trappers, traders, and farmers who brought this pungent, noisy produce to market were every bit as colorful as their wares. They represented many racial mixtures, but Indian blood predominated. They were scarred and ragged, but they carried themselves with an air of independence. This impression was somehow reinforced by the machetes they used so skilfully in handling chores that called for cutting and hacking. In their eyes one could see the living Indio, not the defeated city caboclo. They were proud and self-reliant, though still remote.

Here in the marketplace these visitors from the jungle came into contact with the customs, money, and whiskey of modern civilization. They spent much of what they earned in the market on a drink called *cachaça*, a powerful rum made of sugarcane. *Cachaça* was cheap and plentiful in the city, and was often the reason that the Indio stumbled in taking his first step toward the twentieth century. It was a story with which we, as Americans, were familiar.

We stopped to buy some pirarucú meat from one of the vendors, figuring that if we found it inedible, Suzy might like it. We indicated how much we wanted, and he cut off exactly that much from a long strip with one swipe of his machete. We tried our Portuguese on him, but he spoke a completely unfamiliar tongue. It was Nheengatú, a lingua franca of the Amazon made up mostly of the Indian language, Tupi. Thus, in language as well as in culture, the fisherman was as much a stranger in Manaus as we.

I gradually became aware of the jungle's influence on all things. Man's foothold seemed to depend upon a constant effort to maintain civilized institutions against tropical sloth and decay from within and literal strangulation by jungle growth from without. The magnificent Teatro Amazonas, one of the world's great opera houses, was probably the most striking manifestation of this condition.

The huge domed building was erected at the turn of the century during the peak of the rubber boom. The rubber barons brought the greatest singers of the day to the Teatro, taking pride in the knowledge that the finest of architecture, art, and music were embodied in this imposing symbol of their wealth.

But the rubber boom died, and the economic power of the city, drawn as it was from the jungle, also withered. When we visited the building it was noticeably run-down, though still an overwhelming sight.

We approached the Teatro Amazonas from a broad tiled plaza and mounted one of a pair of great curved staircases. The façade consisted of three pillared tiers that supported an elaborately decorated arch. Inside, the walls that had once resounded to the immortal tenor of Caruso now echoed to the flat voice of a speaker addressing a group of businessmen. The pitifully small gathering accented the emptiness of the vast auditorium.

At the opposite end of the architectural scale were the shabby huts of the floating city.

The port of Manaus and all its waterways were choked with log rafts on which much of the caboclo population lived. On each raft was a one- or two-room shack that housed a family of as many as ten people. In places the rafts were pushed together to form an almost continuous floor of slippery wood covering an area equal to many square blocks. Some sections had been anchored in place long enough to have acquired a look of permanence. There was no census of the caboclo population that I knew of, but some estimates ran as high as fifty thousand, all packed together in this stinking, teeming slum. This was the floating city of Manaus.

The floating city was as squalid as the Teatro Amazonas was magnificent. But, paradoxically, the Teatro symbolized the decline of Manaus from its cultural and commercial peak, while the city of rafts symbolized the upward climb of the Indio toward civilization. We looked at this incredible cistern that supported human life, perhaps the worst human habitation in the world, and insisted to ourselves that the climb toward civilization, our civilization, was indeed upward.

We visited the floating city as more than sightseers, for we knew that eventually we would have to make arrangements there for river transportation. We made one exploratory trip to familiarize ourselves with the place and to dispel any suspicions that the inhabitants might have of us.

At first they were wary, but we knew by then that the door to a caboclo's heart is unlocked by the laughter of his children. Arnie's comic talents elicited such tumultuous laughter from those little human frogs that in a short time the parents came out to talk with us.

The federal government had attempted a few years earlier to make these squatters move, and they had refused. I took this opportunity to ask them why. Their reason was simple:

"What will we do if we leave here? How will we feed our children? At least from the river we can get some food, and some of us have farms in the jungle."

We knew about the farms. They were little patches of cleared land just outside the city. The caboclos worked them poorly, for they were not farmers by nature. The jungle exerted continuous pressure to reclaim the land, and in the long run it usually succeeded.

The river provided a more generous supply of food, but of an unwholesome kind. The caboclos fished and drew their drinking water from the same water in which they bathed, washed their clothes, and deposited their waste. In addition to being contaminated, it also harbored the dreaded piranha and electric eels.

While the river dwellers had taken only one step toward civilization, that step had carried them over an invisible line. They had become part of the city and dependent upon it. That is why their plaint—"What will we do if we leave here?"— carried the weight of truth.

Getting around became easier when Ruey and his brother, José, volunteered to become our guides, instructors, and interpreters. With their help we managed to be on hand for many local events that we would otherwise have missed.

The *Bumba-meu-Boi,* for instance. This was a celebration in honor of the ox, the name meaning "Whoa, my ox." A procession of vividly costumed musicians led the way while a crowd followed, carrying the stylized image of an ox high above their heads. The ritual had a definitely African flavor, as did many of the semireligious folk customs, but it had enough of the Portuguese and Indian character to be unmistakably Brazilian. I was captivated by all of it—the nightmarish colors and patterns, the primitive symbols, the grace of the body movements, the musicality of the speech, the joy and seriousness of the celebrants.

And once we were permitted to witness a *macumba* ceremony, with rituals and dances harking back centuries to the Bantu country of Africa from where the slaves were taken. If I was captivated by the *Bumba-meu-Boi,* I was engulfed by *macumba.*

It took place after dark in a shed slapped together out of rough boards and corrugated iron. The air was so dense with body heat and tobacco smoke that I imagined I could see waves of sound rolling off the drum. The icons and statues bore a grotesque resemblance to traditional figures of Catholic saints. A shaman addressed these objects with incantations intended to give them fetish powers. While he chanted, the devotees stamped and shook to the relentless rhythm of the drum. They screamed, they fainted, they went into trances, they sweated big oily beads that gleamed like purple crosses in my dazzled eyes. On and on they went—midwives, policemen, prostitutes, barbers, clerks—many of them avowed Catholics by day, surrendering themselves by night to the pulsebeat of Africa that throbs in the bloodstream of Brazil.

The purple witch of *macumba* slipped away as the first red streak of dawn sundered the gray sky over Manaus. We left, too, feeling subdued and somehow guilty. While the last of the cultists consummated their nightly ritual, we drove away in silence.

The sound of the dying night was a *macumba* drum.

Catholicism in Brazil is much like Protestantism in America in that it absorbs folk influences and accommodates a great number of local variations, while Brazilian Protestantism has the formal austerity of American Catholicism. This accounts for the existence of this bizarre mixture of Catholicism and primitive spiritualism that was practiced by so many lay Roman Catholics, and even by some priests.

The Alencar brothers took us everywhere, and everywhere we went there were fireworks. This was one of the minor mysteries of that perplexing city called Manaus. The people had painfully little money for food and clothing, but always enough for firecrackers.

Through the Alencars we also widened our circle of Brazilian friends. Not counting Baily, who was an Englishman, the people whom we had met on our own included our driver Miguel, a few of the people who worked at the Hotel Amazonas, some shopkeepers, waiters, and several local beauties.

Most noteworthy among the people Ruey and José introduced us to was Senhor Pedro Vieira da Silva, a long-time resident of Manaus and a gracious, convivial host. On several occasions he provided us with his opinions on how to run the country and with the charming company of his six lovely children. He always greeted us with the *cafezinho*, Brazil's traditional little cup of black coffee.

We also visited Father Stefan, a Salesian priest who headed the brotherhood's fund-raising efforts in the area. We talked at cross-purposes for a while. Arnie and I kept telling the padre about our desire to contact the same Indians on the Rio Negro that the Salesian missionaries were busy converting. Meanwhile, the padre rambled on about the need to replace the chapel roof at the cost of a mere $5,000, how expensive it was to keep the missions supplied, and so on and so on and so on. He was like a housewife complaining about the high price of groceries.

We meandered like that for a while until our conversational paths crossed on the common ground of self-interest. Padre Stefan wanted money, and we wanted help in getting into the interior. He opened negotiations:

"Would you care to contribute to our building fund?"

"I would love to, Padre. I can think of nothing more worthwhile. If I had the money, I assure you there would be no need even to ask. However, if there is any other way . . . You see, at the moment there is this expedition . . ."

"Aha. I see. And the nature of the expedition is scientific?"

"Yes. We want to contact untouched groups of Indians, perhaps the Waica on the Demeni and the Araçá."

"I doubt whether the government would permit you to enter those areas. There has been trouble there, you may have heard."

"Well, then further up."

"Yes, further up it is possible. We have missions in all those areas—very expensive to maintain—they could be of help."

"I would be extremely grateful. Which mission did you have in mind?"

"There are several, of course. Tell me, do you plan to take motion pictures on this expedition?"

"Oh, yes. We have 16-millimeter equipment. We plan to take pictures of the Indians, the animals . . . everything."

"You will also find the missions worthy of photographing, I am certain."

"Oh! Of course, the missions," I fumbled.

"If I could only show the world how much the missions are doing for the poor Indians, it would make my work so much easier."

The light finally penetrated my thick skull. "If you like, Padre, I shall take motion pictures of the missions and then you could show everyone the wonderful work that is being done."

"That is so kind of you, Senhor Salazar. I would be so grateful."

That was my cue. "The missionaries would cooperate?"

"No question!"

"You see, I have a problem of transportation. I understand the regular riverboats do not travel into the interior, while the padres . . ."

"Our mission at Uaupés, the mission of San Gabriel, is in charge of all our work in the prelacy of the upper Rio Negro. There you can make arrangements for a boat to take you up the smaller rivers."

"While we are there we can do our film."

"Precisely, and on your way to San Gabriel you may visit our other missions." Padre Stefan showed me a list of about two-dozen settlements where the Salesians maintained missions, hospitals, and free schools. I wrote down the names, but my mind leaped over Carvoeiro, Barcelos, Tapurucuará, and Umarituba to Uaupés, gateway to the world of the Waica.

We left Padre Stefan with a more or less firm agreement that we would receive the hospitality of the Salesian missions and transportation from Uaupés into the interior in exchange for a documentary film on the work of the missionaries. He promised that he would send a letter of introduction to the river outposts in advance of our arrival.

I came away feeling that I had accomplished quite a lot with one visit, unless I had misunderstood completely what our rambling, typically Brazilian conversation was all about. That, too, was possible.

I insisted that we make the rounds of the hospitals. I had learned, on other expeditions, of the importance of medical knowledge in the jungle. This was my opportunity to learn something of the diseases of the Amazon region and their treatment.

Like all of life in Manaus, the medical situation was a crazy-quilt of good and bad. We visited eight hospitals in which we observed almost as many degrees of cleanliness and efficiency. Only one or two were up to American standards. We saw some operating rooms with shiny new equipment, and others that looked like butcher shops. We met some doctors who were trained in fine schools in the United States and Europe and who maintained the highest professional standards, and others who walked around in dirty smocks covered with blood. We were told that some of the latter were practicing with fake licenses.

Many of the nurses were nuns. They came from all countries to work in the missions along the river. Their objective in Manaus was the same as ours: to learn the language and prepare themselves for jungle life. Theirs would be one of dedication and deprivation. Many missions had no doctors, in which case the nuns performed every medical service, even amputations. For lack of means and knowledge to save infected limbs the hospitals had to perform many amputations. In back of one hospital I was treated to the grisly sight of vultures picking away at a heap of gangrenous arms and legs.

The handling of emergencies was another incredible phase of the hospital system. At one clinic I saw a man who had been brutally cut up in an accident. He was there for three hours and still had not received attention. We heard of another accident in which a body strangely disappeared. It was discovered after two days, stuck to the underside of a jeep. And an Englishman injured in a fight at one of the nightclubs had to wait six hours for an ambulance. The delay cost him an arm. We could not reconcile this apparent callousness with the warmth and generosity of the people we met.

Perhaps the Brasileiro's characteristic acceptance of things as they are accounted for both the friendliness and the callousness. For it is true that most Brazilians demand very little of life. A reporter once asked a thousand Brazilians what they held most important. They said food and sleep. To this I might add *amor* and *cachaça*.

The slow and fast movements of time converged on the day that Jerry Falls, the third member of our expedition, was scheduled to arrive. Until then the days had drifted by unnoticed and uncounted like dust in a quiet room. Then suddenly we were awakened by a stirring in the air to find that an eternity of change had taken place. We had been transformed from gringos into makeshift Brasileiros.

When we saw Jerry, pale and eager, step down from the plane, we realized how far we had come. His clothing and mannerisms were plainly different from ours. And we, who were so new ourselves, could not help wondering whether he would be able to make the transition.

A word about Jerry. Although he was a year older than Arnie and I, he was the fledgling of the expedition. I was the only one with experience in the jungle, and Arnie . . . well, Arnie had been one of the real wild ones in his teen years and was long accustomed to taking care of himself. Jerry was the only one who had had a problem in breaking away from his family. He made a false start once before, when he promised to join me in British Guiana for an earlier expedition but never showed up. He had spent two years since then growing up, and he had contributed money to my latest venture; still, I was a little surprised to see him in Manaus.

We gave Jerry a thumbnail course on the city. Part of it consisted of a trip to the movies. We felt that he was patient and serious enough to pick up some of the language by watching an American film with Portuguese subtitles. We bought a copy of *O Jornal* to see what was playing. In the four-page daily, among government proclamations, social gossip, and lawyers' advertisements, we found the theater listings. An American picture we hadn't seen was opening at the Politeama, so that night we went to see Kirk Douglas in two languages.

Jerry's arrival reawakened our impatience to get started. There was very little left to do but negotiate for a boat. We allowed a few more days for that and for Jerry to become acclimated.

Another event took place during those last few days that reawakened the entire city. Electric power was restored. For years, ever since the generators left by the British had been allowed to go to ruin, the city had been in darkness. For many months the government had been working to build new ones. Now, suddenly, the lights were on again, and civilization had recaptured the night. Firecrackers exploded and dogs howled. Here in Manaus, a thousand miles deep in the Amazon jungle, a lamp had been lighted.

two

WARNINGS AND PREPARATIONS

~~~~~~~~~~~~~~~~~~~~~~~~~~~~~~~~

Ruey had been bird-dogging for a boat for several days. One morning he showed up at the hotel early to announce that he had found just what we needed. We dressed hurriedly, and Miguel drove all of us to the edge of the floating city. There we hired a caboclo dugout to take us to the boat, with Ruey pointing the way.

He was right, as usual. She wasn't pretty, and she stank of fish and feet, but she was just what we needed—about sixty feet long and powered by a 135-horsepower diesel motor. She was called the *Waupes* (wah-pézh), a variant of the name Uaupés, the mission settlement that was our destination six hundred miles up the Rio Negro. The boat might also have been named after the Rio Uaupés, which flows into the Rio Negro about twenty miles past the mission.

The cabin of the *Waupes* looked like a shack along the river. It was a simple wooden structure with a flat roof and tarpaulins hanging over the window openings. The crew was made up of a captain and six rough-looking caboclos, none of whom spoke English. The engineer, or *motorista,* had taught himself diesel mechanics on his father's boat. Other than that he had no training, but he appeared to be quick and competent. The captain was a grizzled old Brazilian, originally from Portugal, who was always in a half-drunken stupor. The only assurance we had that he could pilot the boat from Manaus to Uaupés was that he had done it many times before in the same inebriated condition. We immediately nicknamed him Captain Cachaça.

With Ruey as intermediary, our party boarded the boat to talk business. We made it plain that we wanted to rent the boat to take us as far as Uaupés, no extras, and no side trips. Had I known a little more about the economics of the river, I might have tried to purchase the boat outright and resell it upriver at a profit.

It was only because we had so much cargo—over a ton of it—that we were compelled to use river transportation. Had we been traveling light, we could have hitched a free ride on an Air Force plane making its regular calls along the river.

The Air Force was the controlling military unit in the Amazon basin because of its mobility. It played a broad role in life along the river, transporting supplies and passengers, making emergency rescues, and maintaining contact with military outposts on the borders.

Air Force pilots logged incredible mileage in their Catalina flying boats, DC-3's and DC-4's, most of which were castoff American military planes dating back to World War II. Their work was dangerous. We heard of a commercial flight that pancaked in the jungle only fifteen minutes out of Manaus. The bodies of the passengers and crew were eventually located. They had survived the crash, but had starved to death while trying to cut their way out through the thick vegetation.

But the Air Force managed to hold its own in its fleet of patched-up relics. We called it the Scotch Tape Airline.

When arrangements for the boat were completed, I thumbed a ride via Scotch Tape to the coastal city of Belém to get firsthand information from a man who had been in the Waica region only a month earlier. He was Dr. Eduardo Galvão, a Brazilian ethnologist associated with the Museu Goeldi. His trip had taken him a short way up the Rio Cauaburi, where he was turned back by Waica bowmen. Dr. Galvão offered lots of information and one prediction: "I did not get to meet the Waica and I don't believe you will either."

He told me of other expeditions into the area, of that of Dr. Otto Zerries up the Araçá and Demeni, and of others up the Cauaburi. No one, so far as he knew, had made it to the headwaters of the Marauiá.

Belém seemed less hospitable than Manaus. It was busier, more commercial, more modern. I had no special urge to look around, so I hopped the next DC-4 to Manaus and was back with my friends less than forty-eight hours after I had left them.

We made similar inquiries in Manaus, and did not receive a single encouraging reply. The most pessimistic came from the official at the Manaus office of the Serviço de Proteção aos Indios (Indian Protection Service).

It was necessary to apply to the SPI, an agency of the Ministry of Agriculture, for permits to enter the territory of the Waica. The Service is the official body of the government dealing with Indian affairs. It was founded in 1910 by the great General Rondon, self-declared guardian of the Indians who set the example of nonviolence that all SPI agents follow, and for which many had been martyred. The Territory of Rondônia, in the southern tip of what is called the North Region of Brazil, is named after this national hero. I wished I could have met him.

Since the SPI agent spoke excellent English, we were able to converse at length. He repeated what the *O Jornal* reporter had told us, that the Waica were among the most hostile Indians in Brazil. They had practiced cannibalism at one time, he added, and it was not known to what extent the practice still persisted. Although I didn't doubt the truth of what he said, I knew that it was his job to discourage us. The SPI's policy was to keep adventurers, exploiters and troublemakers out of the Indian territories.

It was therefore his job to ask questions as well as answer them. Who were we? Where were we from? And, inevitably, why were we here? On this occasion the question did not arouse the usual feeling of resentment, because the individual who asked it had the right to ask it, as an official and as a person. To this sincere, dedicated man I gave as true an answer as I was then capable of giving.

I started by telling him of my first expedition, in British Guiana, which was one of those accidents that seemed pre-destined. I had been sent to that country to stay with relatives, in the hope that I would "straighten out" a little. The official raised a questioning eyebrow. Yes, I had been running with the wrong crowd, teen-agers who got into trouble for the sheer mindless fun of it. But they were approaching the age when juvenile fun would soon become adult lawlessness. I was restless and didn't know what I wanted out of life, and this group, a gang if you will, was presenting me with poor alternatives. Eventually I found tinkering with cars, hanging around pool halls, and staging rumbles with other gangs completely disagreeable. I welcomed the trip to Guiana. It crystallized a hundred thoughts and half-formed schemes. About to graduate from military school, and with no intention of entering college, I thought of the trip as a possible beginning for something worthwhile, a fresh start.

"How old were you at the time?"

"Sixteen. Actually, I celebrated my seventeenth birthday on the Rio Essequibo."

"This was not a real expedition, of course."

"No, it was more like an excursion. Money was the main problem. All I had was my own savings. A handful of bearers at a dollar a day ate that up pretty quickly. They pulled a sitdown strike when the money ran out, so I turned back."

"A dollar a day." The official smiled. I knew he would pick that up. Wages like that made it possible for an American teen-ager to head an expedition into virtually any South American jungle, with a full complement of native bearers. But I wasn't ashamed, because the caboclos in Brazil were earning even less, and that wasn't the fault of any American teen-ager.

I explained that from that time on my life had been divided between going off on expeditions and scraping together the money to finance them.

"And where does this money come from?"

"I work, I borrow, I sell photographs that I take in the jungle. Sometimes I bring back animals and specimens for laboratories and museums. Sometimes the others who come with me contribute money. There are always problems, but I never let them stop me. I allow myself a certain amount of time between trips. When the time is up, I take whatever money I have and whoever is ready to come along, and just go. If I don't have enough money for a big expedition I settle for a small one, but I go. I always go."

"Then you have made this your life's work."

"Yes," I agreed enthusiastically, although I had never thought of it exactly that way. "I have been in British Guiana and lived among the Wai Wai. I have lived with the Djukas in Dutch Guiana and the Guaharibos in Venezuela. All along the northern border of Brazil, and many times I was told about the Waica. I wanted to see them before they disappeared."

I knew he was favorably impressed, but he continued to test me. "The Waica may be more dangerous than you realize. Two years ago they attacked four members of the Boundary Commission. Not long ago one of the Waica chiefs got his hands on some shotguns and started raiding other villages. A few months back he chased the Protestant missionaries out of his area." He paused, as if making up his mind, then got up from behind the desk. "Let me show you something."

What he showed me was meant to be his final argument against our going. He led me to a house near his office where a woman was close to death. She was the wife of a rubber tapper who worked in the jungle not far from Manaus. The Indians in that area were supposed to be friendly, but one day, she related, a war party attacked them, suddenly and without provocation. She didn't know what had become of her husband, but was able to drag herself to the encampment of another tapper, who brought her by dugout into Manaus for help.

Her condition was frightful. Her body was full of arrows and infection had set in in a number of places. The stench of dried blood and pus was disgusting.

"These were supposed to be friendly Indians," the agent emphasized.

"But they were Waica?" I asked.

"Then you still insist on going."

"I do."

At that point he resigned himself to our going and started to fill out the permits. I wished I could have got to know the agent better. He was one of the few people who could have understood my feelings about the Indians.

I returned to tell the others about the permits. The news didn't excite Arnie and Jerry very much. They took it for granted that such things were routine.

They had lately developed an interest in maps. There was a big one spread out on the table in my room, with pencil marks indicating the places we hoped to visit. Ruey, José, and other acquaintances dropped in to look at the map and point out unmarked settlements and natural phenomena. The problem was that the only accurate maps were those made from air photographs, and they showed only the important settlements and major landmarks.

Of great importance to us, and overlooked by the mapmakers, were small settlements, sloping terrain, rapids, swamps, small creeks, and variations in the density of the jungle. To complicate matters, some settlements had two names, one given by the inhabitants and a second by the missionaries. Either one might appear on the map. For example, the town of Tapurucuará, which was a key stop for us at the mouth of the Marauiá, was called Santa Izabel on our map, after the mission located there, whereas Uaupés, where the mission of San Gabriel was located, retained its secular name.

And that wasn't the whole of it. There were towns that could not even be pinpointed on the map. There was a lively discussion, for example, over the location of Cabureiro. Some placed it above Barcelos and some below. Not all the confusion could be blamed on poor memory. Some of the small settlements, which were no more than fishing villages or trading posts, actually did move at times.

The phenomenon recalled the golden era of riverboats that Mark Twain wrote about in *Life on the Mississippi*. In those days the pilots who were waiting for assignments traveled up and down the river as the guests of working pilots to keep the changing "shape of the river" fresh in their minds. That was before the days of dikes and dredging. The river meandered as it pleased, and occasionally it would cut through a narrow neck of land where the channel formed a loop, or oxbow. When that happened, a farm or town within the loop "crossed" from one side of the river to the other.

That was more than a century ago. The Mississippi of Mark Twain's time is comparable to the Amazon of today. Except, of course, that the Amazon is bigger.

There were other reasons why villages didn't stay put. Sometimes they were simply flooded out. Sometimes there were raids or food shortages. Or the chief of a caboclo village might decide to move out for his own obscure reasons, and the whole village would follow.

As we filled in our map, we noted that along the entire eight hundred miles of the Rio Negro from Manaus to the junction of the Colombia-Venezuela border, the most sparsely settled stretch was that which passed through Waica country, the three hundred miles between Barcelos and Uaupés. The reason, we were told, was that even the caboclos lived in fear of the Waica.

Paradoxically, it was in this region that the Waica and some of the caboclos were most similar racially. All that distinquished them were a few rags of clothes and a way of life.

We learned that one had to develop an instinct for using correct terminology when making racial distinctions. For example, *caboclo* was a term originally applied only to pure-blooded Indians who had adopted Western ways. It gradually became a general term for all part-Indians and eventually became an even broader term applied to the lower rural classes. It was no longer a racial designation at all, but a socioeconomic label.

My dictionary was of little help in this matter. Although it was more than a thousand pages long and less than a year old, it did not even list the word *caboclo,* and was extremely perfunctory in defining other racial terms. Unable to turn to the Ministry of Education and Culture for enlightenment (for it was this official body that published the dictionary), we had to feel our own way.

We learned never to refer to a Negro by that word, but to use the word *prêto* (black). That is, unless the individual in question was extremely dark, which made him *cor de carvão* (the color of coal), or wealthy, in which case he might be *escuro* (dark), *moreno* (brunet), or even *branco* (white). In the latter instance the term referred to social and economic status rather than race.

Conversely, there were white women who called themselves *mulatas* (white-Negro) to emphasize their sexuality. And although we three were technically *brancos,* we heard ourselves referred to many times as *gringos,* and we learned to live with it.

Our visitors at the hotel invariably cast covetous eyes upon our equipment. Occasionally we did a little business. Photographic equipment was in especially great demand, and we were well supplied. We had a 16-mm movie camera, three different 35-mm still cameras (two Nikons and a Konika), a Polaroid Model 800, a Kodak 620 and a Kodak 120, plus attachments, accessories, and plenty of film.

In addition, we had a typewriter, a small library of scientific books, two battery-powered tape recorders, a taxidermy kit, medical and dental supplies, mineral testing equipment, and a considerable amount of writing material. Prominent among the latter were the old-fashioned ledgers that I used for bookkeeping, for mapmaking, and to record my thoughts.

I was a compulsive keeper of records, and the ledgers became a standing joke. But I had them along for a reason. While the others were preparing for the excitement they hoped might come, I was preparing for the boredom I knew would come.

While we sold off some marginal items to bolster our budget, our armory was kept out of sight under my bed. Even the discussion of selling guns would have been dangerous in our particular circumstances. We were foreigners in a country where many foreigners were agents trying to exploit the political unrest.

During our last week in Manaus we spent a lot of time in the floating city. We got to know our boat, the crew, the caboclos and the river.

The *Waupes* was surprisingly seaworthy. Her hull was made of thick planks that could withstand battering by river debris and gouging by sharp rocks. And she was watertight. I wished I could say the same for the topside construction, for the rainy season was just beginning. It was an uncomfortable time to travel, but the only time when the smaller rivers were high enough for navigation.

I pieced together a fairly accurate picture of what the journey would be like. There would be nine of us in all, crowded into sixty feet of boat along with an engine, food supplies, a cookstove, bunks, tools, personal belongings, and a restless ocelot kitten. Some of our more valuable equipment would be stowed on board, while the rest would be towed in two dugouts covered with tarpaulins. The food would be close to inedible, until we got accustomed to it; the sanitary conditions would be revolting, the routine monotonous, and the rain incessant.

The motorista told me that the trip to Uaupés would take about fifteen days. It occurred to me that the captain must be planning many stops. I asked him how long it would take us to get to Uaupés if we traveled day and night at top speed. He cocked his head, closed his eyes, and calculated. "Three days."

That's all I had to hear. I didn't expect to make it in three days, but I was damned if I was going to let them drag it out to fifteen. "We'll see about that fifteen days," I warned. He shrugged and went back to fiddling with the motor.

He seemed serene, like the river. Where we lounged at the water's edge the Amazon looked as wide as an ocean. In the early evening, the massed rain clouds stood like a wall over the opposite bank, which was no more than a shadowy line. They brooded like mountains above the flat immensity of water. The Booth liner that labored against the current, the rafts, the rickety buildings along the shore: everything there that spoke for mankind was drowned in the vast gray silence of the Amazon.

Arnie and I felt that we owed Jerry a taste of night life, so we made plans to take him out at least once before shoving off. We could have split up to pursue our individual interests—mine being a raven-haired dancer named Denise—but I couldn't shake the feeling that the other two needed looking after. Whenever they were out of sight I became uneasy.

We started at the top, the Acapulco. The atmosphere there was reserved; there was Continental-style gambling, the whiskey came from labeled bottles, the music was quiet, the clientele well dressed, and you had to be formally introduced to the prostitutes.

From the Acapulco we hit the downward trail to the Shangri-La, where we no longer attracted any special notice, and the Veronica, another nightclub like the Shrangri-La. The Brazilians call their nightclubs *café-concertos,* with typical disregard for accuracy. Coffee was not the favorite beverage in any of those places, nor was there the subdued decorum of a concert in the dance music. The dance rhythms ranged from sensual to frenetic. In fact, not all of it was new to us, for the Twist had come to Manaus.

This form of eroticism set to music originated in the Caribbean, where it was danced by children with stylish grace and innocence. The Brazilian version was a mixture of that and the exhibitionism of the American style. Arnie, followed by Jerry, joined the girls at the Veronica in an orgy of Twisting. Jerry was beginning to shed the inhibitions of his strict upbringing. He was sweating and grinding with the best of them.

When I was satisfied that they would be able to take care of themselves, I left. As it turned out, I was the one who needed protection.

I hopped into the front seat of the jeep and told Miguel to take me back to town, but just as he got the motor started a drunken Brasileiro stepped up to my side of the jeep with a 22-caliber pistol in his hand and called me a no-good gringo. He threatened to shoot me for making love to his girl.

The first question that popped into my mind was, which one was his girl. Instead of answering him, however, I turned to Miguel, who was crouching under the dashboard, and told him to get started. Miguel shook his head. Meanwhile, the drunk was

confused by the fact that I was ignoring him. He leaned across
the fender to get my attention. When I saw him in that position,
I reached for the accelerator with my left foot and gunned the
motor. The jeep shot away, sending the drunk spinning to the
ground. As Miguel gained control of the wheel I looked back.
The drunk was lying in the dust, and someone was laughing.

I went off alone the next morning to visit Denise. She had just
awakened after a late night and greeted me at the door wearing
only a loose shift. She smiled up at me, lifted her amazing black
hair with her hands, and stretched her bed-warm body.

She invited me in and padded off barefoot to make coffee. She
surprised me with a gift, much more expensive than the one I
had brought for her. I was a little embarrassed by her immoder-
ate generosity, but that was the way of the Brazilian girl. She
thought with her heart, not her head.

The morning passed. The sun rose over the great Amazon,
reached its blazing zenith over Manaus, and began to arch
westward in the direction of Uaupés. Meanwhile, time stood still
in the little apartment. We existed alone, Denise and I.

As Miguel drove me back to the hotel in the afternoon, I had
the feeling that my expedition was in danger of falling apart. We
were enjoying ourselves too much in Manaus. We had too many
reasons to put off our departure. If we waited much longer the
expedition would rot right there like a seed killed by the too rich
jungle soil.

I strode into Arnie's room, where he and Jerry were chatting. I
said, "Today is our last day in Manaus. Start getting ready."
They looked at each other and shrugged.

three

THE RIO NEGRO

The river was rising that morning late in May when we finally shoved off. The rainy season had begun. We could see the evidence of heavy downpours that were taking place far up the Amazon Valley. Logs, branches, and islands of massed vegetation had been washed off the banks and were drifting downstream. The current was swift, especially out in the middle of the river. The fast water created little whirlpools and herringbone patterns over hidden obstacles. Although I knew it was impossible, the swollen river appeared to bulge in the center like a macadam highway.

The whole character of the Amazon had changed in just a few days. With the quickening of the river, my sense of urgency also increased.

Arnie and Jerry pitched into the job of loading with great enthusiasm. Jerry was a born organizer, and Arnie was the best straw boss in the world. He jollied the crew into working at twice their normal speed, communicating his wishes by means of hand signals. The accompanying babble of English, Portuguese, laughter, and insane noises that he made served only as entertainment.

Ruey became as worrisome as an old aunt during our last hours in Manaus. He complained that we pushed too hard: "Brazilians are not accustomed to working that way." He also regretted that we had rushed our negotiations with the captain, instead of spreading them out over a day or more of eating, drinking, smoking, and chatting. Not that we would have saved a single cruzeiro—we were getting the fastest boat on the river for five dollars a day—that was not the point.

"Your trouble is that you are too impatient," he declared. Ruey was right. I was even too impatient to listen to his complaints.

The caboclos made an event of our departure. The children shouted and danced. They clapped their hands and shook their bare brown torsos in unison to a joyous rhythm that only they could hear. The adults were more decorous. They waved and shouted farewell in the languages of the river, *"Até logo! Até a vista! Cutarantó!"*

Ruey and José looked disconsolate on the dock, Ruey especially so, since he was convinced that we were not yet ready for the expedition. He felt personally responsible for our education in the ways of Brazil. I laughed to myself, thinking that Ruey's was not the first school I had dropped out of.

The sturdy *Waupes* drifted sideways with the current for a few hundred feet. Then the captain swung her around to face upstream and pulled her back into shore to take advantage of the slack water. For a moment the boat stood motionless as he accelerated the motor. In a few seconds the *Waupes* began to breast the current and paraded back past our starting point like a great warship passing majestically in review. We felt like admirals of the fleet.

The feeling did not last long. We were hardly out of sight of the floating city when petty annoyances began to nibble at our high spirits. Arnie, in addition to being naturally restless, had six feet and two inches of body to arrange comfortably in the cramped quarters. To keep himself occupied he engaged in one-way conversations with the crew and tried to study the shoreline through binoculars in the fine drizzle.

Jerry seemed satisfied to pass the time cleaning rifles, and I tried to catch up on my reading.

Before settling down, Suzy investigated every corner of the

boat like any ordinary house cat. When she satisfied herself that her new home was in order, she became mischievous again, springing in kitten leaps at everything that moved. She left red dots on our ankles with her needle teeth, and kept the flies in a perpetual commotion with her quick paws. She did her tightrope act along the edge of the deck while shadowboxing with her reflection in the black water. She amused and annoyed everyone.

On the outskirts of Manaus we saw the first of the hundreds of creeks that flow into the Rio Negro. The crew was vague about most of them, since they were of no navigational importance. The caboclos living along the river and a few that came by dugout from the floating city went up these streams to fish, but for the most part they were unsettled, uncharted, and unnamed.

The first tributaries of any importance that we came to were the Rio Taruma Acu and the Rio Taruma Mirim (the Little Taruma). These small rivers converged as they entered the Rio Negro from the north, which was to our right as we faced upstream.

There were few inlets to our left for the first thirty miles, since much of the rainwater in that stretch of jungle drained off southward into the Rio Solimões, which ran parallel to the Rio Negro. At that point the two rivers were separated by only ten miles of jungle.

Just before the mission of Santa Ana on the north bank, the Rio Negro swung northwest and broadened out to about fifteen miles in width. Hundreds of islands dotted the surface and trailed their vines and branches into the dark current. At about the same point the Solimões turned southwest. That was where the town of Manacapuru dominated the north bank, and a stream emptied the waters of Lake Manacapuru into the Amazon system.

From there the two rivers diverged in direction and in character—the Solimões narrower, deeper, and more densely settled because of the commercial traffic that took ocean liners across the continent from the Amazon estuary on the Atlantic coast to Peru. Into the yellow river emptied the waters of other great rivers like the Purus, the Japurá, the endless, winding Juruá, and the fast-running Içá, all of them lined with settlements and drawing water and commercial traffic from lesser streams. Above Manaus, the Solimões is also the Amazon. To many mapmakers the names are interchangeable.

The Rio Negro had fewer and smaller villages, and not many of the streams that flowed into it could boast permanent settlements. Its dark waters carried a more limited kind of commerce than the Solimões, and very seldom did a boat larger than the *Waupes* venture into it.

If the Amazon system could be seen in actuality as it is seen on a map, it would look like a huge ragged fan, webbed with thick green jungles, patched with brown plateaus, yellow savannas, and blue mountain ranges, and studded with missions, caboclo settlements, Air Force bases, mining camps, plantations, and the thatched *chabonas* of Indian villages.

And if the centuries could be telescoped into seconds, the meandering river and its tributaries would crack like whips, destroying human habitations and gouging out huge chunks of earth and jungle. The seasonal floods that build up in the Guiana rain forests and the glaciers of the Peruvian Andes would pulse along the creeks and rivers, sweeping the debris of jungles and tribal civilizations before them toward the cities of the east and the Atlantic Ocean.

As our little expedition inched its way along the second-largest artery of this enormous complex of waterways, the ancient world of mud, vine, insect, snake, monkey, and Indian that seemed so remote only a day before now enveloped our bodies and penetrated our pores.

Monkeys were with us from the very beginning. Squirrel monkeys congregated in large groups high in the trees and chattered at us with noisy conviction. The Indians called them *saimiri,* which means "little monkey." The jungle was the Indian's home, and the little monkey was his household pet.

Black spider monkeys, using their tails to perform trapeze acrobatics; the black-capped, whitefaced capuchin monkeys, barking at us like dogs; and ragged little ouakaris, staring down from the highest branches, their faces scarlet with anger—all of them paid us visits, followed us, scolded us, then lost interest and disappeared into the trees.

We knew that the jungles of Amazonia teemed with reptiles, but we were not prepared for the incredible specimens that came out to greet us at the very beginning of our expedition. The first was a river turtle called the "matamata," a creature in all ways in a class by itself. Its shell and skin were so covered with scallops, ridges, tubercles, and every other sort of lump and hollow that we could not make out its actual shape. Blackish matamatas between one and two feet long loafed along near the boat, turning their snouts from side to side on long necks, peering into the murky water with tiny close-set eyes. Jerry liked to line them up in the sights of his Winchester. Occasionally he took a potshot at one.

Though the matamata was the eeriest reptile we saw, there were others equally strange that we heard about. Imagine, for instance, the tejus, fast-moving carnivorous lizards that grew to more than three feet in length. They were the scourge of caboclos who raised chickens, just as foxes are the traditional enemies of chicken farmers in the States. Picture, if you will, a farmer shining a flashlight into his chicken coop and seeing a three-foot lizard, black with yellow spots, hurrying off with a hen in its well-developed jaws.

As for snakes, it seemed that the larger the species, the more deadly it was. For example, the harmless South American water snakes that abounded in the Rio Negro were relatively small at two to three feet. It was the six-foot-and-over category that seemed to include most of the crushing and biting varieties. Among those in the heavyweight division we came across a six- or seven-foot emerald tree boa, nonpoisonous but vicious, and equipped with enormous teeth. The giant venomous reptiles, such as the eight-foot fer-de-lance and the deadly twelve-foot bushmaster, these did not make daylight appearances, but the crew assured us that they were always near. The dense hanging gardens that leaned over the river somehow corroborated their existence. In fact, every tropical creature of memory and imagination seemed suddenly to become very real.

And now that we were among them, the people of the river also became more real, and more human and individual.

When the deaf-mute cook learned that I had medical equipment, he invited me to treat a cyst on his calf. Cysts were common among the caboclos, but I had never treated one before. I saw no harm in trying; it wasn't going to get better by itself. Jerry helped me. He wanted to learn.

We couldn't use anything to kill the pain because the cook was frightened to death of the hypodermic. That was a fear shared by many people, including Jerry, who could stand any other kind of pain or discomfort. We opened the cyst with an ordinary razor and drained it. The first cut produced only pus. The second cut drew blood. We cleaned the wound, sprinkled it with sulfanilamide powder, and bandaged the leg.

I never hesitated to handle anything but a terminal case during the expedition, because there were few places along the river where better medical assistance was available.

We ate a tepid supper of rice, salted meat, and noodles. Not the best food we had ever tasted, but acceptable as a change of pace. We bundled up in our hammocks against the dampness and chill of the evening air. We talked a little and sang a few songs, but drowsiness overcame us quickly. I fell asleep with the words of the currently popular song "Sherry" plodding through my brain to the dull throb of the engine.

We awoke during the early hours of dawn on our second day out. A cold rain was beating down hard on the roof. The mist lay close to the water, preventing us from seeing more than twenty-five feet in any direction. We had our breakfast of strong black coffee and hardtack, and tried to get in some fishing off the back of the boat.

From time to time we heard the snorting of pirarucú coming to the surface for air. Then there was a series of great splashes. The first mate, Mario, informed us that we had picked up an escort of *golfinhos*.

"*Golfinhos?*" Jerry asked.

Mario imitated the leaping and diving action of the river creature eloquently with his hand. It was a school of dolphins, perhaps the pink porpoises themselves. We started casting in the direction of the splashes. This agitated Mario considerably. He indicated that the *golfinhos* were not to be harmed.

We yielded to Mario's wishes. It occurred to me that he would have had a difficult time of it had we been in the Guianas, where the Indians considered the dolphin a delicacy.

All we caught that morning were a few piranha. Mario showed us that we did not even need bait. They went after anything that hit the water. The trick was to use a hook about as thick as a good-sized nail, so that the piranha could not bite through it. The other important thing to remember was to beat the fish to death before trying to extract the hook, because those monsters continued to snap at objects even when hooked and landed.

The first mate demonstrated by tempting a hooked piranha with a plantain. It snapped the end of it off clean.

I noticed that the piranha we caught were bigger than the ones I saw in Manaus, which were only about the size of goldfish. Mario smiled and pointed upstream, then held his hands out, palm facing palm, the way a fisherman does when he describes the one that got away. I felt a chill run up my back. Mario's hands were about eighteen inches apart. I wondered how anything could live in the same water as those creatures.

It made me a little queasy to see the cook prepare the piranha for lunch. It had never occurred to me that they could be eaten. In back of my mind was the disturbing thought that one of those fish could have a piece of Indian in its belly. The thought appealed to Arnie's slightly sick sense of humor.

"What's the difference?" he explained. "It's part of nature's cycle. In the long run everything eats everything else."

Jerry butted in, "The cycle is fair enough, but I don't go for any shortcuts."

It was only when the mist thinned out a little that I saw a third boat on our towrope. All I could make out was the black silhouette of a dugout loaded with either freight or people. I asked Mario about it. He explained that the captain had picked up a fisherman's family. This method of hitchhiking was the only way caboclos could return to their villages after drifting downstream, or move upriver to a better fishing or farming spot. Captain Cachaça charged them for the transportation. It was part of his regular income.

We made frequent stops at huts along the bank to sell supplies to hunters and trappers. Between stops there was little to do but sleep. The driving rain limited all other activity.

Lunch consisted of rice, salted meat, and noodles. I began to get the idea that this would be our diet all the way to Uaupés. We could either live with it or start dipping into our own supplies. I decided that we would stick it out. If the crew could survive on this stuff, so could we.

We made one more stop that afternoon to untie the fisherman's boat, and continued on until evening. When the cook began to prepare supper, I checked the pots. Sure enough, it was rice, salted meat, and noodles. I complained to the captain, who spoke to the cook. After that we also got sardines occasionally.

That night we tied up near Cantagalo, a caboclo village of fishermen, hunters, and trappers. The crew scattered among the huts. They seemed to know the place pretty well. No one showed much interest in us, so we wandered about for a while.

We got a close look at the caboclo huts. There wasn't much to look at. The frames were made of planks cut from logs and branches and trimmed with machetes. They were lashed together with coarse vines, or *sogas,* and thatched with palm leaves.

It was easy to look inside, since the windows in most cases were nothing more than square holes cut out of the walls. A typical interior would consist of a bare floor, with perhaps a grass mat covering one small area, tables and stools that were either handmade of rough hewn wood or reclaimed castoffs, and hammocks that served as beds.

The few possessions hanging on the walls included kerosene lanterns, machetes, tin cans that were used as tableware, and a calendar or a religious object.

In one or two huts we saw signs of unusual affluence—a foot-powered sewing machine, a factory-made garment, or a respectable cooking pot. After seeing the caboclo dwellings our boat didn't seem quite so unpleasant, so we went back to it and turned in for the night.

We were awakened the next morning by the noisy climax of an all-night party. Everyone in the village was drunk. Our captain, in keeping with his exalted station, was the drunkest of all. Mario brought some girls aboard and introduced them to us. They offered us *cachaça*. We took a little to be hospitable, but my throat boiled like a volcano.

Even the *cachaça* could not make those girls attractive. Their unskilled use of lipstick and rouge distorted any natural beauty they might have possessed. They wore their party dresses, which only made their bare feet look ludicrous, and their loud voices at that early hour jarred my senses. In all, they were caricatures of the girls we had met in Manaus.

Arnie read my thoughts. He chided me. "Chin up. In a few days these broads will start looking great."

"In a few years maybe even a monkey would look great," I retorted.

Jerry went after Arnie. "I'll bet you could go for one of them right now. Don't be ashamed. I'll get Mario to fix it up for you."

"Learn how to fix it up for yourself first. I don't need any help."

We left it at that. The argument was not really about girls, after all. It was about boredom, wet cigarettes, bad food, and sagging hammocks. The cabocla girls gave us an opportunity to let out some of the steam that had been building up.

Breakfast on land was a welcome change. We ate wild fowl, probably *mutum* (wild turkey), and dried fish. I steered clear of a meat course that looked like monkey. We saw a caboclo hacking up a giant river turtle, the kind that had been on sale in the Manaus marketplace. Those *tartarugas* were a standard food item along the river, though somewhat expensive in the city. At holiday time they sold for astronomical prices. They were to Brazilians what the Thanksgiving turkey is to Americans.

Sick call began right after breakfast. Mario brought me an

infant with an infected toe. Apparently it had started as an ordinary cut that the parents packed with dirt. When I saw it, the nail was off and the toe was no more than a shapeless mass of clotted flesh. I opened the wound and drained it, and gave the infant a penicillin tablet to kill any infection that might set in afterward.

Then there were three youngsters with sores all over their bodies. All I could do was swab the sores with iodine and clean out the ones that looked infected.

The next patient was a man with malaria. He was walking around without a shirt, and until I looked at him he had had no medical attention. I put him to bed and covered him with all the blankets I could scrounge up. Then I applied cold packs to his head and gave him Alarin tablets and a shot of penicillin.

A little girl of about six was next. She complained of numbness in her limbs. I tested her reflexes and found them very slow. From what I knew, her symptoms seemed to indicate polio, although I had never heard of a case of polio in the jungle. All I could do was give her a little therapy. I helped her flex her arms in hot water, and instructed her parents to continue to do this every day.

They nodded, but I knew they would never do it. They expected white man's medicine to work instantly. Before I finished with the girl, I gave her a shot of penicillin as a booster against anything else she might be coming down with.

I treated a few caboclos for minor cuts and headed back to the boat, walking right into the bloodiest family argument I have ever witnessed. Like people everywhere, the caboclos seemed to go out of their way to add to their normal share of suffering.

A caboclo husband found out that his wife had slept with another man during the previous night's party and was battering her face and head with his fists. She pulled out a knife and stabbed him in the shoulder. He spun around and, with a swing of his forearm, knocked out all her front teeth. Their blood splashed all over the ground and sprinkled the toes of the closely gathered bystanders.

With blood streaming from his shoulder, the husband took off toward his hut to get his shotgun. He returned on the run, pushing a shell into the chamber, ready to end his family problems in the simplest way he knew. But Arnie and I disarmed him.

The feuding couple fell to again, and while they battled, their eight-year-old son scampered around them with the shotgun, not knowing which of his parents to shoot. Somehow the episode ended with no fatalities, at least not while we were there.

We remained in Cantagalo most of the afternoon. While the captain was trading for fresh fruits and vegetables, I volunteered to patch up the caboclo and his wife. They were in a surly mood and declined my offer. We pushed off at about five o'clock.

The rest of the day passed quietly. The river was still misty and flat and immense. The flotsam drifting downstream past the boat created the illusion that we were moving faster than we actually were.

This dizzying sensation, the absence of an itinerary, the monotonous diet, the dampness, the drumming of the motor, and the physical confinement combined to create a state of nausea that seemed more mental than visceral. Or, turning it the other way, the boredom seemed to settle in our stomachs like a physical obstruction.

We worked out a shipboard regimen to help maintain our vitality. We played dominoes, sang songs, took exercises, practiced Portuguese, and made an inordinate fuss over ordinary chores. We set a schedule for the taking of our malaria pills, for cleaning our weapons, and so on. And when our activities did not require our being together, we stayed out of one another's way.

The crew showed little interest in what we did, with one notable exception, when I cut Arnie's hair. They thought the baldie style looked rather fashionable, and before I was done I had shaved four more heads.

As we moved along I kept asking about the rivers and settlements. The names had a magic sound to my ear. The Rio Curiau, the Rio Comanau, the Rio Jaú, with its village of Mucura a hundred miles away; the Unini, even longer, with the town of Conquista 150 miles upstream, and Jacitara another hundred miles beyond that in total isolation. At times I had to overcome the urge to ask the captain to take us up one of these mysterious rivers.

On the third day we came to the town of Moura, which was established at the mouth of the Jauaperi as an Air Force installation after the Indian outbreak of 1947. Before the violence had been quelled, four white men were killed and the area was closed off by the SPI. The situation there had not changed in the fifteen years that had elapsed. Moura was still primarily an Air Force base guarding the mouth of the Jauaperi and maintaining a beacon for planes passing overhead. And the Indians of the Jauaperi retained their reputation as the most hostile in the area.

We were anxious to stop at Moura, because Air Force men could always be counted upon to roll out the red carpet. Those whom we met in Manaus tried to extend a hospitality that was far beyond their means. I believe they considered themselves somewhat of an élite, in the sense that they wanted to represent the best qualities of their country, and show their country to visitors in the best possible light.

The personnel at Moura were not as dashing as their brothers-in-arms in Manaus, perhaps because of the monotonous duty and the decrepit facilities, but the community, no more than fifty persons in all, gave us a warm welcome and a fine send-off.

Beyond Moura we came to the mouth of the Rio Branco, the white river, largest tributary of the Rio Negro. Here again, the thought struck me, black meets white in the middle of the Amazon jungle.

The Rio Branco had a special significance for me since it connected with the Rio Tacatu, which served as a natural boundary between Brazil and British Guiana through a long stretch of savanna country. I had visited the town of Lethem on the Tacatu the previous year while on an expedition in British Guiana. I could have made the trip from there to this very spot by dugout, had it been in my plans to do so. To me, as to the Indians, political boundaries had little importance. The Guianas, Venezuela, Colombia, and the northern part of Brazil were all one country, and the only government was nature.

We tied up that afternoon at Cabureiro, also called Carvoeiro. It was downstream from Barcelos, after all. That solved our mapmaking mystery. The reason for vagueness about Cabureiro was also now apparent. One hundred and fifty caboclos—hunters, fishermen, and their families—made up the entire population. They had a church and practiced Catholicism, but lived off the jungle and in general resisted the influences of the outside world.

The *tuchaua,* or chief, invited us up to his hut and proudly served us cold beer out of a brand-new refrigerator. He must have been the leading tycoon of the region, because he was able to keep a generator running constantly just to meet his own personal needs. He had us sit down with him to a sumptuous meal of salad, Spam, and more beer.

Aboard the boat we took Polaroid pictures of the *tuchaua's* family, which we tried to trade for turkeys. However, they did not want to part with their *perus,* as they are called. Then the captain and the chief started to argue. I never found out what it was about, but the argument kept mounting until the captain, spurred on by a quantity of *cachaça,* took a swing at the chief. The chief had plenty of time to step back, and he did, right into the river.

In a rage, the captain ordered the boat to pull out, and off we went, with the *tuchaua's* wife still on board. A cry went up from the shore, and dugouts were dispatched to bring the woman back. When she was safe in one of the dugouts, the noise subsided and we were again on our way.

I learned later that wife stealing was a fairly prevalent form of crime among the Indian tribes in the nearby jungles. It wasn't kidnapping in the ordinary sense, because wives were considered property, like draft animals. While the men fished and hunted, the women tended the fields (usually manioc, but sometimes plantains, peppers, and sweet potatoes, too), took care of the children, did the household chores, prepared meals, and wove baskets and hammocks.

Nor did a wife who was carried off consider herself kidnapped, for she, too, thought of herself as a possession. Among the Indians a kidnapped wife accepted her new home without complaint.

We ate aboard the *Waupes* that evening. After dinner I heard one of the crew calling to me for help. I found him lying in his bunk holding his side. It looked like appendicitis. I applied cold packs and hoped he could hold out until we reached the mission at Barcelos the next day.

There was a momentary halt in the rain the next morning, and we observed the Rio Negro at her loveliest. The sun was bright, the air was cool and clear. We could see towering trees on either bank and their reflections in the slick surface of the black water. The birds welcomed the sunlight with raucous joy. With our spirits buoyed, the *put-put* of the engine sounded reassuring rather than annoying, and even breakfast tasted good.

We took advantage of the break in the weather to film the pageant of nature that passed on either side of us. The trees were magnificent, some rising straight as pillars 150 feet into the air. Others had grotesque swollen bases as tall as a man that looked like huge tumors. There were great hardwood trees and delicate leafy varieties that lost their individual shapes among the bushes and vines. There were a half dozen different kinds all known as *favéira* trees. There were *Hevea* rubber trees and *castanho-do-Pará* trees and trees that no one could identify.

Not that anyone cared to. The crew had seen this carnival of vegetation all their lives. They hardly shared our interest. But they did describe one bizarre species existing somewhere in the jungle that oozed sap exactly the color and consistency of blood.

The riverside forest was garlanded with vines and festooned with white, yellow, and pink blossoms, a richly intricate curtain drawn endlessly past our hypnotized eyes.

And always woven into the curtain were the birds. Brazil, or at least the northern part of it, must be the corner of the world most richly populated with birds. The toucan—one foot of black-feathered body and one foot of yellow beak—was only one of many bizarre species that congregated along the banks of the Rio

Negro. There were kingfishers—magnificently crested green birds with white and pink undersides—that plunged gracefully into the river after fish. There were red hummingbirds, great potoos that looked like parts of decayed treetrunks, black-and-white barred birds, purple birds, blue birds, birds that sang and birds that screeched, birds that cawed and birds that cooed, wading birds and hanging birds, giant birds and tiny birds, common birds and rare birds. It is possible that there was a new species waiting to be discovered there, but in all that feathery profusion even an ornithologist might have overlooked it.

The appendicitis victim let us know by his groans that he was still in pain, but the captain showed no concern. He stopped for firewood; he stopped to trade; he stopped for every reason imaginable; and arrived at Barcelos at six in the afternoon, five hours later than anticipated.

four

BARCELOS AND BEYOND

We helped our patient ashore and made sure he was looked after before we got involved in other matters. He was taken to the Santa Caza (mission hospital) and placed in the emergency ward. There were two other wards for regular inpatients, one for men and one for women.

Barcelos was a modern and self-sufficient community built around a Salesian mission. It was no surprise to see a handsome church in the center of the settlement, and electric lighting and appliances of all kinds. But it was surprising to see a machine shop and carpentry shop that were used to educate the converted Indians for civilized trades. It was gratifying to know that some Indians, at least, had an opportunity to establish themselves with dignity in their adopted society.

We told the head priest and the nuns that we were thinking of stopping off on our way back to visit the Shiriana and Waica Indians on the nearby Demeni and Araçá rivers.

They confirmed that the area had been closed off by the government after diamonds had been discovered, so as to prevent a diamond rush. Before that, however, the Swiss explorer-photographer Furst had been up the Demeni to make television films, and the German Dr. Zerries had explored both the Araçá and the Demeni. It was in this region that the Indian attacks had taken place that Dr. Galvão had told me about.

The sisters, called *irmãs,* gave us some supplies to drop off at the mission of Santa Izabel at Tapurucuará. I was somehow pleased to see that most of the medicine bore American labels. I also asked for, and got, medical supplies to replace those I had used attending to the caboclos and our crew. The *irmãs* did not ask for a donation in return, but we insisted.

They were anxious to know if any of us had colds. Illnesses that seemed minor to us could be fatal to Indians. We heard one comment so often that it sounded almost like a proverb: "A white man sneezes and an Indian village dies." This had happened more than once.

Arnie had got over his cold, but Jerry was still sneezing. We hoped to be free of colds by the time we hit Indian country.

I asked if there were any illnesses that we should look out for. Yes: Infection from leeches and insect bites; yaws, malaria, dysentery and snakebite. The sisters told us that the caboclos and Indians had an antidote for snakebite which they took orally. It was very effective, but no one knew how they made it.

A nun who spoke English asked, "Have you ever had medical training?"

"Not in school. In the jungle. I spend a lot of time reading medical books, especially the practical things like surgery, giving injections, treating infections."

"Have you performed operations?"

"Oh, yes. I saved the leg of a Wapashana boy in British Guiana by removing pieces of gangrenous tissue."

"How did you know how to cut without practice?"

"I had practice, on steaks."

The sisters burst into laughter; first the ones who understood English, then the others as my reply was translated into Portuguese. I felt a little foolish, watching them enjoy what they thought was a joke. But it was the truth. I practiced surgery by cutting up raw steaks with a scalpel before cooking them. It gave me the feel of the blade against the texture of flesh.

I often wondered how long it would have taken me to learn the same thing at Monsignor Clancy High School or Richmond Hill High School or New York State Military Academy. Probably a year, and then I would have forgotten it anyway. The curriculum would start with half a dozen books on anatomy, and each book would begin with a long-winded introduction that would bore me to death.

In my own way I had learned to cut umbilical cords, extract teeth, set bones, and do a hundred other things that could mean the difference between life and death for some poor savage. That kind of education was good enough for me.

I protested to the nuns that I was very serious about my medical work. In their gentle way they showed that they understood, and asked me what kinds of cases I accepted.

"All but the terminal ones," I told them.

They knew what I meant. Indians had a habit of blaming the doctor if the patient died, even when the case was hopeless from the start.

Every missionary had this experience: An Indian would be carried into the Santa Caza, delirious and close to death. There would be signs that a witch doctor had attempted treatment and had sent the patient to the nearest missionary to transfer responsibility for his death. The missionary might also want to turn the patient away to protect his reputation among the Indians; but, being a priest as well as a doctor, it was his duty to save the heathen's soul and dispatch it heavenward from a properly baptized corpse.

So it was that the Christian life of many a converted Indian consisted entirely of a few tortured hours on a cot in a Santa Caza, and it was often the duty of the missionary to inform the family of the departed, standing its pathetic vigil outside, that it had lost both the body and the soul of its loved one.

There were exceptions, when the missionaries and nuns performed genuine miracles of healing. And on the other side of the ledger, we saw horrible scars that indicated successful operations performed by witch doctors. The cosmetic results were usually bad because they used no sutures. They usually packed the cut with dirt or cobwebs.

We decided to postpone our inspection tour of Barcelos to the next day, as the prospect of sleeping in a real bed dulled our curiosity. So, after a simple supper served by young Indian girls, we turned in for the night. The last thing I did before going to my room was inquire about our patient in the emergency ward. The report was that he was feeling better. Apparently it was not appendicitis after all, and he would be well enough to continue with us the next day.

I remember lying on my back and looking at the whitewashed ceiling ribbed with streaks of light from the setting sun, the gray-white of civilization and the blazing orange of the jungle. I heard the evening mass above the noise of the early crickets. The profoundly formal Latin phrases sounded frail and pathetic on the lips of the little Indian children. I heard in their chant the two voices of Brazil. I listened to the ghostly discourse there on the mist-shrouded banks of the Rio Negro: the God that healed and punished and the god that deluged the earth with teeming life, the eternal word and the fleeting song, the angry and the amiable, the austere and the lavish, the priest and the Indio. Fred Salazar could hear these voices.

When we awoke the next morning the rain was coming down and there was a cold breeze above a low-hanging mist on the river. We spent a few hours washing our clothes and fishing while the motorista brought an engine part over to the machine shop to be repaired. About noon we said good-bye to Barcelos.

Did the sisters warn us about insict bites? No warning could have prepared us for the plague we suffered that afternoon. Swarms of *piums*—we called them "peons"—came out of nowhere. At first we were only a little annoyed; they didn't seem to be biting. Then we discovered red welts on our arms where they had buried themselves in our skin.

We put alcohol on the welts to keep them from festering. This also had the welcome effect of making the piums pull their heads out. Plucking them out was impossible. We always retrieved the body and left the head, a very unhappy compromise.

We got out the insect repellents to protect us against future attacks. The nets were of no use; the piums were so small they flew right through them. While I dabbed and smeared all the exposed parts of my body, I glanced up and caught the captain grinning surreptitiously. The piums didn't seem to bother him at

all. My first thought was that he had enough alcohol in him at all
times to thwart the insects. Then I realized that they did not
bother the rest of the crew, either. It must have been that their
skin was hardened by outdoor living or that there was an
accumulation of dirt that served as a protective barrier.

The boat continued to make several stops each day, with our
unanimous consent. We needed that relief from the depressing
routine. The captain took advantage of my seeming laxity to
take on passengers for short stretches. He also took advantage of
the language barrier to ignore my occasional objections. I was
fearful on several occasions that my friends would take matters
into their own hands.

We were now beyond the protection of law. This is a strange
thing for novices in the jungle to comprehend. They do not
realize what a mainstay of their lives the law is until it is taken
away, and then they suddenly realize they are far, far from home.

The awareness can have as profound an effect on a rebel like
Arnie as on a peaceful citizen like Jerry.

For the first time Arnie understood that beneath his disdain
for laws, lawyers, courts, and cops was a deep appreciation of
their power. His flouting of the law was his perverse way of
recognizing it. It was as if he said, "I can take on the biggest and
strongest force that the world can throw at me," and what is
bigger and stronger than the law? Without that appreciation,
coupled with his belief in himself, the open battle between Arnie
and all forms of authority would never have taken place.

For that very reason he welcomed playing the role of authority: What were those caboclos up to? What was the crew
whispering about? Behind the façade of the reprobate hid a
policeman and a moralist.

Jerry had been anticipating this situation for some time. The
constant cleaning of rifles was part of it. He was a practical type.
If the law wasn't here to protect him, he wanted a rifle handy,
and in good working order.

Actually, there was a law of sorts on the river, but it hardly
intruded upon the way people chose to live. There were lawyers
and judges with no formal training in law. A judgeship seemed

to be a family affair. If your cousin was a mayor, you could be a judge. It was as blatant as that. The courts were barrelhead courts like those of the Old West. Only a major crime like murder would be tried by the prefects at Barcelos, Tapurucuará or Uaupés. Criminals convicted for long terms were then sent to Manaus, and difficult cases were sometimes referred to the higher court there.

The jails in the little river towns were flimsy. Any American teen-ager who had ever been in jail could break through the mud walls of an Amazonian lockup in less than an hour. Normally, though, he would not have to, since the doors were usually open and the turnkey drunk. The reason for all this apparent carelessness was that there was no place to run to. The jungle is the final jailer.

Prisoners were usually well treated. They could come and go during their sentence, but might be required to do chores as restitution. As often as possible the mayors and sheriffs tried to settle matters out of court. They realized that after the fuss had died down they would have to go on living with the accused, whether guilty or not. Sheriffs, or *delegados,* seldom tried to be heroes. Those who did were often found shot in the back or were forced by an irate community to hie themselves back to Manaus.

I could see a change wrought in my friends by their few days on the river. The apathy that had begun to set in back in Manaus was giving way to self-discipline and wariness. They were alert to any unusual behavior by the crew, which, because they outnumbered us, made them uneasy. The ragged passengers also kept them on their toes. There was no telling whether they were chance pickups or cohorts in some violent plot. We were all well aware that the easiest way in the world to dispose of someone was to "lose" him over the side of a boat on the Rio Negro.

Our suspicions proved unfounded. As Ruey undoubtedly would have explained, the social and commercial detours were merely the Brasileiro's way of making the journey pleasant. All the captain wanted to do was exactly what he was doing: Drink constantly, stop frequently, take on passengers for their company and a few cruzeiros, and do a little trading for the pleasure of cheating a caboclo.

Swindling the caboclos was favorite pastime along the Rio Negro. There were traders who made a profession of it. They were a breed apart. As voracious as the piranha, they preyed along the entire length of the river as far as Iauaretê on the Colombian border. They came to steal and they came armed. They traded pots, pans, needles, knives, combs, brushes, and other manufactured articles for bales of jute, skins, raw rubber, and other jungle products. If a caboclo wanted more than he was offered for his produce, the trader raised his own prices accordingly.

Some of the great fortunes of Brazil were started by traders. The fortune of the Sabbas, one of the leading families of Manaus, is said to have been founded by a trader who sold sewing needles along the rivers. Today the family trades in factories and oil refineries. I compared them in my mind with the Astors of North America. In two centuries of Western Hemisphere history the way to make a fortune in the wilderness had not changed, but the hunting grounds had moved from Hudson's Bay to Amazonas.

The saying "They'll steal your eyeteeth" was painfully true of the white visitors in the region. The traders took the caboclos' possessions, the missionaries took their souls, and the itinerant dentists took their teeth.

Tooth decay was a chronic problem. It was caused by the high acidity of farinha, the staple of the caboclo's diet. The enormous suffering caused by rotten teeth accounts for the esteem in which dentists were held.

Following is the translation of a lesson in Tupi, from a manual prepared by Brazilians interested in reviving the native language and the traditon of which it is a part:

"TEETH PULLER (TEETH EXTRACTOR)

"The valient [sic] teethpuller who died on the 21st of April, 1792, in the defence of Brazil. What is his name?

Joaquim José da Silva Xavier
Why was he called Teethpuller?
Because he knew how to extract teeth."

Here is an example of a man's reputation as a dentist eclipsing his fame as a patriot!

The lesson helps explain the susceptibility of the caboclos to dental quackery. The itinerant dentists who visited the settlements were mostly frauds. They carried the tools of dentistry and claimed the knowledge, but most of them could not even stop the bleeding after an extraction.

After Barcelos we passed the town of Piloto on the left bank. Virtually all the settlements on this part of the river were on the left, as the settlers sought to keep the river between themselves and the warlike Indians of the north. Beyond Piloto the Rio Caivini flowed in from the south, the Rio Caivini with its lonely settlement of Saroroca.

A heavy rain greeted us on the morning of our seventh day. Water poured into the boat from all sides, and the churning current tore huge chunks of earth off the banks. The rain let up a little before breakfast, but by that time the hammocks and all our clothes were thoroughly soaked.

The last two days before Tapurucuará were uneventful. We had one meal at the casa of a *tuchaua,* who proudly showed us all his wealth and told us of his great family. He gave us a sweet drink made of cane sugar mixed with fermented manioc, and loaded us down with plantains, oranges, lemons, cashews, and fish to take along on the boat. He was typical of the river dwellers we had met. He was friendly and generous, and had no ax to grind, as did some of our acquaintances in Manaus. I don't think we were called "gringos" once during our entire voyage.

The river became narrower as we passed Santa Ana, Tomar, and São Joaquim. We passed the mouth of the Rio Prêto (the dark river) on our right and the Urarirá on our left. There were whirlpools and dangerous-looking eddies as we picked our way among the islands between the mouths of the Rio Jacaré and the Igarapé Jaú (Jaú Creek), which were pouring their waters into the mounting flood.

The captain said he would keep going all night so as to make Tapurucuará by eight o'clock the next morning. I wished him well. If we adhered to his schedule it would mean one less meal of salted meat, sardines, rice, and noodles.

With that pleasant thought in mind I settled into my hammock, while the bleary-eyed captain guided our boat through the mist and darkness, between islands and rocks, and on through the night, past the Rio Daraá and the Rio Jurubaxi, toward the mission of Santa Izabel at Tapurucuará.

five

THE MISSION OF SANTA IZABEL

When I awoke the next morning and saw sunlight glinting off
the white walls of the mission of Santa Izabel in the distance, my
faith in humanity went up a few notches. Captain Cachaça had
come through.

For the first time in days I was filled with anticipation. Santa
Izabel and the community of Tapurucuará lay close to the edge
of Waica country. I hoped to see full-blooded Waicas among the
converts, and perhaps a few from the surrounding area who still
retained their primitive ways.

All along the Rio Negro up to this point the banks were
strewn with caboclo settlements of all sizes, from a single hut to a
community of hundreds. What we had not seen was the original
untouched Indian. The few places below Tapurucuará where
they still existed—the Rio Jauaperi, the Rio Demeni, the Rio
Araçá—were closed off by the government. Santa Izabel was the
perfect place to watch the transition of the Indians from primitive jungle dwellers to caboclos who would eventually populate
the miserable river villages and the floating city of Manaus.

That transition is a remarkable thing. It is subtle and cata-
clysmic at the same time. A mature Indian who has never before
worn clothes puts a hat on his head, and for the first time in his
life he is naked. A savage with a wooden spear says three words

in his primitive language and strikes fear into the white man's heart, while his fellow tribesman, armed with a machete, greets the stranger in broken Portuguese, and the white man loathes him.

Conversion is conquest. Assimilation is subjugation. The Wai Wai of the Guiana rain forests who clung to their tribal ways through the years of the rubber boom still earned the white man's respect. Other Guiana Indians who became rubber tappers earned fifty cents a day.

The irony was that the tribes that had been swallowed up were killed with kindness. The doctors, nuns, and missionaries who healed, educated, and converted the Indians turned them from independent hunters and warriors into drunkards, thieves, and lowly laborers. Who had helped the Indians more, the director of the Salesian mission at Tapurucuará, or the infamous white demon known as the "Ear Cutter" of the Rio Xingu, who collected Chavante ears in a pouch like rabbits' feet, and who was largely responsible for the hostility that has kept the Chavante independent in recent years?

The boat entered a channel between a large island and the north bank of the river. On the island was a post office and a government administration building. On the bank was the mission, a solid two-story structure like the other missions we had seen, made of brick and cement and painted white.

The religious settlement of the mission of Santa Izabel included a wooden church, the only building remaining from the original mission; the Santa Caza, the dormitories, the school, and the workshops. Nearby were the homes and shops of the secular community of Tapurucuará.

In back of the settlement lay cultivated fields tended by Indian children under the direction of the priests. Beyond the cleared land, unseen among the trees, were the huts of Indians who had come down from the jungle highlands to settle near the mission, and deeper in the jungle were their mysterious cousins, the Waica.

There was another point of interest, directly across the river. It was the Protestant mission. Competition for souls was fierce on that part of the Rio Negro.

The three of us went straight up to the mission to meet the director and the nuns. We were surprised to find that we were expected. An Irish brother named Thomas Hanley, who spoke both English and Portuguese, read a letter from Padre Stefan of Manaus, informing the director that three young explorers—two Catholics and a Protestant (Arnie)—were coming to take motion pictures of the mission. Brother Tom offered to help us in every way possible.

He began by inviting us to breakfast. We said grace, thanking God for His favors, such as food without insects and a table that didn't rock. Next to godliness, the mission table shone with cleanliness, for everything had been scrubbed by obedient little brown hands.

After eating we toured the mission. As we walked, Brother Tom told us its history. It was founded in 1940 to convert the caboclos to Catholicism, to give them medical help and to teach them trades. One at a time, with the help of the converts, permanent buildings were erected. The fields were cleared for planting so that the meager diet of the caboclos could be supplemented by fruit, beans, and green vegetables. Generators were installed to provide electric lighting and power for the workshops, and for refrigerators and other appliances used by the staff.

Recently some two hundred head of Brahma cattle had been brought to Santa Izabel in the hope that they could be bred locally for their meat. When I saw the herd it was down to about eighty head of skinny, sickly animals. Insects were eating them up alive. Occasionally the director ordered one killed and the meat distributed among the caboclos. Soon there would be no cattle at all. Only a person who has suffered the voyage from Manaus to Tapurucuará could know what a noble experiment that had been; what a monumental effort and what a bitter defeat.

The mission ran its own store, one of three at Tapurucuará.

The mission charged lower prices than its competitors, and accepted fish, wild animal meat, and other jungle produce in place of money. There was also a loan system. The caboclos could borrow outboard engines and pay for them by working for a specified length of time. In effect, the mission traded mechanical labor for human labor.

Being a well-established mission, Santa Izabel did more than serve the caboclos. It was the base of operations for missionaries who went into the surrounding jungles to convert the savage tribes. This was a far cry from dealing with docile rubber tappers.

The wild Indians spoke a variety of languages that bore no similarity to other known tongues. Even from village to village, among Indians of the same racial stock, there was often a language barrier created by generations of isolation. In addition, there were the dangers of disease, snakebite and infection, and the awesome rapids that had taken countless lives on every river in the region.

And the Indians themselves. They were sometimes hostile, sometimes playful, sometimes suspicious, always unpredictable. They used powerful drugs and deadly poisons. Most frightening of all, they were said to be cannibalistic. This terrifying thought lurked behind the humor of a joke then making the rounds:

"The padre has succeeded in partially converting the cannibals."

"What do you mean by partially?"

"On Friday they only eat fishermen."

There were two priests working out of the mission at that time. One was making the rounds in his *lancha* at that very moment. His name was Padre John Badelotti.

Brother Tom told us about Padre John, an amazing man among men, but little more than average among Salesian missionaries. He had traveled to the far corners of the earth on missions of salvation, and had not set foot on his native Italian soil for twenty-three years. If he died in the service of his faith without ever seeing his homeland again, he would not be the first of his order to do so. Before coming to Brazil he was missionary to Krishnazar, India. He left there because the Indian government would not allow him to have half of his diocese in India and the other half in Pakistan.

Padre John had been assigned to take over the primitive mission established by Padre Antônio Goyz on the Cauaburi, and to expand the work begun by Padre Antônio in that area.

Meanwhile, Padre Antônio was breaking new ground on the upper Marauiá. That was completely virgin territory, since no border commission, trader, SPI agent, explorer, scientist, or prospector had ever ventured up that river.

Padre Antônio was the Albert Schweitzer, Henry Hudson, and Wyatt Earp of Waica country all rolled into one. We met him at lunch. He was tall and powerfully built, with the black flowing beard of a biblical patriarch. He wore canvas sneakers and a plain white cotton cassock, under which he sometimes carried a revolver. He was in Tapurucuará at that time because of an attack of malaria.

Padre Antônio spoke with wit and simplicity. It was easy to see how he could inspire respect among the savages. He vibrated authority in every word and movement. He must have literally put the fear of God into every one of them.

We asked him how he went about contacting the Indians.

He answered, "You don't contact them. They contact you."

That was precisely his technique. He would travel along a river or overland through the jungle until he came across signs of the Indians' presence—a vine bridge, a patch of sweet potatoes or an abandoned hammock. He would then pitch camp, and wait. And wait. And wait.

With luck, an Indian would eventually show himself. Padre Antônio would win his confidence by giving him gifts. When the lucky owner of a hat or comb returned to his village, the news would get around, and soon other Indians would be visiting the padre's campsite. The missionary would distribute additional gifts among them and leave quickly, while their curiosity was still high.

The padre said that on his next visit, with God's blessing, he would find gifts left for him by the Indians. After that it was a

matter of perseverance, experience, courage, and good sense.

"Never show you are afraid. Never show you are undecided. Never show you are ill. When they know you as a strong, courageous person, they will respect you and believe what you tell them. At the same time you must show generosity; give them food, clothing, tools, medicine."

"And in return?"

"In return they attend mass, send their children to the mission school, and settle down around the mission to learn to live like Christians."

"What if they don't cooperate?"

"Then I stop giving them gifts. If they want them badly enough they come around. Eventually they learn to value the rewards of a civilized life."

This method of indoctrination had a familiar ring. I thought of shifty-looking men who waited in cars near the schoolyard in Richmond Hill to distribute bennies, goofballs, reefers, pot, and everything else with a frivolous name that meant narcotics. They also would demonstrate the value of their commodity by withholding it when the need became overpowering.

To put it plainly, the good padre got the Indians hooked on Catholicism.

Sometimes the parallel was followed all the way to its tragic conclusion. Just as addicts turned to robbery and murder to get their fix, the Indians often robbed and killed to get the things they had learned to want and could acquire in no other way.

A group of Macu Indians that had been induced to settle down near Santa Izabel were a living example of what could happen. During the day they learned how to farm, how to use tools, and how to pray to their new God. At night they drank and fought.

Yet I liked and admired the padre. He was a warm, robust human being; a man of the cloth and a man of the world, in the fullest sense of each. Moreover, he had a sense of purpose. If I questioned his motives and criticized the results of his work, what could I say for myself? Were a few stuffed animals and some film footage a more worthy reason for coming to Tapurucuará? If I should transmit a deadly virus to these Indians, will I have left them a better legacy than the missionary?

And what could I say for Arnie and Jerry? Why were they here? To prove their courage? To flee authority? Assert their independence? Get rich? Or was it possible that they were merely caught up in my enthusiasm?

After long nights of talking with them in New York, in Manaus, in mud villages all along the Rio Negro, I still did not know the answer. I could only feel dim forces at work in all of us. I suspected that in every man there is a creature—an angel or a devil or both—that compels him to do and become what he must. The creature in each member of our little party had turned his feet toward the jungles of Amazonas. All the rest—the cameras, guns, taxidermy kits, mineral testing devices—all this was rationalization.

After lunch we took a dugout across the river to visit the Protestant mission, which was operated by the Seventh-day Adventists. We were warmly received, but the missionary did not have much to offer us. The physical setup was much smaller and more rudimentary than the Salesian mission. It was not as well supplied, nor was it part of a system as well organized as the Catholic outposts.

The Brazilian government was strictly impartial in its attitude toward the various evangelists, but the population being predominantly Catholic, it was the Catholic missions that got the most assistance. As always, the personal attitude outweighed official policy.

We asked if the Adventists had had much success in spreading the gospel.

"A fair degree. We have a handful of converts. Some were taught Catholicism first," the missionary said, nodding toward the other side of the river, "but we managed to win them over."

"Doesn't Protestantism appeal to the wild Indians?"

"Perhaps, but we do not have the means to send missionaries off into the jungle. We must do our work near the river, and therefore we concentrate on the caboclos. I believe the Indians who leave Catholicism for our religion do so because they want to be treated more as equals. I also feel that they do not have the patience for those long masses."

For all that, the Protestant mission seemed hard put to hold its own. There is something to be said, after all, for good organization and sufficient funds.

When we returned to the Salesian mission we were rebuked by the director.

"Since you accept our hospitality, it is proper that you remain on this side of the river."

We didn't make a fuss about it, but as we walked away Arnie múttered to himself, "Isn't that a blast?" Jerry and I felt the same way.

The sisters, however, were as friendly as ever. It seemed that nothing in the world could disturb the gentle disposition of those graceful, gracious ladies.

Ladies? No, women. Despite their vows, despite my lifetime of thinking of nuns as a separate kind of human being, I saw in the sisters of Santa Izabel all the warmth and strength and beauty of womankind. They knew love, the kind of love that enabled them to endure the severest life in order to serve others. They knew motherhood. What care and understanding did any mother give her child that the sisters did not lavish on two hundred children?

After the sophisticated girls of New York, the painted women of Manaus, and the raucous harridans of the Rio Negro settlements, their fine, pale faces framed in luminous white hoods reminded me that true beauty is only a reflection of deeper virtues.

They took us to meet the children. We were introduced to the girls during their afternoon *merinda,* or snack. From the youngest age group on up, the girls and boys were kept apart at all times. There were separate dormitories; the school and dining hall were partitioned off; they bathed in the river at different hours; and the boys took their specialized training in the machine and carpentry shops while the girls attended nursing classes in the Santa Caza.

The girls sang for us, and we sang for them. A stranger with a new song was as welcome as Santa Claus. Arnie clowned and made ferocious faces. He stroked his young beard diabolically and leered around the room as if looking for a victim. The little girls squealed with delicious fright.

Among the glowing brown faces I saw several that had what I believed were characteristic Waica features. They were small-boned and their skin was the color of coffee. They had round heads topped with perfectly straight black hair. Their faces were broad, their cheeks high and prominent, and their eyes were just a bit slanted. Their noses and chins were well shaped, and their lips were very expressive and perhaps a little fuller than those of the average European.

I found them lively and responsive. My guess was that they were the equal of other racial types in raw intelligence. Madre Irmã Emma Guidotto agreed with me. She said they were good learners. Why, then, I wondered, had they remained at such a primitive level of development?

One of the more interesting theories I had heard was that they were descended from a highly developed civilization that had been destroyed by disease or an enemy nation. If so, where were the ruins of their ancient culture? In the Venezuelan mountains to the north? To the west in Colombia? Somewhere nearby in these jungle highlands? This was the kind of mystery that drew scientists into the wilderness gripped by a low-pitched hysteria somewhat akin to gold fever.

Irmã Alice Zinato, the head nurse, sought us out and asked us to take along supplies for the Santa Caza at Uaupés.

I had become so engrossed in this wonderful Amazonian microcosm that the mention of Uaupés struck my ear like the sound of an alarm clock. It was growing late, and I had hardly spoken to the crew of my boat all day.

I found them lounging by the river in the quiet of late afternoon. The soft sunlight, the shimmering water, and the exhilarating cool air had put them in a heavy-lidded stupor. The piums had taken a holiday, and the diesel engine was still. A stately silence reigned over Tapurucuará like a benediction.

None of us felt like pushing on. The deadliest rapids of all northern Amazonas lay ahead of us. The Cachoeira Joana Boni, the Cachoeira Taubi, the Cachoeira Cocal, and other rapids, named and nameless, dotted the Rio Negro between Tapuru-cuará and Uaupés.

So dangerous was this stretch of river that in the old days, when the area was a link in the trade route between Colombia and Brazil, the traders coming down from the highlands chose to follow tiny streams to the headwaters of the Rio Iá and down the Rio Cauaburi to the Rio Negro, right within range of the poison-tipped arrows of the Waica Indians, just to avoid those terrible rapids.

Still we chose the black river to white linen that night. I didn't want to be sidetracked before reaching Uaupés. There, at the last major settlement on the Rio Negro, I would complete my film record of the river journey and lay my plans for the latter part of the expedition.

The captain said it would be wise to get started immediately, for the next sixty to seventy miles of river could be negotiated by night. After that we would need daylight to make it through the "white water."

Arnie and Jerry climbed aboard reluctantly. We shoved off without ceremony, and the *Waupes* headed straight into the equatorial sunset. On both banks we saw tiny caboclo communi-ties made up of huts as shabby as any on the river. The inhabitants survived by collecting jute, Brazil nuts, and animal skins, and by tending their little *balata* plantations and selling their produce at the nearby trading posts.

The last horizontal rays of the sun reddened the underbellies of the rain-swollen clouds and set the treetops afire. In the deep shadows at the water's edge we saw lanterns winking in the windows of palm-thatched shanties. The warm light and cool shadows put me in a nostalgic mood.

I thought of my home, a modest home on a tree-shaded street, with a collie puppy whining on a leash in the backyard and a light burning over the front door all night, blinking patiently through the maple leaves, waiting for the wanderer to come home.

six

RACE FOR LIFE

The crew lit the lanterns and Jerry started to putter around the stove. He had taken to overseeing our meals in the last few days, to make sure that after he got through rejecting the fish and anything else he didn't like there still would be something left worth eating. He taught himself to make a fine pot of coffee, and it was his idea to add condensed milk to the rice, which replaced the muddy taste of the water with a rich, sweet flavor.

We could feel the current trying to turn the boat around, but the captain held her true to her course. The river was getting narrower all the time. We could judge the approximate distance to shore by the lanterns. Some of them shone through the windows of huts, and others bobbed along on the heads of tappers making the rounds of their rubber trees.

We dropped off to sleep quickly, but several times during the night we were awakened by the violent rocking of the boat as we skirted a whirlpool or rammed a floating log. Somehow we never got accustomed to living on the boat. There was always one thing or another to rob us of sleep, make us uncomfortable or arouse our fears.

The Rio Teia branched off to our left as we came away from Tapurucuará. In the darkness we passed the mouth of the Marauiá to our right, the doorway to Padre Antônio's jungle parish. Then the unexplored Rio Abuera, which ran parallel to the Marauiá, and the little village of Castanheiro—chestnut tree—a village named after a tree in a land named after a tree.

Toward dawn we passed the mouth of the Cauaburi and the island of Jerusalem, an outpost of the mission of Santa Izabel used as a supply depot for the traveling missionaries.

With daylight came the rain. The cabin was awash, and islands passed by like gray ghosts shrouded in sheets of water. In the midst of this deluge we came to the Cachoeira Joana Boni, a riot of white foam and leaping spray. The boat lurched and tipped. It seemed to have made up its mind to turn itself sideways to the current, which would have ended the expedition right there. We struggled through whirlpools that would easily have sucked a small dugout under.

In some spots the current was so strong that the boat stood dead still with the engine going full blast. The captain would jockey her to one side until he found slower water, and then the *Waupes* would start inching ahead again.

Old Cachaça was either a man of unbending habit or greedy beyond belief. With all his problems of navigation he still insisted on making numerous stops. We were not inclined to argue with him. Our lives were in his hands.

More islands, more rain, more rapids, and we finally stopped at a tiny settlement for lunch. The rain had let up, so we went ashore to walk around in the mud and stretch our legs. A caboclo woman came up to us and looked from one to the other, asking, *"Doutor? Doutor?"* I knew I had another medical case on my hands.

I fetched my medical kit from the boat and we all followed the woman to her shack.

The moment we walked through the doorway the stench of putrefaction assaulted our nostrils. It emanated from a little girl lying very still in a hammock. I took one look at her and wanted to run out. A blue-black substance was oozing from between her lips. She didn't seem to take notice of our entrance.

I pieced together the story of what had happened. An itinerant dentist had pulled two teeth and left the girl hemorrhaging. She had been losing blood for three days, and was unable to eat. Between loss of blood, infection, and lack of nutrition, she seemed just about ready to die.

I turned to the others, who knew by now what our position would be if we undertook to treat her, and failed.

"What do you think?"

"Forget it," Arnie said. "She's as good as dead already." He couldn't look at the mother as he spoke. She didn't understand what we were saying, but from the way she hung on our words I surmised that she thought we were discussing the girl's care, not her abandonment.

I asked Jerry, "How about you?"

"I'll go along with whatever you decide."

Arnie guessed that I had decided to take a chance. "That makes one-and-a-half against one-and-a-half," he commented wryly.

"I think it's two-and-a-half against one-and-a-half," I replied, nodding toward the mother. Just then another girl came in and put her arm around the woman's waist.

"The odds keep going up. Okay, suit yourself, but I don't want any part of it. I'm no *'doutor,'*" and he ducked out of the hut.

I forced myself to clean up her mouth a little with wet gauze. Then I sent everyone out of the room but Jerry so that I could give her a shot of penicillin without getting into an argument with the family. Meanwhile, Jerry was preparing hot saltwater. Both of us were gagging from the smell in the room.

The saltwater was supposed to stop the bleeding, but it didn't. The only thing I could think of was sulfanilamide powder, which was not supposed to be used orally, but at this stage I had nothing to lose by trying. It was too late to turn back anyway. I put the powder on a wad of gauze and packed it into the open wound where the teeth had been pulled. I made her close her mouth on the gauze so she wouldn't swallow it.

In fifteen minutes the bleeding stopped.

Now the job was to keep her alive. The thing she needed most was a transfusion. The only place where she could get one was Uaupés, so I spoke to the captain and asked him how long it would take us to get there. He said about a day and a half, perhaps two days.

"And what if we went full speed, right through the night?"

He shrugged, *"Amanhã."* Tomorrow.

We carried the girl as gently as we could to the boat and set her down carefully in a hammock. She could hardly open her eyes. The mother and sister asked to come along. I was happy to have them; if the worst happened, I wanted them to see for themselves that we had done our best.

Once again it worked out that we would not come to any rapids until the following morning, but there was still considerable danger. The fast current drove logs downstream like battering rams. There were also rocks here and there just beneath the surface of the swollen river.

During the night I got the girl to take some condensed milk mixed with warm water. She had to drink it through a straw. Every time she dozed off I checked her pulse. The pounding of my heart almost drowned it out. When she awoke for a few minutes I gave her more milk. She took about three cans of condensed milk that way through the night. Jerry spelled me occasionally. Arnie looked like he wanted back in, but we didn't ask him.

Eventually I dozed off with the roar of the engine in my ears, wondering whether the girl would be alive when I awoke.

In the morning I found her sleeping peacefully. I thanked heaven, and looked for things to keep me busy until she opened her eyes. After some hot coffee and hardtack I exercised a little, fed Suzy, made some entries in my log, and took some photographs of the shoreline. Along that portion of the river the banks were covered with dense undergrowth, and where there was no foliage there was heavy moss like green velvet covering the earth, rocks, and lower portions of the trees.

At about ten o'clock I went to look in on our patient, and was shocked to find her awake and sitting up. I felt proud of Jerry and myself for helping God perform a miracle.

We fed the girl coffee and milk, and I repacked the wound with clean gauze. She had improved so remarkably that it looked like she might not need a transfusion. All the same, we kept the boat going at full speed, and that morning we made no stops at all.

There wasn't much conversation because it was almost impossible to be heard over the combined roar of the engine and the rapids. Otherwise, Jerry and I might have yielded to a petty inclination to rub salt into Arnie's wounded pride. I knew better than that. I knew that any two-against-one relationship could develop into quite a nasty situation among three men forced to spend so much time together. But it took a lot of restraint to keep my mouth shut.

Nevertheless, every remark and every movement seemed to betray our thoughts. Every time I moved toward the medical kit for any reason, Arnie looked away and Jerry looked at Arnie. Every time someone scored a bloody hit on a pium there was an ominous pause. I had a hard grain of rice stuck between my teeth that must have been planted there by the devil himself, but I refrained from picking at it. Instead, I worked at it with my tongue. I concentrated so hard that I didn't realize Arnie was staring at me. When I looked up and our eyes met, all three of us burst out laughing. We were buddies again.

The rain let loose at about two in the afternoon. It was a torrent, a rain to end all rains. We spent about an hour fretting about the downpour before the river gave us something more serious to worry about, the Cachoeira Taubi, the beginning of a two-mile stretch of rapids that were so frightening that I had to force myself to look.

There was nothing but turmoil as far ahead as we could see. The water churned, roared, spouted straight up into the air, threw flakes of foam about like a mad animal, gyrated in great, slick circles, tore at the earth and rocks, and galloped eastward at breakneck speed like the hordes of hell let loose upon the world.

I might say that we were at the mercy of nature, but in nature there is no mercy, only justice. Anyone fool enough to attempt those rapids deserved what he got—a watery death or the scare of his life.

The captain had made this trip countless times, but I could see

the veins standing out on his neck. The engine was always in full throttle, yet there were long moments, longer than at the previous rapids, when the boat just stood still and shuddered as if it would never leave the spot.

The last rapids were the Cachoeira Cocal and the Cachoeira San Gabriel, practically at the front door of the mission of San Gabriel at Uaupés. It was there that several missionaries had been drowned.

We could see people coming down to the banks as we catapulted through the last of the rapids. Someone must have been looking for us from the church steeple. All at once we found ourselves in calm water, and the roar of the rapids was just a whisper over our shoulders.

We had covered the two miles in about an hour. That meant that the boat, with its 135-horsepower engine, was held by the river to the speed of a middle-aged man taking a Sunday stroll.

After a few moments the crew began to talk again. I had been gripping the side of the boat so tightly that it hurt when I finally opened my hands.

About a dozen caboclos were waiting to help us beach the boat. We hopped out into ankle-deep water just to feel something solid under our feet. A moment later the gangplank was set into place and, to our amazement, the little girl came walking down under her own power.

The eyes of her mother and sister were brimming with tears. Whatever can be said of the caboclos, no one can claim that they do not love their children dearly. We cheered for the girl as she walked up the bank toward the hospital. I felt like crying myself.

The noise of our shouting carried up to the mission, and soon I saw a priest and some other people hurrying down to see what the commotion was all about. I wiped my eyes with my forearm just to make sure they were dry. After all, I was Fred Salazar, explorer, come to face the savage Indians of Brazil.

seven

BECALMED

~~~~~~

We escorted the girl to the Santa Caza, where a genuine *doutor*
was in charge. We told him the story of the last twenty-four hours
as he looked at her mouth. He complimented us on doing a fine
job. We could see for ourselves that the girl's big dark eyes were
full of life. She could not speak with her mouth full of instruments and cotton, but those eyes were laughing a conspiratorial
laugh. She seemed to be saying that we three had played a
wonderful joke on the doctor.

The girl's mother and sister remained outside to tell the local
citizens all about the miraculous recovery. From there the news
would spread like wildfire. That much we knew for certain. The
entire Rio Negro was one big back fence with caboclos gossiping
over it from one end to the other. What else did they have to do?
When they got to work on a story, they filled all the gaps
between the hard facts with the mortar of their imaginations.

Our reputation was in good hands. That is the other side of
the coin when you treat a sick caboclo. Heads, you're a hero;
tails, you've had it.

Arnie and I went back to unload the boat, while Jerry looked
for help in transporting our tons of cargo up the slope to the
mission. I enjoyed the perspiration of labor after the oozing

sweat of anxiety. I kept thinking that the river would be nice and cool after a little exercise in the sun.

As we worked, it suddenly dawned on me that our voyage on the *Waupes* was over, and that our alcoholic, eccentric captain had delivered us safely to our destination. In addition to the remainder of our fare, we owed him a debt of gratitude.

Looking back, I could see how my feelings about him had changed from suspicion and disgust to trust and respect in only eleven days. And that was another thing to think about. Eleven days. The motorista knew what he was talking about when he said the trip might take fifteen days. If not for the girl it would have taken a minimum of twelve, and that was without any serious motor trouble.

Ruey was right after all. You simply can't force a Brazilian to hurry.

My reverie was interrupted by the sound of a truck lurching down the hill. Now what in the world is a truck doing here? I asked myself. As far as I could see, there wasn't a single road in Uaupés worthy of the name.

The vehicle turned out to be the possession of a Dom José Gonçalves, a resident of Uaupés and owner of a business monopoly that dominated the entire upper Rio Negro. He had entertained hopes at one time of building a road somewhere in the area, or of getting the government to build one for him. Since the road did not materialize, the truck remained at Uaupés to test Gonçalves' ingenuity at thinking up ways to use it.

The caboclo who drove the truck must have harbored an ambition to someday get up enough speed to drive straight across the river. He raced down the hill as if that day were the day. The truck came to a stop sliding sideways in the direction of the water, with the tires churning up mud.

We loaded the truck and took our supplies to the mission. The director, Padre João, made a room available for storage, then invited us to eat as soon as we were done unloading. Needless to say, that did not take long. Anything he put on the table would have been a feast after the flybait we had been eating on the boat.

The dinner surpassed our most gluttonous dreams—meat, fruit, properly cooked rice, and coffee. Lots of everything. We reeled away from the table short of breath.

In the evening we asked Padre João about a boat, fully confident that he had been informed of our needs by Padre Stefan. But the director started to talk about Dom José, as if he thought we were planning to hire another commercial boat like the *Waupes*. I got a sinking feeling in the pit of my stomach; we had come all those hundreds of slow, miserable miles to find out that our plans had fallen through—Padre Stefan had not written ahead.

"Up the creek without a canoe," Arnie cracked. Leave it to him to make a joke out of everything.

But when we got to talking among ourselves, the sinking feeling lifted. While the mission wasn't prepared to supply us with transportation, that didn't mean none was available. We could work out a new plan without giving up our ultimate objective.

For example, we could take small dugouts or go overland in the direction of Colombia. We could photograph the tribes in that area, then work our way back down the Rio Negro, stopping off at Tapurucuará or any other place that gave us access to the interior where we could contact the Waica.

So the next day was one of busy preparation. The mission bells rang at 5:00 A.M., signaling that mass would begin in half an hour. Although our bones still ached from the banging around we took aboard the *Waupes,* we forced ourselves to get right out of bed. The luxury of awakening in a bedroom put us in high spirits.

"A hot shower! *Magnifico!*"

"Something's wrong: the room doesn't rock."

"I feel stuffy. Open a window and let in some water."

We ate our breakfast in the same mood. The meal consisted of strong coffee, the first soft bread we had seen since Manaus, and that rarest of luxuries, fruit jam. Jerry kept saying, "Pass the jam," even when it was right in front of him.

The better part of that day was spent splitting up our supplies and recrating the food and equipment that we would take with us.

That evening we studied our maps and got as much information as we could about the Indians in the area. One of the mission padres was considered the leading authority on those Indians, having studied them for twenty-five years. He was writing a book on one of the tribes, called the Tucanos, near the Colombian border.

The following day dawned bright and cold and clear, so I decided to shoot some motion-picture footage. I got out of bed with my teeth chattering, washed and dressed quickly, and hurried to breakfast. I was still at the table when a gust of wind swept through Uaupés, heralding another torrential downpour.

That was when we began to lose our momentum. It always seemed to happen that way on an expedition. You're going along according to plan, collecting specimens, shooting footage, covering ground; then something happens. It could be illness or money trouble or just having too good a time, as in Manaus, and suddenly you're standing still.

My partners and I killed the afternoon playing games with the children, talking about home, and singing songs. About two in the afternoon the rain abated and we set up the cameras. We got some good shots of the rapids. Then the children began to swarm around and get in the way, so we wound up taking their pictures. The lovable little scamps kept us busy for nearly two hours, and then the rain chased us indoors.

It wasn't until evening that we got around to asking the director again about a boat, any little boat that we could have for a few days. He wanted to know where we planned to go. We pointed out a spot on the map where there were supposed to be Indians. It was the Cachoeira Pari near the Colombian border, the last navigable point on the Rio Tiquié, a tributary of the Rio Uaupés, which fed into the Rio Negro not far from the mission. The director put us off. He said he would let us know the next day.

The word is *amanhã*. According to the dictionary, it means "tomorrow." But on the Rio Negro they don't read dictionaries, magazines, newspapers, or even calendars. That was the first of

many times that we were to hear *amanhã* at Uaupés. It seldom
meant tomorrow.

Amanhã came and so did the director. His polite way of telling
us that he had no boat was to announce the imminent arrival of
an Air Force Catalina. That is what I call changing the subject on
a grand scale. He asked if any of us cared to hitch a ride back to
Manaus. I suspected that he wanted all of us to hitch a ride back
to Manaus, but I played innocent.

However, as long as we were going to be stuck there for a
while, I figured it wouldn't be a bad idea for one of us to go back
for some things we needed and to pick up the mail. Jerry was the
likely choice because he loved to bargain with the Brazilians and
take advantage of the soaring black market in U.S. dollars.

According to the director, Jerry could return on another Air
Force flight on Sunday, four days later. By that time I hoped to
have something worked out for the next leg of our expedition.
The plane took off under a direct sun that beat down so hard
that it seemed to pin the huge gray wings to the shimmering
water like a moth mounted on a silver platter. We watched the
lumbering craft lift itself off the river and swing around in the
direction of Manaus. In three hours Jerry would be walking on
paved streets.

The plane that took Jerry away deposited an Air Force ser-
geant named Raymond Becerria, who came to stay a while at
San Gabriel for some obscure reason. We took to each other
immediately.

While Raymond went about his business that morning, I decided to give Arnie a taste of what a jungle expedition was all
about. We took some heavy gloves, ropes, poles, and cages and
headed into a wooded area that looked like good reptile country.
We wore our boots.

We got a pretty good haul of snakes and lizards, and Arnie got
a good look at the jungle from the inside. He was amazed at how
dark and cool and quiet it was. He said it was like walking into a
movie on a summer day. But how much more like a cathedral
was that living cavern bathed in eternal green twilight.

The sunlight stunned us when we emerged. We headed back

to the mission to take a dip in the river. Our specimens were left writhing in a reed cage in the coolest spot we could find. We put on our trunks and headed for water.

That was Coney Island day for us. We wound up with terrific cases of sunburn. Odd as it seems, that was our first sustained exposure to the sun in all our time on the river. The rain and insects kept us under wraps a good part of the time. At other times, particularly mornings, we needed our clothes to keep warm. A strange kind of equatorial jungle, this.

The sunburn robbed us of sleep that night. Or was it that old itch to get started again? Probably both.

"No loafing today, old man," I told Arnie in the morning. "Today we break out the rifles and we hunt."

"Who's arguing? I'm bored stiff around here."

We rounded up Raymond, who was game for anything, and together we went into the jungles behind the mission. I had hopes that we would bag something big, like a jaguar, but we walked half the morning without seeing anything bigger than a macaw.

We came to a small Indian farm, where we rested and quenched our thirst. The woman of the house gave us some cassava bread. Raymond asked the farmer if there was much game in the area. He said that game was very scarce except for monkeys.

After tracking for another hour without success, we decided to head back to the mission. It looked as if all the game in the area had been killed or frightened off by the Indian hunters.

I saw the pattern here that I had seen at Santa Izabel. The Indians were losing their ability to live off the jungle and were becoming dependent upon the mission. Whether they realized it or not, the Indians, when they lived as nomads, did pretty much what a good farmer does when he rotates his crops. They gave nature time to replace what man had taken away. In a hunted-out jungle, there isn't even the beginning of a new generation of animals.

Fish got to swim, birds got to fly, and guns got to shoot. Walking all day with loaded rifles was a strain on our trigger fingers, so we fired off several rounds and called it target practice. With that out of our system, we headed back to the mission for lunch. If the Indians couldn't live off the jungle, how could we?

Lunch carried us over the midpoint of the day and from there we coasted downhill toward evening. That is the way a day can sift through your fingers when you're becalmed in the tropics. In the words of O. Henry, we had eaten of the lotus.

While we were marking time, a rare opportunity came our way by courtesy of Raymond and the Brazilian Air Force. One morning he told us that a Catalina would touch down at Uaupés and then continue on to Taraquá.

"If you want to come along, I promise you a surprise."

"What kind of surprise?"

"Are you interested in the Waica?"

"Definitely."

"Then take a ride with me. This will fascinate you."

We didn't need much convincing, since there wasn't anything at Uaupés worth staying for.

Raymond knew his way around the little mission town of Taraquá pretty well. After greeting a few friends he took us directly to a hut on the outskirts of the settlement. While we were walking he told us what was in store.

"Doña Helena."

"Who is Doña Helena?"

"She is a white woman who was captured by the Waica when she was a little girl. She became the property of a chief, who made her his wife and had several children by her. Later she was captured by another chief, who also made her his wife, and again she had a family. Then once again she was captured. In that way she lived as a Waica captive for more than twenty years, moving from village to village, from the Cauaburí to the Demeni to the Araçá.

"She is believed to have had fifteen children in all, several of which have become chiefs. The hostile Waica chief who is causing all the trouble with his shotgun in the Rio Araçá area is supposed to be her son."

I asked Raymond how the woman had found her way to Taraquá.

"She eventually convinced one of the Indians to run away with her. I am not too clear about that, but perhaps she will tell you. She has been living here for about five years and has learned to speak Portuguese again. I will introduce you to her."

Doña Helena showed every bit of the suffering she had endured during her captivity. I have seldom in my life seen a face so expressive of weariness. She spoke very little, and sat silent when we asked her questions about her life with the Indians. Realizing that our interrogation was stirring up painful memories, we cut our visit short and bade her a courteous farewell.

All the warnings of Dr. Galvão, the *O Jornal* reporter, and the SPI agent were reawakened in my mind. I had always been prepared for the possibility of injury or even death, but the thought of an imprisonment like Doña Helena's made my legs feel weak.

We returned with the Catalina to Uaupés, and resumed our wait where we had left off.

At least we got to know Uaupés a little better.

The town itself was shabby. Dom José's house was the nicest of all, and still it was little more than a wooden shack surrounded by palm trees. The "Dom" before his name, it must be said, was a title of respect. Gonçalves was prefect of the upper Rio Negro as well as a *magnata,* a tycoon. He was a big man physically, too, and had sired a big family that lived a life of comparative luxury in his rambling house.

Gonçalves' store was nearby. We got the impression that the staple of his business was cheap whiskey. There were always a few men standing around or sitting on the floor with drinks in their hands. Gonçalves made his big sale when a rubber tapper came in to trade the yield of a couple of months' work for supplies, tools, and trinkets.

His trading posts in the hinterlands did a thriving business in rubber, jute, skins, nuts, and other produce, and his little fleet of *lanchas* was kept busy taking new trading goods to the outposts and bringing the jungle products back to his headquarters at Uaupés. From there Gonçalves' big boat made regular trips to the market in Manaus. That, in brief, was Dom José's mercantile empire.

We asked Gonçalves if any of his boats were for rent. He told us that the big boat, the only one that could be trusted with a heavy cargo in fast water, was on one of its regular trips to Manaus. There was no telling when it would return.

He was somewhat of an agrarian, too, this Dom José. His cows roamed free around Uaupés like the sacred cows of India. I wondered how he had succeeded where the padres of Santa Izabel had failed.

The mission was consideraly more impressive than the town. All the buildings were made of brick, stone, and tile, and all of them faced onto an enclosed courtyard. Most of the labor that went into the construction of the mission was supplied by converted Indians and caboclos who were trained in the manual arts by the padres. The missionaries, no strangers to toil, did their share of the work, too.

Typical of mission settlements, the focal point of San Gabriel was the graceful white church steeple. The surrounding area was farmland, and behind that was the jungle.

Like Dom José, the director of the Salesian mission was at the hub of an organization that had outposts on nearby rivers and a small fleet of boats to hold the operation together. The two enterprises, the ecclesiastical and the temporal, sometimes worked at cross-purposes, but on the whole they coexisted nicely.

For the activities of the next day, Saturday, I lowered my sights from jaguars to insects. I knew I could find plenty of those. Among the trees just out of sight of the settlement we spent about three hours taking pictures of hundreds of varieties of spiders, moths, butterflies, wasps, bees, beetles, and other tiny creatures in which the area abounded. Their colors were magnificent, comparable to those of tropical fish.

Their sounds also were strange. There was one beetle that emitted an ear-piercing whistle that lasted for minutes at a time.

We made it back in time for lunch. At the table, Arnie dropped a remark about something I had noticed myself, that the food was getting a little worse each day. Either the mission pantry was not as well stocked as we had supposed, or we were overstaying our welcome. We didn't ask which and nobody told us. I told Arnie, "What the heck, they have a couple of hundred kids to feed."

Lizard collecting was the after-lunch activity. The lizards

seemed harmless enough, but they made a castanet sound like that of a rattlesnake. When we tired of that we washed off the dust and lizard stains in the Rio Negro and went back to the room for a nap. That is one of the later stages of lotus-eating.

In the hammock, swinging cool and comfortable, I told myself that tomorrow would be different. Tomorrow the plane would bring Jerry back and we would get rolling again. Tomorrow. *Amanhã.* I was beginning to use the word myself.

The sound of the church choir woke us the next morning. I attended mass. If my mother could only have seen me. When you're living at a mission, going to church seems like the most natural thing in the world. It's almost literally like rolling out of bed. In New York, to get to church you have to pass movie houses, friends' houses, and bars, and if you walk slowly and it gets to be one o'clock, the bars open and your friends are hanging around, and what the heck.

It being Sunday, all work in the village stopped. The change is immediately noticeable to someone who has spent years in Brazil, if he studies the situation carefully.

We lounged around waiting for the Air Force plane from Manaus. To pass the time we played games with Suzy, oiled our rifles, and talked, and Arnie whanged away at the guitar.

The distant roar of the Catalina's twin engines brought us to our feet. Yippee! Here comes Jerry and here comes transportation. When the plane leaves tomorrow we can hitch a ride back to Tapurucuará. That solves everything, we thought.

But Jerry was not aboard. We asked the pilot what had happened to our friend, but he didn't know what we were talking about. I was worried.

Arnie and I talked things over. It didn't make sense to wait in Uaupés forever. Out best bet was to take advantage of the transportation that was available. We could either get word to Jerry that we had moved on to Tapurucuará, or he would find out where we were when he returned to Uaupés. He could catch up with us with little trouble, since he wouldn't be loaded down with supplies. We convinced each other that we were doing the right thing.

"Okay. That's it. We won't worry about Jerry. He must be in Manaus; there haven't been any plane crashes."

"Jerry can take care of himself."

"Yeah, he knows how to keep his nose clean."

And so on. It wasn't easy.

We went to bed early in order to be up early, and the mosquitoes were waiting for us. We were awake half the night, itching, scratching, and swearing that we would never go on another expedition as long as we lived.

Our hides were a mess in the morning. We were still flaking from sunburn, and now there were red welts on top of that. Arnie spoke for both of us as we sat down to our meager breakfast, "Let's get the hell out of here."

But when we went down to the river, the Catalina was already revving its motors. We climbed aboard to talk to the captain. He apologized, explaining that the plane was full.

"With your cargo aboard, senhores, my plane could not get off the river. *Perdão.*"

"So's your mother," Arnie muttered bitterly.

The flying boat roared off with our latest hopes and left us in silence and in the doldrums. Alternating anticipation and disappointment had worn out our ability to rebound. We spent the rest of the day in our hammocks, staring at the ceiling and trying to figure a way to get out of Uaupés. We weren't even thinking any longer of going further up the Rio Negro. We had our minds set on Tapurucuará. For the moment, that was home.

When we asked that day about boat transportation, no one even said *amanhã.* I don't think they liked the way we reacted to the sound of the word. They just said a boat would be coming along soon, in as reassuring a tone of voice as they could manage.

So just for spite a boat showed up the next day.

It was Gonçalves' boat with its payload from Manaus. To our surprise, there were also two young foreigners aboard, an Italian and a Frenchman.

eight

THE ADVENTURERS

~~~~~~

Armand and Guilio were adventurers, not explorers. I make this distinction because in Indian country the difference can be critical. To an adventurer, an expedition is a picnic. Everything is funny, nothing is serious.

Guilio spoke English, so he did the talking for both of them, but Armand did the thinking. I sometimes got the uncomfortable feeling that I was talking to a dummy.

And they smiled. Oh, how they smiled! All the sunny skies of Cannes and blue waters of Capri were in those smiles. Like Greek masks, they had an existence of their own, independent of the smooth young faces that wore them.

Apparently they were promised a look at the "real" hinterlands, unfrequented by foreigners, because they showed genuine disappointment to see us there. I think they felt a little better when they learned we were explorers. That made us belong, somehow. In fact, they immediately volunteered to join the expedition. I talked it over with Arnie, but the final decision had to be mine. I said okay.

Both Europeans spoke Portuguese. That was their main value to the expedition. That, plus two extra pairs of hands to drag dugouts over rapids, chop trees for temporary camps, and share other heavy duties. The logistics of a jungle expedition are such that picking up two additional members so close to your destination is a very fortunate accident.

I figured it this way. All the cost and trouble of bringing them into the area was already taken care of. That was the expensive part. From here on in it would cost us a little in food, but that was all. It seemed well worth it. But you can figure and figure, and still not know what little hidden minus will come along to cancel out all the big pluses.

For the moment we were all in good spirits. There was a boat in Uaupés; that was the important thing. All we had to do was work out a deal with Gonçalves. As we walked up the hill to his store I said to myself, Please don't tell us *amanhã*, even if you mean it.

He didn't. He said, *"Sabado ou Domingo,"* Saturday or Sunday. Today was Tuesday. *Amanhã* was getting further away all the time.

Well, we could kill a few days getting to know the new members of our expedition and breaking them in to the jungle. In the back of my mind was the thought, even then, that things might not work out with them. The delay gave me time to find out if they were going to be troublesome. If so, I could hand them their walking papers before we got into Indian country.

Both had impressive credentials. Armand was an engineering student at the University of Paris. Guilio was a physics student at the University of Rome. They were both on six-month holidays. Gonçalves' boat had picked them up at Tapurucuará, where an Air Force plane had deposited them. They had been living in São Paulo and other cities in the south, and were the guests of the governor on this little excursion.

They carried newspaper clippings about themselves from various Brazilian newspapers. I was impressed. Not because I thought they were celebrities, but because I knew they were moving in pretty high circles. In Brazil, a call from a high muckamuck will bring a newspaper reporter on the double, even if only to interview two visiting foreign students. As far as I could see, there is no other way their visit could have caused a ripple in the newspapers. Still, it seemed a little childish for two educated men in their twenties to flash their press notices like that.

Armand and Guilio made their presence felt right away. They stopped people to talk to them in Portuguese. The point they seemed to be making, without saying it, was, "We are your kind; we are your friends." The poorer and shabbier the caboclo, the more they tried to ingratiate themselves with him.

They took a walk along the river to the Fortaleza, where ancient cannons lay rusting at the water's edge. Portugal's colonial army had placed them there to blockade the river against Spaniards coming down from Colombia. I wondered if the adventurers were disappointed that the Conquistadors had been to Uaupés before them.

We had the pleasure of their company that evening. And it was a pleasure. Singing and joking together established a certain camaraderie. I really hoped things would work out. They knew that I was the leader of the expedition, but I wasn't certain that they had accepted me as their leader.

We got them up early the next morning. It had been raining steadily all night. The ground was muddy in some places and spongy in others. Everything was soaked. The trees dripped, and the rainwater was draining off into the river in little rivulets that had formed overnight. In all, it was an ideal day to initiate the European scholars to the Brazilian jungle.

Arnie and I gave them a jolt when we got right up from the table after breakfast and told them we were ready to go hunting. Guilio passed the message along to Armand, who expressed annoyance. When Guilio translated Armand's answer, I noticed that he even mimicked his grimace.

"It is raining. We will wait until later. Okay?"

The "Okay?" was his own idea. I could see for myself that Armand wasn't asking. He was telling. Poor Guilio. He felt he had to placate everybody.

I was firm. "It will be raining later, too. This is the rainy season. If you can't stand the rain you might as well forget about the expedition."

Guilio translated.

There was a long pause. Armand studied his cigarette. He knew I had put him on the spot. Either he backed out of the expedition and lost face or he came along with me as boss. Finally he gave his answer to our uncomfortable intermediary. As he spoke he made a little gesture in our direction as if to say, "Let them run along."

Guilio said, "You go and get ready. We will be along shortly."

Well done! Armand had turned the tables. Now it was we who were at his command. If we went, we were obeying his order. If we stayed, we were abandoning our plans, which was what he really wanted. But I wasn't finished.

"I want you both to be ready in five minutes. If not, we go without you." I signaled Arnie and we walked out before the Frenchman had a chance to reply.

On the way up to the room Arnie asked, "Is that the way it's going to be with those guys?"

"I don't think so. Frenchie just has to learn who's boss."

Even though I had no expectation of coming across big game, I decided to take the rifles. Imagine the impression we would have made on the Europeans coming down the stairs with nets and lizard cages. They would have had a good laugh, and that would have been the end of it.

They were waiting for us downstairs wearing ponchos and rain hats. I was surprised to see Guilio playing with a revolver. It never occurred to me that those two might be armed. Armand must have instructed him to have the pistol out when we came down, just to show us we weren't dealing with children.

I could tell that Arnie didn't like the whole business—the subtle innuendoes, the jockeying for position. But I was having a little wicked pleasure. The ace in the hole was mine. I had the equipment, the experience and, with Jerry, the numerical advantage. No matter what Armand pulled, we would go through with the expedition as planned. He could come along on my terms or not at all.

So off we went in a steady downpour, carrying machetes and Winchesters. We were walking only a short time when the rain stopped. That made it perfect. We were soaking wet, and the sun came out to make everything sticky. I kept them going under those conditions for about two hours.

When I called a halt, Armand and Guilio started to look around for a dry place to sit down. I told them we weren't stopping to rest, but to cut down some trees with our machetes, just as if we were on an overland expedition.

I said to Guilio, "Tell Armand that in the jungle you don't rest until you've put up your camp for the night."

While we were hacking away, Arnie whispered, "You never told me that before."

"I never thought of it before," I whispered back.

The adventurers showed a lot of grit. I'll concede that much. They stayed with the chopping for an hour.

"That's enough," I called out, inspecting the wood that the Europeans had cut. "We've got enough now for a base camp, but you've got to learn to cut the right lengths. But don't worry, you'll learn," and I started walking again. Guilio didn't bother telling Armand what I said. He just followed, and Armand fell in behind him.

We came to a stream, and I saw a dugout on the bank, either abandoned or left there temporarily by an Indian. I decided to borrow it, to see if we could spot any game along the stream. We had no luck at all. In weather like that, animals don't have to come down to the stream to drink.

We paddled back to where we had found the dugout and beached it; then we returned by foot to the mission. That evening everyone was friendly. We talked, sang, and played the guitar. I ended it early so I could hit the hay. Breaking in the adventurers was tiring work.

Armand and Guilio were up before us the next morning. They came into our room wearing their smiles and exuding Continental charm. I told myself, Well, that settles it; they really want to come along. I smiled back.

Now that we were friends, I introduced them to the less glamorous aspects of exploring. I brought out the reptile paraphernalia and we went lizard hunting. Crossing the quadrangle that passed for Uaupés' town square, we ran into Gonçalves. Seeing us reminded him of something. He stopped and fished a piece of paper out of his pocket. It was a penciled note addressed to me:

"Stuck in Manaus. Lucky to be alive. Will tell you about it when I see you. Wait for me. Jerry"

A note from Jerry. Where did it come from?

"Guilio, ask him where he got this."

"*O telégrafo,*" Dom José said, pointing to a wooden shack.

"A telegraph office!" Arnie exclaimed. "Why didn't they tell us that before?"

Obviously because we didn't ask. But now that we knew, we were back in business. We sent a message to the telegrapher in Manaus, in case Jerry came around to check, and another note to Jerry in care of Ruey. Both were the same:

"Leaving for Tapurucuará Sunday. If you can't get to Uaupés before, then meet us there."

I asked Arnie, "What's today?"

"Thursday the fourteenth."

"Eleven days. That's how long it took us to get here and that's how long we've been sitting here. Let's keep bugging Gonçalves about the boat. If we don't we might stay here forever."

Hearing from Jerry was a relief. I knew when I read the telegram that I had never really felt right about leaving Uaupés without him. I felt better about it now.

We whiled away the next two days sorting out our supplies and figuring out how long our staples would last in the jungle with five mouths to feed. I wasn't kidding myself that we could supplement our supplies with game. If Waica country were anything like the area around Uaupés, we wouldn't be able to live off the land for more than a day.

If Gonçalves got fed up with our questions he didn't show it. We kept asking him when the boat would be ready, when the next Air Force plane was due, and whether there had been any telegrams. He didn't vary his answer once during the entire two days:

"No telegram today; no boat before Sunday; no plane before Monday."

Guilio dutifully translated the report. Sometimes Armand acted sullen toward him, as if he resented his working for us. When he was in one of those moods, Guilio got very upset and apologetic. We began to wonder what kind of hold Armand had over him.

Other than observing their strange relationship, I didn't learn much more about them at Uaupés. They spoke to each other in French, so I couldn't pick up much of what they were saying. Armand was generally taciturn and Guilio was solicitous, and both were quite obviously on their good behavior.

Sunday finally rolled around. I was happy to hear the choir and the bells. Those sounds meant farewell to Uaupés. Arnie sang as he dressed:

"I hate to see us go, I hate to see us go, I hope to heck we never come back, I hate to see us go."

The choir answered, "Aa-amen."

We laughed. Arnie grabbed the guitar.

"Let's see if we can do that again. He listened for the next Amen and headed it off with a fast "I-hope-to-heck-we-never-come-back-I-hate-to-see-us-go."

"Aa-amen."

Applause.

We loaded the truck and told the driver to take us down to the river. He spun the wheels, and the truck shot away down the hill. Part of the path to the river skirted the edge of a small cliff overlooking a pile of boulders. I closed my eyes and held tight to Suzy's leash.

That scare was followed by a shock, when I got my first close look at Gonçalves' boat. If that was the one he trusted, the others must all have been at the bottom of the river. It was full of leaks and had to be bailed out constantly. The power supply was an old steam engine. Speak of the Mississippi, that engine must have pushed the first sidewheeler past Memphis.

Old Gonçalves didn't miss a trick. The steam engine burned anything he put into it, so he didn't have to keep it fed with gasoline or diesel fuel. But what a risk to take! One day that old pufferbelly was going to blow a boatload of people to kingdom come.

The first good news I got was that Dom José himself was going to make the trip. That made me feel a little easier about the boat. The *magnata* liked himself too much to want to drown.

Armand liked himself a lot, too. Too much to strain himself helping load the cargo. I let him know that I noticed by telling him to watch our things while we went back to the mission to say good-bye. He shrugged as if to say he hadn't planned to go with us anyway.

Padre João gave us his blessings. When we bowed our heads we all noticed the same thing at the same time. The director was wearing a pair of shoes that Arnie had thrown away. At the time it was hard to keep from laughing, but in retrospect it was touching to think that the head of the mission practiced such stringent economy on himself, while extending so much generosity to others.

When we returned to the boat, Gonçalves and his crew were nowhere to be seen. An hour passed before he showed up, accompanied by about twenty people, mostly caboclos. Arnie remarked that he hoped all of them weren't coming along. He was joking, but those twenty turned out to be the crew.

Guilio asked one of the caboclos how long the trip to Tapurucuará would take. He held up five fingers. I winced. Five days on that noisy, leaky, stinking scow would make our first trip seem like a Dayline cruise up the Hudson. I was amazed that the Europeans would consent to go after having traveled on that boat once before.

We shoved off and headed into the rapids. I really didn't believe we would make it. The water came up inside the boat almost to the floorboards. "If we don't crack up we'll sink anyway!" I shouted to Arnie, pointing to the floor. He shook his head in wonder.

Going downstream through the rapids presented different problems from going up. And I would say the dangers were greater.

Coming upstream, the trick is to get up enough power to counter the force of the current. You either have it or you don't. In any event, you never move so quickly that you can't pick out the danger spots, if you know what to look for.

Heading downstream, the current pushes you so fast that you don't have time to look for anything. The pilot has to know the river or he is out of luck. And even though you have more speed than you need, you have to keep the engine going in order to control the boat. If the engine should cut out, the boat would become just another log in the river, and would smash to bits against the first boulder in its path.

Needless to say, we made it through the rapids a lot quicker than the first time.

We stopped at Mercês, just beyond the rapids and on the opposite side of the river from Uaupés. Mercês was a fairly important settlement, one that we had glimpsed in passing on our hasty upriver journey. Our presence—Arnie's and mine—caused quite a commotion. Our fame as healers had preceded us down the Rio Negro. We passed up the food from Dom José's commissary for the feast set for us by the caboclos.

We kept going until sunset, and tied up at a little landing where there were two smaller boats. These also belonged to Dom José, and would be hitched to the big boat when we pulled out in the morning. Gonçalves said we could move our cargo into one of the small boats and put up our hammocks there. We welcomed the opportunity to get out of the overcrowded steamer, but now we had new problems.

The worst problem was the smell. The boat had been used only for cargo until then. Think of what that cargo might have consisted of—animal skins, fish and raw rubber, among other things. We had to pull the tarpaulin off and air the boat out for half an hour before we could come near it.

Five days on this tub? We would surely go crazy. As darkness fell it started to rain again, just to make our misery complete.

We made many stops the next day, at a fair-sized settlement called Umarituba on the north bank and at many smaller villages. That was when we learned that our fame as doctors had spread up and down the entire river. I could picture the cabocla mother holding up the little girl and pointing to the empty space in her mouth as she told her hair-raising story.

They had a welcome prepared for us two miracle workers at every stop. The caboclos offered us pigs, turtles, and all kinds of other wonderful gifts and delicacies. We couldn't eat all the food, but the glory—ah, the glory—we did eat that up.

As for our European friends, they ate bitter gall. They didn't know what to make of this latest turn of events. When they spoke to the caboclos, I could tell by their gestures that they were brushing aside any references to our achievement.

But the stops were not for the purpose of letting the villagers honor us. Gonçalves was trading for hemp. I saw some of his transactions and learned how he got to be a rich man. At the same time I saw how the caboclos managed to stay poor.

As the sun descended behind us we tied up at a deserted cove. We shared Dom José's dinner—rice, beans, and salted meat. Captain Gonçalves must have belonged to the same maritime union as Captain Cachaça.

Dom José's oldest son, a slim, bright-looking boy of about eighteen, came to our rescue that night. He said that on the following morning he would be picking up another boat with an outboard motor. In that boat we could travel nonstop to Tapurucuará, and make it there before sunset. He asked if we would like to come along.

Would we! The expedition was unanimous on that one.

The next morning we had to decide what to take along in the *lancha* and what to leave in the care of Gonçalves and his seedy-looking associates. We decided to take our most valuable possessions—guns, cameras, and the like—and everything else that was packed small. We took a shrewd guess that they wouldn't steal anything big, because it couldn't be hidden anywhere on the big boat. The most they might do is trade off something at one of the villages. But then we would be waiting at Tapurucuará, and they would have a hard time explaining the absence of a large crate or drum.

The speedy outboard skimmed down the middle of the Rio Negro with young Gonçalves at the controls and a silent little

Indian boy at his side. The rest of us—Armand, Guilio, Arnie, and I—were sprawled out with our shirts off, enjoying the breeze and soaking up the sun.

We stopped at a village at midday and took a cool dip. Our lunch, the first meal since the night before, consisted of biscuits, farinha, and sardines.

We all dozed comfortably as the boat sped toward Tapu-rucuará, all except the young captain, who remained steadfastly at the tiller.

At about five thirty we came into view of the mission of Santa Izabel, a vision that remains fixed in my memory as one of the most welcome sights of the entire journey.

Several Indian boys ran down to the water to help us unload. The director, the priests, the nuns, all of them were there to greet us, but no Jerry Falls.

nine

GOING TO JERUSALEM

∿∿∿∿∿∿∿∿∿∿∿∿∿∿∿∿∿∿∿∿∿∿∿∿

The boys formed a sort of bucket brigade to help us with our cargo up the hill to the mission. It was like a relay race. Each barefoot youngster ran his allotted distance up the slope, dropped his bundle, and dashed back for another load. Arnie and I kept the assembly line fed until the boat was empty. Meanwhile, Armand and Guilio strolled up the hill with their hands in their pockets.

The rain had stopped, and the insects were quiet in that magic moment of peace that holds the river spellbound at dusk. As we approached the mission, the diminished sound of boys' laughter coming up from the beach reminded me of evening on the campus of Coindre Hall. Brother Tom came out to meet us. He smiled with a compassion that embraced each of us singly and all of us together—the explorers, the adventurers, the Indian waifs dancing in the mud, and all God's creatures spinning out their allotted time under the red Brazilian sky.

"Welcome back, my young friends."

"Hi, Brother Tom. We decided to take you up on your offer, if it's still open. We'd like to stay for a while."

"What must you think of us, Fred? We have not changed our minds in these few days. The mission is your home."

"The padre-director wasn't too happy with us last time when we visited across the river."

"Then all the more reason to have you here, my boy. We wouldn't want you staying with the Protestants, now would we?" Brother Tom had a great ability to put us at ease. Moreover, he never condescended or made us feel that we owed him anything.

"Come, follow me. Have you eaten? There'll be a little something in the kitchen if you don't mind eating cold food."

The coffee was hot, and that made the meal just fine. Brother Tom sat down with us but didn't eat. He joined in the conversation, showing Armand the consideration of speaking to him in Portuguese. When we were finished, Brother Tom showed us to our rooms.

"There are nets over your beds because of the malaria. Be sure to use them. There's little enough of the fever left to go around without your taking some away with you. And be quiet, or you'll wake your friend."

"Jerry!" I shouted. "Is he here?"

Brother Tom rolled his eyes toward the ceiling in mock exasperation. "Now you've done it. I'll bet you've awakened the poor boy, and him so tired from traveling."

We rushed in to see Jerry. What a reunion! Brother Tom took Armand and Guilio to their room while we filled one another in on what had happened in the last twelve days.

Jerry's flight to Manaus was uneventful, except for some low-level acrobatics by the pilot. Once there, it didn't take him long to pick up our mail at the Hotel Amazonas and do the shopping. "Guess what! I got six hundred cruzeiros to the dollar. That's fifty more than the top price when we left. By the time we get back we'll be able to buy out the whole place."

His troubles began when he started looking for a return flight. "Every Air Force flight was full. I checked every day. I was almost ready to blow a bundle on a Pan Air ticket, but I decided to hold out. Finally I got a flight on one of the Catalinas, and it pancaked in the river just outside Manaus. They had to tow us back."

"We asked the pilot at Uaupés. He said there weren't any crashes," I said.

"I guess they don't count that as a crash. Nobody got hurt.

The crew didn't even get excited. It must happen all the time."

"Baloney," Arnie argued. "They were just as scared as you. You didn't expect them to bust out crying, did you?"

In a few minutes it seemed as if we had never been apart. Jerry was curious about Armand and Guilio, whom he had glimpsed through the bedroom door. He had an amazingly astute and suspicious mind. "I think they're Communists. They've got them all over the place in the East, you know, stirring up the plantation workers."

"They're going to have a tough time stirring things up over here," I answered. "Nobody cares about politics on the river."

"I still think they're Reds. Everything you told me sounds like Reds."

"Nah," Arnie interrupted, "they're probably queers. Guilio is Frenchie's girl friend."

"So what are they doing up here?" Jerry countered. "There's nothing special here for queers."

Arnie kept saying, "Look, you haven't met them yet. We have."

And so it went. My friends' voices were like a lullaby. The mosquito netting enveloped me like a cocoon, and I slept.

The following day Jerry was all for making up the time he had lost in Manaus, and he talked us into going hunting. He demonstrated his amazing marksmanship by picking off a brilliantly colored bird on a high branch with his .38.

Jerry took the bird back to the mission. For want of something better to do with it, he passed it through the partition to the girls' side of the mission school. To do so he had to use a device we called the jungle Automat. It was a big tin can set vertically into an opening in the partition. Part of the side was cut away, and there were nails in the top and bottom, so that the can could pivot. This ingenious contraption permitted objects to be exchanged without physical or visual contact. We heard giggles on the other side of the wall when the bird was passed through.

That night we were served something that looked like a big jelly roll. It was made of baked dough with diced meat inside. That was the disposition of Jerry's bird.

We fell in with the rhythm of mission life, and could sense the appeal of that life for the Indian children. There was a regularity of work, study, play, rest, and prayer. They were shielded from the ravages of nature by walls, windows, mosquito netting, and medication, and the meals were tasty and nourishing. In addition to the three regular meals, there was a midmorning *merinda* and a midafternoon *merinda*. The sisters seemed forever to be serving meals and snacks. I could see why many of the children were sorry to leave the mission when their time came to face the outside world.

Armand and Guilio became pleasant company during our stay at Tapurucuará. They showed an interest in our activities, although they did not always participate.

Our schedule included hunting, trapping, and fishing. The only large animals around the mission were sloths, and a few deer that showed up in the morning to munch manioc leaves on the mission farm. We set traps and caught quite a few birds, reptiles, and smaller rodents.

Fishing was not quite so good. We borrowed a dugout and looked around for a good spot, but the river was high and the big fish were hanging out on the bottom. Once in a while we found a school of dolphins on our tail, but we left them alone.

Gonçalves showed up after four days with our heavy cargo. Everything seemed to be in order. Dom José's caboclos were too drunk on *caxiri*, their homemade liquor, to care about stealing. Perhaps they regretted the lost opportunity when they sobered up.

Then the rain sealed us indoors. We saw no point in getting soaked just to wander around in that meager jungle, hunted out and picked clean as it was.

We caught up on old news from the collection of *Time* magazines that belonged to Brother Tom. After a while we just slept, all five of us, each in his own private limbo. Waiting had become a way of life.

But Brother Tom was a man of quiet purpose. In his quicksilver mind he had figured out a way for us to get started on our expedition without having to wait for one of the padres to return.

One afternoon he told us to prepare our things. The monthly

supply boat was due to arrive the following morning. We could hitch a ride to Jerusalem, where the boat would drop off supplies for Padre John. When the padre came down from the Cauaburi to pick up his supplies, we could return with him as far as his mission, then strike out into the jungle on our own: ". . . if you've a mind to," Brother Tom added casually, which was his way of minimizing his thoughtful assistance.

We fell immediately to work breaking down our supplies for the Cauaburi trip. Now, at last, we felt we were surely on our way. Armand and Guilio pitched in. They even allowed us to pool their belongings with ours to make the cargo more compact. One thing I remember doing was giving Guilio a carton of cigarettes out of the supplies Gonçalves had returned to us. This was in return for several packs I had borrowed during the last few days.

The supply boat appeared the next morning out of the mist, right on schedule. We watched the unloading and were astonished at the amount of food needed from the outside to sustain the mission for a month. We spoke with the captain, and the padre-director put in a word for us. It was agreed that the next morning when the boat pulled out we would be aboard.

We finished packing and tried to make the most of our luxuries during the last twenty-four hours at Santa Izabel. We stuffed ourselves with food and napped in the afternoon, but my mind was too full of plans to sleep soundly that night.

There was an incredible rain the next day, so heavy that a few miles from the mission the big supply boat had to lay over for several hours until the pilot could see well enough to steer. This was the first time any of our pilots had given quarter to the weather. Even Suzy couldn't escape. She crouched in a corner shivering, her fur sticking out all over in wet spikes.

We got started again late in the afternoon, and the same thing happened a second time. There was such a solid wall of rain that we could not see the shore at all, and on the surface of the river the separation between air and water became indistinct.

As miserable as we were, the accommodations were better than on our first journey upstream. The boat was bigger, permitting us to stretch our legs, and the vibrations of the motor were not so strong. After a while Suzy got her sea legs back, and prowled the vessel like an old salt.

The boat was unloading at the island of Jerusalem when I awoke early the next morning. We had to clamber over slippery rocks to remove our supplies. We got little help from the adventurers. They roosted on dry land while we struggled with boxes and sacks in water up to our knees.

The only inhabitants of Jerusalem were a caboclo named Eugenio Souza Tavares, known as the Old Man of the Cauaburi, his wife, his children, and a couple of billion piums and mosquitoes. Tavares worked for the missionaries, and the piums and mosquitoes worked for each other. The piums had the day shift and the mosquitoes the night.

The piums were just coming on duty when we landed, and they greeted us with all the appetite that a good night's sleep had given them.

Tavares showed us the hospitality due us as guests of the padre-director of Santa Izabel. He turned half of his house over to us. We took some of our supplies indoors and left the remainder against the side of the house, covered with tarpaulins. We hung our hammocks side by side on the sheltered porch and called it a bedroom. That was standard procedure for overnight visitors along the river; the host supplied the roof and the guest supplied the hammock.

Eugenio was polite but formal. He never volunteered information; he rarely smiled; and he seemed to worry about his children when they were near us. No doubt he developed a suspicious attitude toward strangers because of the kind of visitors that had come to Jerusalem over the years. We heard of trigger-happy prospectors in search of gold, and unscrupulous traders venturing beyond the mouth of the Cauaburi in search of new customers. At that time a German machinist, wanted for murder in Manaus, was said to be living somewhere on the river.

Most outsiders were potential murderers, for each man was his own law, and it was said that on the Rio Negro no white man had ever been convicted for killing an Indian. Whether that was true or not, most people believed it. Eugenio had good reason to keep his distance.

I felt that a gift was in order. For whether Eugenio worked for the mission or not, the house was his and he was putting us up. I gave him a machete, for which he thanked me graciously. Later I saw Armand hefting the machete critically and talking to the caboclo about it in Portuguese. I asked Guilio what it was all about, but he just shrugged.

That was as good as a translation. I knew Armand was telling Eugenio that the machete was no good. I sat there doing a slow burn while they talked. Finally I walked across the room, took the machete out of Armand's hand, and buried it with all my might in one of the heavy logs that supported the roof. An inferior blade would have shattered against the hard wood. I was satisfied that I had made my point, but a violent act like that only made the Tavares family fear me more.

Eugenio kept his back to me as he pried the machete out of the wood. Armand looked at me with raised eyebrows, very cool and superior. For the second time he had turned the tables on me, and I didn't like it.

Jerry had worked up quite a hatred for the Europeans in the few days he knew them. I could see what was on his mind by the way he unconsciously let his hand drop to the .38 at his side now and then. His confidence had increased considerably since we put Manaus behind us, and a certain aggressive quality was beginning to show itself. It had a lot to do with carrying a gun. That was the great leveler.

Routine is a great antidote for tension. There was too much to do for us to remain at one another's throats. For one thing, we had to eat. Jerry cooked a meal of coffee, rice, corned beef, and plantains for all of us.

While we were eating, itchy red spots began to develop on our arms. They were the first pium bites. It had taken a while for them to develop. I got out the alcohol and we doused ourselves with it. I felt it sting here and there where the bites were bleeding.

Arnie held out his left hand and said, "Hey, look at this." He

had so many pium bites that the whole hand was swollen and misshapen. I bathed it in alcohol and gave him a shot of penicillin.

Padre John's boat wasn't due for a couple of days, so we decided to explore the island. There wasn't much to explore. It was about two miles long and a half mile wide. Nothing much grew on it but typical Rio Negro flora—numerous varieties of trees whose upper branches were lost in a tangle of vines, and creepers and pungent blossoms carpeting the rocky ground. There were millions of the infernal insects—wasps and cicadas most prominent—and because of the insects a good number of small birds that thrived on them. We spotted several manakins, green on top and yellow underneath, with a little white crest. They were busy decimating the insect population. We wished them luck.

The river around the island was dotted with rocks. In the dry season that stretch of water was nothing but one big set of rapids. There was no reason in the world to put people on that desolate island except that it was only two hours from the mouth of the Cauaburi. If Eugenio's supply depot weren't there, Padre John would have had to make a two-day round trip to Tapurucuará in his little boat every time he needed supplies.

Eugenio used some of the provisions for his own needs, but he helped feed his family by setting fish traps all around the island and by raising chickens. We saw how little the Tavares family had to survive on, so we didn't invite ourselves to their table.

It was impossible to sleep that first evening at Jerusalem. The hungry mosquitoes were out in full force. We slapped at the whining sound around our ears and writhed in our hammocks until we saw that it wasn't going to do us any good. We took a stroll down to the river, and to our surprise there were no mosquitoes at the water's edge. Elated, we got our blankets and curled up on the flat boulders near the water. We slept about four hours that way until a cold drizzle woke us and forced us to return to the mosquito-infested house.

The next day was just another bleak day like any other in the rainy season. We sat around playing cards and listening for

Padre John's boat. During breaks in the rain we cleaned our equipment and did a little target shooting. The air was so damp that the silica gel we used to absorb the moisture in our packing crates had all turned pink. We emptied the bags of sandlike grains into a frying pan and cooked the moisture out to make them absorbent again.

While we were working, one of Eugenio's youngsters came running up with his toe bleeding badly. He had cut himself fooling with one of our hunting knives. I guessed that he had been playing "territory" the way he saw us do it, and had got his foot in the way when he threw the knife into the ground.

I sprinkled some sulfanilamide powder on the cut and wrapped the toe in gauze. Eugenio seemed pleased. That afternoon he invited Jerry to come with him on his rounds of the fish traps. That was his first overt act of friendliness. They returned later with enough fish to last several days. I was surprised to see Tavares deplete his fish traps like that, since the catch would have stayed alive in the water until he needed it. It may have been his way of letting us know that he had enough food for everyone.

But it was only the adventurers who helped themselves to Mrs. Tavares' cooking. They made a big show of feeling more at home with the caboclos than with us. It was getting plainer all the time that those two did not belong on our expedition.

We were swimming in the river in the late afternoon when a dugout with three caboclos appeared. They brought word from Padre John that the missionary's boat was undergoing repairs and would not arrive at Jerusalem for at least another week.

That about ended our hopes of going directly up the Cauaburi from the island. Another week at Jerusalem would deplete our vitality and our supplies to a point where we would not be in shape for an extended expedition. We decided to return to Tapurucuará and start all over again. Eugenio said we could return on the supply boat that was due from Uaupés in two or three days, probably the same boat that brought us to the island.

That was when the trouble began to come to the surface. Waiting had been tedious in Uaupés and Tapurucuará, but the food was good and the beds comfortable in both places, and there was some diversion. At Jerusalem there were only discomfort and desolation, excellent soil in which to sow the seeds of conflict.

For one thing, the guns were all too handy. We carried them around, cleaned them, fooled with them, and shot them off for practice.

One of Eugenio's chickens paid the supreme penalty for walking in front of our target. It caught a bullet right in its quizzical eye. We made restitution to Eugenio and cooked the chicken. I prepared it with brown rice the way my mother made it. As usual, our Continental friends would have no part in the work, but when they smelled the chicken cooking they condescended to eat with us.

Out of spite, I gave Guilio a large portion and Armand a little piece of wing. The Frenchman refused to eat, so his sidekick put his plate down, too.

"To hell with the both of them. I hope they starve," Arnie said.

But they didn't. Guilio gave some of his chicken to Armand and both ate in silence.

Armand got his revenge in the afternoon during another round of target practice. One of my shots ricocheted off a rock, and the next thing I heard was one of the children crying.

"Oh, my God, I've hit a kid!" I exclaimed.

The boy went running to the house as the Old Man came out.

As it turned out the child was only frightened, but Armand took advantage of the situation by holding a big speech in Portuguese for Eugenio's benefit. The gist of it seemed to be that the gringo had no respect for the life of the caboclo. There wasn't much I could say at the time. I really wasn't too proud of myself.

Guilio must have mistaken my crestfallen appearance for a sign of defeat, because he began to act a little bolder with me. In the evening he confronted me and asked for the return of the cigarettes I had borrowed. I reminded him that I had given him a carton at Tapurucuará. He denied ever having received it. He kept putting his hand out and asking for "my cigarettes." Every once in a while he would tug at his belt to remind me of the gun and knife he carried. Finally I lost my temper.

"Listen, you crumb. If you keep bothering me I'm going to put a bullet right through your thick skull."

Guilio blanched. He believed I meant it, and I did, but I am happy it never came to the test. I like to believe that I would have settled the question without guns even if challenged.

That ended the Euro-American alliance right there. The two parties did not speak to each other for the remainder of our stay. Armand and Guilio separated their belongings from ours and kept to themselves.

The next day was our fifth on the island, and Eugenio said the supply boat was due that afternoon. We started to pack our things and move them down to the water.

Jerry asked, "What if it doesn't stop for us?"

"Why shouldn't it stop?"

"You never know about these guys. They could go right by us and never give it a second thought."

"The bastards," exclaimed Arnie.

"I wouldn't let them get away with it," Jerry said.

"What would you do about it?"

"Put a couple of bullets through the bow and sink them."

That was the state Jerry had reached. All the props had been pulled out from under his orderly world. All he had left to lean upon was his rifle.

We ate and played cards near the shore that day so as not to miss the supply boat. In the evening we covered the boxes with tarpaulins and continued to watch from the house. Half the night passed that way. At two in the morning we decided that the boat was not coming and went to sleep.

Eugenio woke us at 5:00 A.M. He pointed upriver and tapped his ear.

"Arnie, Jerry," I called, "Eugenio hears the boat. Let's get down to the river." I decided that I owed it to Armand and Guilio to wake them up so they wouldn't be left stranded, but they were gone. We found them waiting down by the river. They had heard the boat coming and slipped away, hoping to leave us on the island.

By the time we got our things on board we weren't ready to trust anyone. The adventurers were yapping away in Portuguese with the crew. There were six of them, making the odds three against eight.

We kept to ourselves at the stern end of the boat. Jerry had a plan worked out whereby we could take the boat if we had to. We were outnumbered but we had most of the guns. It was decided that we would take turns standing watch.

That is the way we spent the journey back to Tapurucuará—sullen, suspicious, and almost sleepless.

When we were children we used to play a game called Musical Chairs, or Going to Jerusalem. The players went round and round a line of chairs, and there was one more player than there were chairs. When the music stopped, everyone would race for a chair. The player left standing was eliminated.

Our expedition had made one round trip to Jerusalem, and two players had been eliminated.

ten

VIVA KENNEDY

The supply boat docked on the island side of Tapurucuará before crossing to the mission. The church steeple looked as welcome to us as the Statue of Liberty as we waited impatiently to cross the channel.

The director and a priest were standing in front of the mission when we got there. I explained what had happened, and asked for permission to move back into our quarters until we could find transportation. They were quite cordial, and not a bit concerned to hear that Padre John was stuck somewhere on the Cauaburi with a damaged boat.

That evening at dinner there was a wall of silence between us and the Europeans. The missionaries acted as go-betweens for all communication, such as, "Padre, would you please ask Armand to pass the salt." The padres put up with this nonsense good-humoredly.

Guilio lodged his complaints against us with the padre-director, who was also Italian. I knew even less of that language than Portuguese, but it was pretty plain that he was telling the padre a pack of lies and exaggerations. I couldn't tell whether the director believed him.

I waited until after dinner to get the padre alone to tell him our side of the story. He said it wasn't necessary for me to explain. He said that many of his countrymen were given to making up lurid tales. So Guilio, instead of finding a sympathetic heart in his countryman, had found an understanding one.

We managed to keep busy during the days that followed. I completed my film record of life at the mission. The final scene was shot on a Friday, when morning mass was followed by a festival procession. Now I knew what the firecrackers of the previous evening were all about. They erupted anew after the procession and continued throughout the day.

Our stay at Jerusalem taught me an important lesson. We had underestimated our needs on that last false start. I was amazed at how much we had eaten, even accounting for Armand and Guilio, and at how much of our food and equipment was ruined by the rain and humidity. Next time we would take everything along. That meant recrating our equipment all over again.

An Air Force plane took Armand and Guilio back to the coast. They showed no reluctance to leave. Up to the very end there remained a barrier of mutual contempt. We never found out what motivated those two. It would be a great irony if someday I learned that they had no great secret at all, but were impelled by the same forces that guided the rest of us. But I somehow doubt it, if only for the reason that they changed their minds so casually.

Padre John showed up at last in his launch. The trim-looking twenty-five-footer was bigger and better outfitted than I had expected. I knew immediately that the padre's mission could not be near the headwaters of the Cauaburi, because that launch could never get through shallow rapids, and it was far too big for even two men to portage.

I wondered who could have helped him repair the boat in an area where the inhabitants were barely familiar with dugouts. Jerry guessed that the mysterious German machinist must have done the work. From there his mind leaped nimbly to the theory that Padre John also was German, perhaps even a wanted war criminal. I realized then that on his trip to Manaus Jerry had been told about Nazi war criminals hiding out in the jungles. We had heard the same stories, but had not run into any likely suspects. To consider Padre John Badelotti a likely suspect was complete lunacy, but Jerry was acting a little moonstruck at the time.

He asked the padre several times if he were German. The padre kept insisting that he was Italian, but Jerry would always come away with a narrow, knowing look in his eyes. It was embarrassing for Arnie and me.

Padre John in no way fitted my concept of a Nazi war criminal, except for his intensity. His eyes were penetrating. As tired as his face might be, his eyes always shone with a searing awareness of what went on beneath the surface of things.

In all other respects he was a typical Salesian priest. His beard was as long as Padre Antônio's, but almost snowy white. He wore the same simple cassock and canvas shoes as the younger missionary.

He had no qualms about taking us with him on his return trip. He only pointed out that we would need dugouts of our own if we wanted to continue beyond the mission. He suggested that we borrow them from Tavares, who was to accompany the padre as far as his mission outpost.

We asked if Eugenio, the Old Man of the Cauaburi, was familiar with the river beyond the mission. Padre John smiled. "Eugenio has guided missionaries and others on that river for fifteen years. No one else knows it as well as he."

From that point on, Eugenio Tavares became part of our plans. We asked Padre John whether it would be possible for him to come along. The padre recommended the idea most heartily. I knew that his vote would be decisive. Eugenio's fate was sealed.

Padre John also suggested that we take one of the Indian orphan boys with us. The Waica might be less suspicious if they saw the bearded strangers in the company of one of their own race. "I have a particular boy in mind," the padre added. "He can cook and do many other useful things. He has learned his lessons well. You will be happy to have him with you."

We wouldn't have dreamed of turning him down.

What could go wrong this time? I couldn't think of a thing.

Still, we had been nibbling around the edge of Indian country for so long without going into it that I was afraid to be hopeful.

The three of us tried to hide our impatience. We owed it to the padre to let him rest and refresh himself for a couple of days. Everything else being taken care of, we loafed around the mission and visited the villages that lay within walking distance.

Then one morning we were awakened by firecrackers.

Arnie croaked, "What, again? What holiday is this?"

"I don't know," I answered. "It's hard for me to keep track of all the religious dates."

Jerry looked at his pocket calendar and sat up in his hammock. "Religious dates? What religious dates? This is the Fourth of July!"

We dressed quickly and ran out to watch the boys shoot off their limitless supply of fireworks. When they saw us they began to shout, "Viva America! Viva Kennedy!"

Our President was an inspiration to all the people of South America, even to those Indian children in a river settlement adrift in the backwash of modern history.

A Catholic President of the United States of America. "Viva America!"

And a handsome, magnetic young man at that. "Viva Kennedy!"

Long live Kennedy. How could anybody have guessed that his brilliant flame would be snuffed out less than seventeen months from that date. "Viva Kennedy!"

We decided to celebrate in style. We started by polishing off a bottle of palm wine. Then we gave all the children candy and made the rounds of the nearby settlements. Everywhere we went it was palm wine all around, a din of firecrackers, and "Viva Kennedy!"

In the evening we built a big bonfire down by the river and showed the Indian boys how to roast wieners on sticks. We told them it was a very important part of the July Fourth celebration. We were high on palm wine by that time.

We went back to one of the villages in the evening with Padre John. He acted as interpreter as the villagers told us of their hardships, particularly hunger. I felt tears well up in my eyes. We eat and our brothers are hungry, I said to myself as I took another swig from the bottle. What a wonderful, sad evening that was! The Indians were drunk and feeilng sorry for themselves. We were drunk and feeling sorry for the Indians. The padre was sober and probably feeling sorry for all of us.

He led us back to the mission and tried to get us to go to bed. I balked at the entrance to the building. Holding up one finger I intoned philosophically, "Padre, you can lead a souse to hammock but you can't make him swink. I mean swing."

"It is time you went to sleep."

"First we want to swimp. I mean swim." I staggered off to the river with all my clothes on. The others followed, and we had a grand, cool dip. We got rid of some of the alcohol in the river, enough to disinfect the Rio Negro as far down as Barcelos.

"Viva Dietrich!"

"Viva Falls!"

"Viva Salazar!"

eleven

THE RIO CAUABURI

We spent part of July 5th regretting July 4th. It took gallons of strong coffee and the entire morning to reduce our heads to normal size. The rest of the day was devoted to packing. Again! I began to feel that we would wear out our equipment just packing and unpacking it.

Padre John was planning to leave the next morning. To the padre, that meant 5:00 A.M. We loaded the boat during the evening and covered everything with tarpaulins. Before dawn the next day we met the padre, his motorista, and his little Indian acolyte by the river. He said a prayer and we pushed off quickly.

This was the fifth time we traveled the stretch of river between Tapurucuará and Jerusalem. The first time, aboard the *Waupes,* was our introduction to the wonders and frustrations of life in Amazonia. The second, aboard young Gonçalves' little *lancha,* was a pleasant excursion. The third, with the adventurers on the supply boat headed for Jerusalem, was filled with hope and doubt. The fourth, returning with the adventurers to Tapurucuará, was passed in silent anger. And now trip number five was getting under way in a spirit of confidence and expectation.

We had our coffee aboard the boat, then stretched out on top of our supply boxes. Our cargo took up virtually all the floor space of the padre's launch. Even though we were crowded and damp, this was in many ways our pleasantest voyage. For one thing, there was no one on board of whom we had to be suspicious. We could relax, sing, talk, play with Suzy and, when we were tired, just doze off.

Padre John had the motor wide open. He wanted to reach Jerusalem by the next morning and continue immediately on to the Cauaburi. We offered to take turns steering the boat, but the motorista allowed himself very little rest. I don't believe he trusted our ability to stay out of dangerous water.

The water level on the Rio Negro had not dropped at all, and our little four-horsepower diesel labored hard against the current, but by the time the sun came up we had put quite a bit of distance between us and the mission. The day was clear, and we studied the shore for signs of life. There were a few rubber tappers about and the brightly colored birds that we had come to expect, but no animals.

In the afternoon a wind whipped the surface of the river into whitecapped wavelets, a familiar storm warning. We sealed all the openings with tarpaulins and huddled in the cramped cabin as the clouds tore open and unleashed a torrent. The motorista strained to see through the whitish gloom while the rest of us crawled around looking for a comfortable corner. Eventually we surrendered to the discomfort and lay across the boxes, listening to the rain hammer at the roof a few inches above our sweating bodies.

It poured that way for three hours. When it stopped we threw open the tarpaulins and let the hot clammy air out of the cabin and the cold clammy air in. The sun was starting to set, and we were still chugging along against the powerful force of the river.

We ate on board that evening and kept pushing ahead all night. The moon was out, giving the motorista plenty of light to steer by. He kept to the middle of the river and stared unwaveringly at the water ahead, a damp cigarette drooping from the corner of his mouth.

Jerusalem came into view as the sun cast its first somber gray light against the horizon behind us.

Eugenio's keen ears had caught the sound of the little diesel, and he was waiting for us on a flat rock by the water's edge. Padre John spoke to him about coming along as our guide. He looked over the padre's shoulder as they spoke, and nodded without enthusiasm. He seemed strangely neutral about making a trip on a dangerous river to meet a tribe of savages whom he had no interest in seeing.

The Old Man of the Cauaburi went back to gather his things while the padre directed us to hitch Eugenio's two dugouts to the larger boat.

Eugenio returned with a cloth sack slung over his shoulder and his oldest son, a boy about sixteen, at his side. The boy seemed to know the Indian youngster, whom we named Junior. The two of them chattered and joked in a patois of Portuguese, Tupi, and local Indian dialect. Our permanent party now consisted of six—three Americans and three caboclos. Fair enough.

We were on Jerusalem less than two hours, just long enough to catch the last of the mosquitoes and the first of the piums; then we pushed off again.

An hour later our convoy swung north into the mouth of the Cauaburi. I felt a tingle run up my back. Arnie and Jerry must have felt the same electricity. After dragging up and down the river for six weeks, laying over at missions and settlements, always hemmed in by the banks of the Rio Negro, the door to the jungle had suddenly swung aside. We crossed the threshold and left the twentieth century behind us.

The current was faster than on the Rio Negro and the banks were closer, but the scenery was otherwise the same thick foliage that we saw all along the big river. The Cauaburi also was black like the Rio Negro. The padre explained that the water turned that color in the upland swamps during the dry season, when it soaked the dyes out of rotting foliage.

About five miles up the river we came to the first rapids. At the foot of the rapids we pulled in at a small landing where there was a thatched house. An Indian family lived there and tended a small farm in the nearby jungle. They had been settled on that spot by the mission to help travelers pull their boats through the rapids when there were not enough men aboard to do it alone.

I had this portrait taken in the village of the Kohoroshanitari Indians. The outfit is typical. I was seldom without the protection of my revolver or the companionship of Suzy, my pet ocelot.

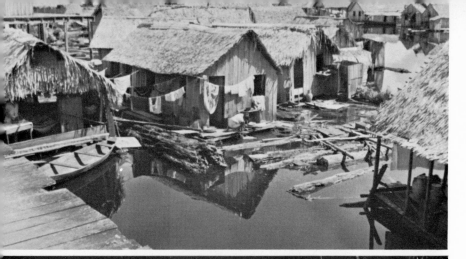

ABOVE LEFT: The floating city of Manaus. Thousands of palm-thatched huts built on crude rafts formed a slum colony in this harbor halfway up the Amazon. Indians and part-Indians, collectively referred to as *caboclos,* made the floating city their home, and used the stagnant water for drinking, fishing, bathing and for the deposit of wastes. In the center, a woman launders clothes in the river while another housewife, left, does her ironing. The floating city, as shown here at the time of the expedition, no longer exists. The government has destroyed the rafts and relocated the *caboclos* to land settlements.

BELOW LEFT: One of the supply boats that we used for transportation on the upper Rio Negro. Arnie Dietrich is playing the guitar for an audience of two, Suzy and me, while Jerry tries to sleep on top of the cabin (*left*). The boxes and baskets on the cabin roof are animal traps.

ABOVE: The mission of Santa Izabel at Tapurucuará as seen from Padre Antonio's motor launch. The whitewashed cement structures are typical of the missions along the Rio Negro. Mission outposts on the smaller rivers are either thatched huts or simple wooden shacks. Fronting the water, left to right, are the main mission building, the chapel and the girls' dormitory. All were built with the help of converted Indians who were taught manual skills by the padres. At right a trader's boat lies at anchor.

ABOVE: Two Waica Indians relax in the shade of the *chabona* wall. The hammocks are temporary ones made of palm leaves. Permanent hammocks are skillfully woven of twined cotton. Both of these braves have shredded tobacco leaves tucked behind their lower lips. This is a custom in all Waica groups. The Indian in the hammock is wearing an armband and a cotton waistband. His body is decorated with red dye from the *urucú* plant. The smoke curling up behind him comes from a wood fire that is kept burning constantly in his family's section of the communal shelter. In the background a naked baby crawls in the dirt, and at right a newly acquired machete lies on the ground next to a bunch of plantains. This scene, photographed in the Kohoroshanitari village, is typical of all the Waica settlements.

RIGHT: A Waica woman gives her neighbor a haircut. The typical tonsure consists of a clean-shaven circle on the crown of the head, with the rest of the hair trimmed evenly in the shape of an inverted bowl. The barbering, always the job of the woman, is done by pinching the hair between two slivers of bamboo or bone. Note the tufts of hair on the ground, left foreground. The giant arrows at right are among the few possessions of the Waica brave. They are left unguarded because among these Indians, who place little value on material possessions, there is little chance of them being stolen. This attitude begins to change when outsiders introduce machetes, mirrors, combs and other strange treasures. And with the introduction of clothing and religion, the innocent nakedness seen here also disappears.

ABOVE: Kamboe paints designs on his body with red dye taken from the waxy seeds of the *urucú* plant. We followed him and a band of his fellow Kohoroshanitari braves to their plantation, where we watched them go about these preparations. The ritual for which they were preparing turned out to be a wild dance in which all the participants were under the influence of a drug called *abana*. The vines at left are sweet potato plants, and the logs strewn on the ground at right are the remains of trees burned down to clear the land for farming.

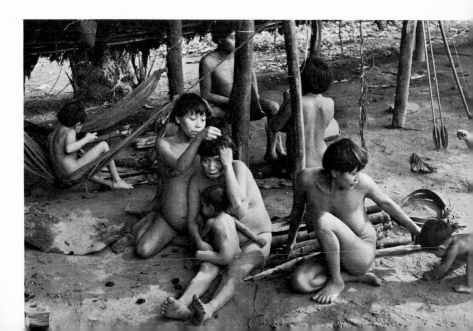

On most occasions when we first entered a Waica village, the women and children were nowhere to be seen. When the men came to trust us they brought their families out of hiding. Women were prized possessions, and the bachelors of one village would often raid another village for brides. There were moments, like the one captured here, when I felt almost like a member of the family.

The Waica had no need for protective clothing. This young brave could travel barefoot with no discomfort over the same rough terrain that tore my sneakers to shreds. His matted hair was all the protection he needed from the elements, while Jerry, Arnie and I had to keep our heads and bodies covered for protection nearly all the time.

After making camp in the abandoned village near the Imeri Mountains, I took time out to practice archery with one of the bearers. At that stage of the overland journey, I was wearing boots instead of sneakers because of the extremely rocky ground and the abundance of snakes. This village had been attacked only hours before we arrived, and part of the *chabona* wall was burned to the ground. We did not encounter the inhabitants or their attackers, but suffered several natural calamities before we left that desolate spot.

The Waica were extremely agile. They could climb up a perfectly straight tree trunk without the aid of implements, as this one is doing, and travel swiftly and easily through the thickest jungle. At the same time, they had such a strong aversion to water that none whom we saw knew how to swim properly.

A Waica beauty about eighteen years old. In perhaps two years she will start to show signs of aging, and by the time she is thirty will look like a wrinkled old woman. Waica women generally have the good sense to keep their mouths closed, but when they open them, they reveal teeth that are filed to points like those of the piranha. That is supposed to make them beautiful.

A handsome Waica brave. The only flaw that mars his looks is the condition of his teeth. The limited Waica diet, high in starches and low in protein, causes an abnormally high rate of tooth decay. The same is true of the more civilized Indians who live along the Rio Negro. These *caboclos* practically worship dentists, and often are taken in by quacks.

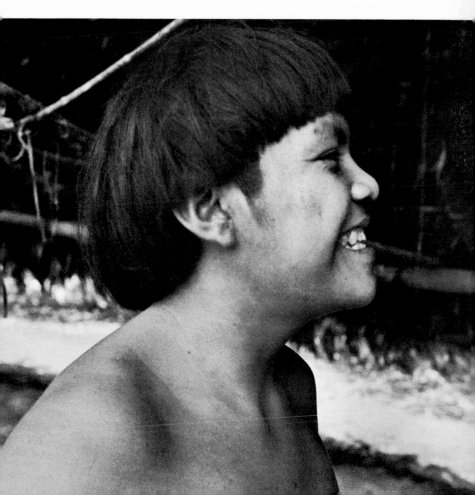

Kohoroshanitari warriors dance and brandish their weapons while under the influence of *abana*. Kamboe brings up the rear in the two left photographs. The Waica use *abana* to prepare themselves psychologically for an attack on another village. They inhale the drug in the form of snuff through a tube inserted into the nostril. Normally, another warrior will help by blowing into the other end of the tube. While under the spell of *abana* the braves are extremely dangerous. The young boy at right in the above picture has the good sense to watch from a distance.

A portage on the Marauiá. The approaching dry season caused a drop in the water level that made our work all the more difficult. Newly exposed sandbars spawned millions of sand fleas, which added to our misery. The parrot on top of the boat, which belonged to Padre Antonio, was a pet of his pilot, Babette.

Jerry Falls poses with Padre Antonio at a temporary camp on the Rio
Marauiá. Jerry was never without his rifle, and the missionary kept a
.38 revolver under his cassock. Even the friendliest visitors to the
dangerous jungles of Amazonia come armed.

Waica Indians at the turning point. This little group waits for a handout from Padre Antonio at his mission outpost. They no longer are
able to live off the jungle. Although they still use traditional Waica
weapons and cut their hair in the typical Waica style, they have begun
wearing clothes and attend Mass regularly. The bespectacled gentle-
man in the foreground has progressed to the next stage of becoming
civilized. He makes his home at the main mission at Tapurucuará and
assists the padre in his work.

Those Catholics living on Cauaburi had been given their allotted task almost as soon as they had been given their new religion. Helping boats over the rapids was surely an unusual way to find grace.

We went ashore to stretch our legs. The padre said mass in an old abandoned hut. The roof had caved in and the walls had collapsed on two sides. The third was about to go. There wasn't much to the little church but a single wall and an altar under the sky. The strange little congregation stood awkwardly in the tall grass studying the padre's brilliant white robe with its huge embroidered cross, while the priest intoned the old Latin phrases.

We shared the Indian family's breakfast—manioc, plantains, and coffee—and left them some canned food in return; we could tell that their farm was not very productive. Then we faced the uninviting rapids.

The motorista headed the bow of the boat straight into the main current and maneuvered his way in and out of whirlpools and around rocks. The river seemed to be on a steep incline, and the boat just fought its way up.

At various stages we came to wide, flat rock formations over which the river flowed like a silken sheet. The problem there was finding a channel deep enough for the boats. Several times we got out on either side and pushed, with one man up ahead or on the bank pulling a towrope.

At the worst rapids we were forced to unload our supplies, portage them along the shore, and haul the boats over the rocks through sheer might and main. Padre John labored with the rest of us, his cassock trailing in the water. As I squished along behind him, I asked if we were in any danger of being attacked by piranha. He assured me that the river was too fast for piranha.

Our heads were bowed to the river. There was hardly a moment to raise our eyes to the changing sights. Late in the afternoon, when we were beyond the rapids, the padre pointed to a clearing on the right bank where we were to make our camp. All at once I realized that we were in a different world. We were no longer on a river surrounded by jungle, but in a jungle through which a river ran. I cannot say at what point the change takes place, but it does take place.

Perhaps it is when you look up at the sky from the boat and see treetops out of the corners of both eyes. Perhaps it comes when you are standing in the middle of the stream and know you can walk to either side. No matter. I knew I was in the jungle. I was in a state of uncanny joy as we put up our hammocks. The feeling that I always felt in the deep jungle crept over me.

I recalled my first expedition. I remembered walking through the rain forests of British Guiana, somehow thinking that I had been there before. The mossy rocks were like the threshold of an ancient home, and the bearers wore the amiable, anonymous faces of household servants sent out to welcome home a member of the family.

I remembered walking on and on, anxious to get somewhere without knowing where I was going. I remembered coming to a village of pointed huts that loomed in the mist like a gathering of hooded ghosts. Several Wai Wai warriors, powerful and imposing in their fantastic headdresses, came out to meet me.

I knew I had arrived. I looked deep into these brown, timeless faces and fell forever under the spell of the Indio, a free and doomed race.

"What are you thinking about?" Jerry interrupted my reverie.

"I was just thinking it's good to be among the Indians at last."

"That's a funny thing to say. All we've seen so far is peons and mosquitoes."

"But we're practically there. Can't you feel it?" Jerry gave me a funny look.

There was nothing at the landing that offered shelter. We had to provide our own—a mosquito net strung over a hammock, with a tarpaulin handy in case of rain.

Arnie and Jerry were very careful with the supplies and equipment. They had already learned that there is a thin line between carelessness and disaster in the jungle. A box of cereal left open a crack means the loss of several meals to insects and mildew. A mosquito net carelessly arranged means waking up with an arm clotted and ugly with bites. They were still going through their initiation, as I had gone through mine, but hopefully, by the time we reached the Indians, all that would be behind us. For the most part I let them learn by themselves. I didn't want to stand over them like a mother hen. The only thing I reminded them about was their malaria pill.

We had dinner, and everyone retired to his hammock to engage in lonely combat with the swarms of bloodsucking insects.

I slept very little that night. The mosquitoes were not the only reason. I was renewing old acquaintances. The smells of the jungle drifted through the netting and awakened memories—the heady fragrance of night-blooming flowers, more seductive than perfume on a woman's shoulder; the rank smell of the swamp with its thousand generations of dead plants and insects breeding new life; the cool breath of the fast-flowing river, as heady as champagne. Every shift of the wind brought back a little more of the jungle.

And the noises. The whisper of the hurrying water, the belly croak of a bullfrog, the endless shrill whistle of a giant beetle, the sawing of high branches in the breeze, and the enormous insect chorus. A billion instruments directed by a mad virtuoso.

I hung in a dream limbo between sleep and wakefulness most of the night. I saw young people gyrating to a monotonous rhythm in a cavernous ballroom. They looked like the crowd at Sunnyside Gardens on that insane night of the rock-and-roll show, part of a scheme to finance an expedition once, a long time ago. Wait, it wasn't New York, it was Manaus, and the prostitutes were dancing to an orchestra of Wai Wai Indians. No! Indians don't belong in a nightclub. Come, I'll take you back. What? You can't come? You belong in church? But this is not a church. It's wrong. It's all mixed up. Everything is out of place.

Coffee perking and the busybody chatter of monkeys awakened me. It was a tired awakening, but pleasant—the world of the jungle was more secure than the world of dreams. I looked through the mosquito netting and I liked what I saw—the green jungle, two lean, bearded young men who were on their way to becoming explorers, four caboclos who were helping me reach my destination, and a Salesian missionary preparing for Sunday mass. My expedition.

We ate cereal mixed with condensed milk and stood patiently through Padre John's Sunday service. The expedition was making a good Catholic out of me. I wondered about the thoughts going through Arnie's head. He was a Protestant surrounded by Catholics. Even the Indians were Catholics.

Eugenio was at the helm when we pushed off again. We were heading for the worst set of rapids on the river, although it didn't look that way at first. The Cauaburi widened out and became peaceful for a distance of several miles, then split up into two broad channels around a craggy, overgrown island. We took the right fork, which was the shorter.

The day was mild, the air bracing, and the scenery breathtaking. We drank it all in, the lush green loveliness bathed in sunlight, until we began to notice streams of white foam, like soapsuds, floating past us on the black water.

"We are near the rapids," Padre John informed us.

The second set of rapids was too dangerous to attempt by boat. We pulled the launch and dugouts tight up against the shore and unloaded everything. The portage was difficult, since we had to cut a path for ourselves through tall foliage that grew right up to the water.

We went back and hauled the boats over the rocks. The padre cautioned us to hold on tightly to the side of the boat as we waded. Just a step away and we could have been caught by the current and dashed to death against the rocks. The river was deceptive; most of the rocks were hidden under masses of foam. It looked really inviting to my sweating body, like a bubble bath.

Standing in cold water and perspiring in the sun didn't do Jerry's cold any good. The only member of the party that seemed to be thriving was Suzy, who could always be seen stretched out on a box in the sun, licking herself and blinking at our peculiar endeavors. She was part of a multitudinous animal audience—the rest were monkeys, macaws, and an occasional immobile tree sloth—that witnessed our awkward efforts to do what was so easy for them, get from one place to another.

On the other side of the rapids, the padre told us it would be best if we moved all of our things into the dugouts, because he planned to remain for a while at the next camp while we continued on by ourselves. He had "business" in the area. Perhaps there was an Indian baby to baptize or a sick caboclo that needed attention. He didn't tell us what his plans were or invite us to come along, and we did not ask. That was one of the differences between him and Padre Antônio. He was less communicative, more of an "old line" priest who kept his distance.

Only occasionally did he volunteer information, such as that afternoon, when he remarked, "Just about here we cross the equator." Put that in your geography book, I thought, addressing myself to a dozen teachers of my youth, who told me all about the equator and taught me nothing.

Never did they say that the equator divides upper Amazonia into two worlds, ancient and modern, that the sun is hot and the air is cold, that the water is black and the foam is white, that the names of the towns and rivers on the map don't mean a damned thing, that when you get there the town might be gone and the river might be known by six other names, or that there might be a hundred other rivers nearby with no names at all.

The boat made good time on the last leg of that day's journey. We passed the mouths of many rivulets that carried rainwater down from the Sierra Imeri range into the Cauaburi. It was starting to look like real mountain country. Here and there we could see a few misty peaks to the north and northwest, the general direction in which we were headed.

We came to a sizable caboclo landing at midafternoon. There was a row of huts, as well as several dugouts. This was the padre's lower base camp, which he used when he worked the lower Cauaburi area and the Rio Maiá, which branched off eastward from the Cauaburi a few miles upstream.

I was curious about the caboclos who lived at the landing. A few seemed to be pure Indians, but many others looked like Portuguese-Indian halfbreeds. They were living evidence of the furthermost penetration of the Portuguese colonists of centuries before, a brief invasion of soldiers and energetic traders. All other signs of their visit had disappeared.

At Padre John's recommendation we added four Indians to our crew to help us paddle and portage. I call them Indians rather than caboclos because they had adopted very few of the ways of the outside world. While they wore short pants that the padre had given them, the typical feathered bands of the Waica were still on their arms. Their language also was Waica, and they were as racially pure as any Indians we had seen on our expedition.

We looked over the settlement while Eugenio visited with his acquaintances and the padre busied himself around his hut. It was a simple palm-thatched dwelling like all the others, too small to house us for the night. There were still a few hours before darkness, so I decided to move right out.

Arnie asked, "What's your hurry?"

"I can't see anything worth staying for. The mosquitoes are the same here as anyplace else on the river."

"Maybe worse," Jerry added.

We rounded up our four Indians, Eugenio, and the two boys, the younger one having attached himself to the Tavares family like another son. The padre blessed us and wished us a safe journey. We were now on our own.

It was a strange feeling to glide silently along in the dugout after traveling for so many days to the accompaniment of motor noises. The jungle seemed closer, and we seemed totally isolated.

Arnie asked Jerry, "What's half brown and half white and hairy?"

"I don't know," Jerry replied. "What is half brown and half white and hairy?"

"Fred's expedition!" Arnie laughed so hard he nearly tipped the boat. Junior and young Tavares joined him, though they hadn't the faintest idea of what it was all about.

Eugenio pointed out a clearing on the left bank as the sun began to descend. We paddled over to it and beached the dugouts. I noticed that on the opposite side the river branched off toward the east. I asked Eugenio about it in the broken Portuguese that had become our common language. He informed me that it was the Rio Maiá.

We put things in order for our overnight camp and warmed up some food for supper. Just as we sat down to eat we heard a drum in the distance, a steady hollow knock. I couldn't imagine that it carried a message; just the same monotonous knock, on and on and on. It was in no way similar to the rhythms we had heard elsewhere in Brazil, with their African complexities. It was closer to the drumbeat of the North American Indian. I knew we were now in a region almost completely unaffected by the outside world. We were in the land of the Waica.

twelve

THE MEETING

~~~~~~

We took turns standing watch that night, just in case the Indians decided to pay us a visit. Not that any of us got much sleep. The drum kept beating all night without interruption. I dozed off just as dawn came.

We ate a nervous breakfast that morning. The confidence we had gained from three days of mastering the Rio Cauaburi evaporated in the cold morning mist. The hollow knock of the drum kept reminding me of Padre Antônio's words, "You don't find the Indians; they find you." They had found us, and we had not found them. I didn't like it.

I couldn't tell what Tavares was thinking. He seemed too calm. I wondered whether he thought his job ended when he dropped us off somewhere at the headwaters of the river. We had two dugouts, but I would put a bullet through one of them before I would let him go back without us.

The mist was the thickest we had ever seen when we pushed the two dugouts into the water. The six members of our party, two of the Indians, and Suzy were in one dugout, and the other two Indians were with the supplies in the second which was tied alongside.

Eugenio pointed the way and manned one of the paddles. Arnie, Jerry, and I took turns with the Indians at the other paddles. The two youngsters helped out occasionally, but for the most part they passed the time playing with Suzy. They giggled and chattered and climbed around like little animals.

Macaws, monkeys, and insects beyond our range of vision provided a background of small noises as omnipresent as the gray mist that chilled every bone and branch. Occasionally we heard the splash of a big fish. Other than that there was only the gurgle of the water under the paddles and the regular wooden knock of the invisible drum.

I couldn't imagine how Eugenio saw to steer through the mist. My best guess was that he simply headed directly into the current and trusted to good memory and keen eyesight to avoid rocks.

There wasn't much conversation. We were all squinting into the mist to try to get our bearings. When it thinned out a bit the curtains of jungle emerged like gray walls. I looked for Indians in the foliage, but the harder I looked, the more I imagined grotesque faces staring back at me.

Finally I told Jerry to put aside his paddle and make some coffee on the Sterno stove. The smell of coffee and the familiar sounds of preparation had a comforting effect on us, and soon we began to relax. After a while the mist began to show silver and gold edges under the first strong rays of sunlight.

In an hour the sun had risen past the treetops and was shining full upon the river. The olive-gray world of morning had bloomed into a brilliance of shimmering blue sky, ragged white peaks, and an infinite spectrum of greens and browns that plunged from the translucent green-gold of the highest leaves to the opaque brown-black of the mud. Red and white orchids bloomed in clusters close to the ground, and macaws flying in perfect formation cut pink arcs in the clear air around us. The vivid panorama was reflected perfectly in the river, creating a double world between which the dugouts passed as if suspended.

Toward noon boredom and irritability set in. Our clothes remained damp despite the warmth of the sun, and the noises around us diminished to a buzz as the jungle began to doze for the afternoon. Meanwhile, the drumbeat continued.

We passed the mouth of the Rio Iá, the river that had once

been part of the commercial route from Colombia, and a few miles past that we spotted Padre John's jungle mission. It was nothing but a thatched hut like thousands of others we had seen. We didn't even bother to stop.

We had lunch on shore. Tavares got out some cold *mutum,* which he probably picked up at the settlement where Padre John left us. I guessed it wasn't maggoty if the Old Man gave it to the boys, so I helped myself to a piece and the others followed suit.

After lunch we pushed off again, reluctantly. Paddling against the current was tiring. Life at Tapurucuará had made us soft, and the mosquitoes and sleepless nights on the Cauaburi had weakened us. Eugenio indicated in pidgin Portuguese that we would hit the next rapids in about three hours. I figured that that was as good a place as any to make camp. I didn't want to put an unreasonable strain on anyone when we might have to call upon all our physical reserves at a moment's notice.

Also, I didn't want to show up at the Waica village all worn and haggard. Again Padre Antônio's words came back to me: "Never show you are afraid. Never show you are undecided. Never show you are ill."

When flecks of foam began to appear on the surface of the water, we stepped up our rhythm. The end of the day's tiring labor was in sight. Where the river turned sharply to the west at the foot of the rapids, we paddled straight ahead at full speed and skidded onto a bar of smooth pebbles. We hauled both boats onto higher land and made ready for the night.

Suddenly we realized it was quiet. I didn't even know when the drum had stopped. Somewhere along the way the pounding had gotten all mixed up with the rhythm of our paddles and the pulsebeat in our ears. The silence started us wondering all over again. I had come to like the idea of those Indian hands keeping busy on that drum. What were they up to now?

I demonstrated the movement of the Indian drummer's hands, and asked Tavares, *"Que ha?"*

With hand motions and his cryptic Portuguese he explained that the Indians downstream were talking to the Indians upstream. Now they were finished talking—*"Acabado."*

I asked him what would happen next. He shrugged.

That was the kind of information I was accustomed to getting from Eugenio. The only time he showed concern was when the boys were out of sight. And he smiled only when he felt obligated to do so.

We set up a night watch again, and again the mosquitoes came out to make sure that the guard did not nod. None of us did, as a matter of fact, for any appreciable length of time. It is the nature of mosquitoes to create an illusion of numberlessness, like a nighttime crowd on Times Square, but I felt certain that the swarms were thinning out as we got higher into the mountains.

I compared notes with Arnie. "Do you notice? There seem to be fewer mosquitoes up here."

"Don't kid yourself. The same mosquitoes have been following us since Jerusalem. They're not bothering you because they've decided whose blood they like best. Mine."

Jerry suffered more than either of us. His cold was still plaguing him, and because of a poor appetite and selective eating habits he was losing weight. His pants and shirt hung on him like the clothes of an old man. On top of all that his skin was raw and red from the sun. Jerry had the kind of complexion that doesn't tan. What I didn't like was that he was suffering silently. I like it when a man who has problems lets off steam. It cools him off and lets you know what's going on in his head. The quiet ones are likely to pull some crazy stunt, like jump overboard or turn on someone with a gun.

I kidded with him a little, and he responded in kind. That put my mind at rest. I didn't like being uncertain about a man who could handle a rifle so well and who always had one with him.

When we finally bedded down in our hammocks, I noticed that for the second night Tavares' was hanging right over the smoldering remains of the campfire. I figured that it was his way of keeping insects away. I thought of giving the Tavares method a try, but it seemed like an awful lot of trouble when I could get better protection from the netting.

Exhaustion overcame anxiety, and we slept soundly through an uneventful night. Jerry and Junior were busy with breakfast when I awoke. There was talk in the camp; that was a good sign. And no drum.

We checked out the boxes in the second dugout. The dampness had penetrated considerably. There were beads of moisture on the underside of the tarpaulins, and green specks of mildew on some of the crates. We dried everything out as best we could and oiled our metal equipment. While we worked we left the tarps hanging over the breakfast fire. When everything was once more secured, we pushed off again into a sea of morning mist.

Jerry continued to sneeze, and there were red rings around his eyes. Other than that, he seemed in good shape. Arnie had no complaints except for the ones we all had—itching and dampness; we could hardly keep a cigarette lit. All things considered though, I felt we were in fit condition to meet the Waica.

The river was extremely narrow at this point. In several places trees had fallen into the stream and blocked it almost completely. I noticed that Eugenio was keeping the boats close to the left shore. The reason became clear a little later when through the mist I perceived the mouth of another river to the right. Eugenio was following the left fork. I asked him about the other river.

He answered, *"Ai Cauaburi."* Then, pointing up the left fork, he added, *"Ai Maturacá. Ai Waica, Kohoroshanitari."*

Apparently we were now on a different river, the Maturacá, but what was Kohoroshanitari?

"Êles Waica. Ai chabona dos Kohoroshanitari." The Kohoroshanitari were Waica Indians, and their village, or *chabona,* was to the left on the Maturacá.

We were getting the deluxe tour. Eugenio had a particular group in mind, the Kohoroshanitari. Their village lay somewhere up the Rio Maturacá, in the direction of Cucuí, a boundary marker between Brazil and Venezuela. Cucuí was the anchor of a borderline that was otherwise unmarked for hundreds of miles. It was accessible by way of the Rio Negro, where the river swung northward beyond Uaupés and then doubled back to the east and northeast. We knew that at least one expedition of the Border Commission had tried getting there the hard way. That is, by way of the Cauaburi and Maturacá. It had cost them four lives in an Indian ambush.

The Maturacá was little more than a mountain freshet. The trees leaning over the river nearly touched above our heads. Some of these looked as if they were about to give way to the pull of their own tremendous weight. The soil was gradually being washed out from under their high-standing roots. There was more life in the trees here—more birds, more sloths, more monkeys. Occasionally an otter would poke its head up from the grassy bank or a big turtle would slip into the water with a splash.

We took a few potshots at the animals. When we missed they just stood still and stared at us. They had never heard the sound of a gun before.

The day grew warm, and the animals retired to the shade. We were left alone to toil in the sun. At about noon we came to a stretch of river where a number of trees had been felled. We pulled in to have a look. It was some sort of plantation. There were sweet potato vines climbing on the trimmed trunks of young trees. Charred tree trunks lay all around the clearing. Eugenio pointed out footprints in the brown earth. We were on a Waica farm.

Eugenio instructed Jerry to shoot his rifle into the air. Now that we were close to the village, he didn't want to come across a hunting or foraging party by surprise. Like any jungle creature, the Indian was most dangerous when taken unawares. Jerry obliged with two shots. When the echo died away the place seemed even quieter than before.

We had our lunch right there on the edge of the clearing, just so we wouldn't have to make another stop. Nobody ate much. Even the boys were quiet.

All eyes were on the shore as we continued moving up the Maturacá. The towering peak of Mount Oneri was to our left, but all signs of human life were to our right. We saw several more patches of cleared land dotted with charred stumps, and flat ground at the water's edge where the grass had been trampled underfoot.

Suddenly Eugenio stopped paddling. He straightened up on his knees and motioned to Jerry without turning his head. The Old Man had heard something up ahead.

Jerry fired off two rounds, cracking a high branch with the second shot. The river became unnaturally still. It was a silence teeming with the memory of voices we had mistaken for bubbling water and sighing leaves.

Coming around a bend in the river, we saw a spot on the right shore where the Indians had been gathered just a few moments before. It was flat and muddy and showed many footprints. The still water in the cove was cloudy where the bottom had been stirred up. A broad leaf upon which an Indian had been sitting was still in the process of regaining its flat shape, so recently had the weight of his body been lifted.

The same thing happened several times during the next two hours. Each time we detected a faint babble of voices around the next bend. And each time we came to the landing and the Indians were gone. We listened hard for the sound of movement or voices in the bushes, but the Waica, if they were nearby, had "frozen" liked hunted game.

Signs of Indian life became more plentiful as we moved on. Broken vines hung into the water at various points. They were probably the remains of crude bridges. There were clearings of various sizes and narrow paths that led down to the water. There were even rudimentary enclosures, strikingly similar in construction to the caboclo huts farther downstream. We were somewhere in the vicinity of a large village, or, to use Eugenio's strange word, a *chabona*.

Without warning we came upon a great clearing, empty and quiet, with a broad path leading uphill into the jungle. We had not heard the sound of activity on the bank. No doubt Waica couriers bearing news of our approach had outdistanced the boats. The Kohoroshanitari must have moved back into the shelter of the trees.

I could feel my heart pounding as we pulled the dugouts ashore. We held a short meeting.

We would carry only gifts; I ordered the guns left behind. They wouldn't do us much good against a whole village of Indians, and if the Indians knew what a gun was for, the sight of our rifles could very likely start a panic.

The only one who needed convincing was Jerry, but he finally relented and put his Winchester under a tarpaulin in the dugout. We put a rope around Suzy's neck to make sure she didn't follow us or stray into the bush.

On a hunch I asked Eugenio if he had ever been to the Kohoroshanitari village before. He shook his head, but when we started up the path he marched along with a confidence that could have passed for familiarity. I found myself thinking about this strange man who was our guide. There was a genuine pathos about him. Torn between old habits, beliefs, and temptations on one hand, and new skills, obligations, and restrictions on the other, he seemed to have turned within himself in search of sustaining values. His stubborn independence showed in the back of his bony neck.

We followed the steep trail for about fifteen minutes, breathing heavily, more from tension than from the climb. Then the ground leveled off and we continued through a heavily overgrown area. Not a sight or sound betrayed the presence of another human being.

Jerry said once, "Where are they?"

Arnie replied, "What did you expect, a brass band?"

The path brought us out into a tremendous area of cleared ground. The destruction of trees and bushes was clearly human work, done with the help of fire. Charred wood was everywhere.

About a quarter of a mile away was a structure that looked something like a primitive football stadium. It was the home of the Kohoroshanitari. Eugenio continued across the open field, and we followed him. I never felt so exposed in my entire life. Not a sight or sound except for the noises of the birds in the trees behind us.

The tense silence was suddenly broken by a scream that froze the blood in my veins. It came from somewhere among the trees. Eugenio said it was only a *macaco,* a monkey. Then I realized it was a howler monkey, a tough baboon-sized species whose terrifying screech we had heard once or twice before. But never so close, and never under such trying circumstances.

As we got closer to the *chabona,* I noticed that it was enclosed by a wall of poles that leaned inward. The poles were tied together by rope. The barrier was about twenty feet high and formed a giant horseshoe-shaped lean-to big enough to hold an army. I was hoping it didn't.

The path led us straight up to an opening in the wall—no door or gate—just a separation. As we were about to enter, Eugenio stopped short. Directly in front of him was a ball of cotton impaled on a stick. It was covered with blood.

The message seemed plain enough. The Kohoroshanitari were inviting us to stay out. We stopped to discuss our next move, conscious that somewhere nearby a whole village of Indians was waiting for our decision.

It was evident that the inhabitants of the village had left in a hurry. Small wood fires smoldered at intervals of a few yards all around the enclosure, under the shadow of the wall. Heavier posts that supported the wall were hung with plantains, gourds, and baskets, and between the vertical braces were strung hammocks made of loose twining. I noticed a colorful bird in a straw cage swinging gently on a red string. The smell of dung and burned fat hung heavy in the air.

The Indians were waiting and we were waiting. I didn't come this far to turn back and I didn't like the idea of leaving things up to them. Jerry looked white under his sunburn, and the fun had gone out of Arnie's eyes. Even Tavares didn't look too happy. I pointed to the gifts, and Tavares nodded. Better get started with the public-relations campaign before one of us did something foolish and touched off a shower of arrows.

I unslung the cloth sack and walked up to the red ball of cotton. I rummaged around and fished out various gifts, one at a time. Looking over each one carefully, I placed it on the ground as if it were a rare treasure.

I passed a comb through my hair, smiled, patted my head, and put the comb on the ground. I tried on a bead necklace as if there were nothing more desirable in the whole world. Jerry told me not to get carried away with myself, but somehow I felt that the Kohoroshanitari appreciated the performance. I stopped while the sack was still half full, leaving something to their imagination. If their imagination were anything like that of their caboclo cousins, they would figure me to have at least a herd of elephants tucked away in that sack.

I rejoined the others, and we sat down to wait. We put on a show of indifference that was almost comical. Seldom had an audience been treated to such a magnificent display of yawning, stretching, and scratching as those hidden Waica. A drama critic in their midst would surely have let fly with the first arrow.

Time went by. Our indifference became labored. We found ourselves glancing frequently behind us into the jungle and across the clearing to the far side of the village. Then, almost between blinks of the eye, a semicircle of armed Indians appeared within the perimeter of the arena, bringing us to our feet.

I couldn't even tell where they came from. They seemed to materialize out of the shadows. There must have been a hundred of them. Each carried a drawn bow, with the arrow angled down at the ground. That was a hopeful sign.

They edged toward us, but we didn't move a muscle. At this point we had no choice but to brazen it out.

The Indians were small in stature; none of them was more than five-foot-four or so. They were the color of cocoa powder and had almost no hair on their bodies except for thick pubic hair and the straight black hair on their heads, which was a tonsure cut in the shape of a shallow bowl with a clean-shaven circle on the crown. They wore no clothes except for a plain cotton waistband, from which a cord was looped under the genitals, and an armband, which some had decorated with feathers.

Their weapons were fantastic in size. Both the bows and the arrows were well over six feet long, a full foot longer than the archers who used them. A black enamel-like sheen on the tip of each arrow indicated a coating of deadly poison.

The semicircle closed until the Indians were shouldering one another, and the far ends of the line began to drift disturbingly out of my range of vision. We were surrounded on three sides. Arrows rattled dryly against one another in the tightly packed formation as the warriors moved still closer. Then one raised his hand and they all stopped. He pointed gravely at the trinkets on the ground and said, *"Warishana."*

The Old Man understood him. The word was from the same dialect as that spoken on the lower Cauaburi. Tavares translated: *"Belo."* Beautiful. He turned to the tribesman. *"Shorema."* Friend.

We repeated, *"Shorema."* And that, as far as we knew, was the first communication between the Kohoroshanitari and the outside world.

The spokesman was taller than the others and had stronger features, although he looked younger than most. While the other Indians turned their attention to the trinkets with exclamations of *"Warishana!"* he inspected us with disdain and suspicion. He was undoubtedly the chief of the village.

He noticed me studying him, and he met my eyes with a hard, narrow look. I recognized in that look an attempt to stare me down, just like the look you would get from the leader of any street gang. This was language I understood. I stared right back.

The visual fencing was interrupted by Tavares, who suggested that we start distributing the gifts. The Indians were gathered around the glittering pile demanding, *"Eba! Eba!"* Give me! Give me! I remarked that it was surprising that they didn't help themselves. Eugenio rebuked me with a look. I understood what he meant. Taking without permission is the white man's way. The Kohoroshanitari had not learned it as yet.

We began handing out gifts. As soon as the things on the ground were gone, we fetched more out of the bags. Each Indian thanked us with an expressive, rapid-fire *"Enehapewe!"* They showed great patience and consideration for one another during the gift giving, and were surprisingly quick to grasp the purpose of each object.

The chief looked reproachfully at his docile warriors. Their weapons were scattered on the ground like toys while they celebrated noisily with their necklaces, kerchiefs, bracelets, hats, combs, mirrors, and other new treasures. He seemed displeased by their lack of dignity. Turning his back on us, he headed toward a large thatched hut, separated from the communal lean-to, which was undoubtedly his house. A few cronies followed him. I guessed that he wanted to receive his tribute in a way befitting his office.

We gave the royal household time to prepare itself for the meeting of the heads of state. Meanwhile there was one Waica brave, a handsome, serious fellow, who remained emptyhanded. He kept pointing to me, saying, *"Warishana! Eba!"* I laughed, thinking he wanted to take me home. He gestured with increasing animation, insisting, *"Eba! Eba!"* All at once I realized it was my wristwatch he wanted. Although it was an expensive watch, I decided on an impulse to give it to him.

In taking off the watch I instinctively noted the time, then thought to myself what an irrelevance a timepiece was in a place like this. It was five o'clock in the afternoon, but what century was it? I knew the number of the year, dated from an event that was the most important moment in history to the inhabitants of Santa Izabel, only a hundred miles away. But to this Waica, was there such a thing as a year, or only rainy season and dry season, and times for loving, killing, and playing, according to the calendar of nature?

I had been living for only five days by the cycles of nature, and the watch had already become a mere ornament. But it had a certain significance, passing from my hands into the hands of this jungle man. It was appropriate that the last moment of his ancient, primitive civilization be counted by those mechanical fingers.

Taking the watch, the Indian exclaimed, *"Enehapewe!"* and turned to run. He took a few steps, and halted. He looked back and pointed to himself, saying, "Kamboe." I returned the introduction. Pointing to myself I said, "Salazar. *Shorema.*" Kamboe flashed a grin and bounded away like a hare.

We found ourselves alone, almost ignored. For the moment the Indian men were busy with their new possessions. Rangy dogs with smoke-colored hair loped about the village, barking excitedly. In front of his house, under the shelter of its overhanging roof, the chief reclined in his hammock, his royal retinue gathered about him. There were no women or children to be seen.

Tavares recommended that we wait until the gaiety died down before approaching the chief. We selected his gifts—a knife, a pair of shorts, an ornate hand mirror, and a metal cup—one from each of us. When the noise subsided, we marched four abreast across the clearing, leaving the boys and Indians behind, the gifts held out before us. We stopped a few feet from the chief's hammock. He reminded us of his status by allowing us to wait while he finished talking with his advisers. Finally he looked our way and motioned impatiently for us to get started.

The Old Man said a few words, then signaled me to hand the knife to the chief. He showed no interest in the gift, or in the three that followed.

Afraid that our welcome was wearing thin, Tavares launched immediately into his prepared speech. He told the chief of our voyage up the river, and expressed the wish of all of us to remain in the Kohoroshanitari village. While he spoke, the chief studied each of us from head to toe. When Tavares finished, the Waica leader reached into the shadows behind him and brought out a double-barreled shotgun. He spoke to Tavares, who shook his head emphatically. They argued a little, but it was over in a moment.

Eugenio explained that the chief had gotten the shotgun in a trade with another Waica chief. The weapon had been making the rounds that way because of its magic power. This could have been the very gun used by the Indians in the Demeni area against the missionaries. The chief wanted us to make the fire tube work for him. We weren't certain whether he knew exactly what ammunition was, but that was what he was after.

This could have been the very reason he allowed us into the village, to have us make the fire tube work. I was thankful for having left our guns with the boys. The sight of them to this chief could have provoked a hostile greeting.

The chief was annoyed, but he didn't give up. Had he known more about the shotgun, he might simply have polished us off and ransacked our belongings for shells.

He instructed one of his men to lead us to a place where we could hang our hammocks. He made his distrust plain by assigning us to a deserted corner of the village.

Arnie, Eugenio, and our four helpers went back down the path to start bringing up the supplies. I told them to keep the guns out of sight and to discourage the Indians from poking around among the boxes. Jerry and I remained behind with the boys to make it clear that we were not changing our minds about staying. We didn't want to go through that reception all over again.

We found ourselves surrounded by squatting Kohoroshanitari braves, placid and curious. I tried to ask them for firewood by using sign language, but the Indians just smiled and nodded approvingly, as if I were pantomiming for their entertainment.

The Old Man returned with the two boys, each of them burdened with supplies. Arnie had remained with the boats. Tavares asked the Indians to help with the rest of the cargo, and a number of them bolted down the path as if they had been invited to a picnic. This time Jerry went with them.

Tavares stayed to ask for firewood and water. I made up my mind to spend as much time with him as possible so that I could pick up some of the Waica language. My dependence upon the interpreter was becoming annoying.

The beachhead of modern civilization in the Kohoroshanitari village took shape quickly. In this corner of the jungle where the only metal artifact to date had been the chief's secondhand shotgun, there was now an aluminum pot filled with boiling water, tin cans and brass can openers and several kinds of steel knives. Elsewhere in the village were objects of metal, plastic, paper, glass, and other foreign materials, harbingers of the day when this beachhead would become a colony.

The Indians, who lived on a bland and limited diet, were aroused by the aroma of sausages. Jerry offered them an open can, and they ran off to eat the exciting delicacy in private. A few remained behind to stare at the wonders that emerged from the boxes. Tavares asked them to bring more wood for the fire: "*Orehe, kiewaka.*" They continued to stare as if hypnotized, making no move to comply.

The novelty of the occasion had worn off enough for their normal indolence to reassert itself. While we were considering how to handle the problem, two Indians came back for more sausages. They held out the empty can and demanded, *"Eba."*

Tavares told them that first they must bring us *"orehe."* They shuffled undecidedly for a moment, then ambled off toward the trees. By the time they reached the opening in the *chabona* wall, they were racing at top speed.

They returned quickly with armloads of dry wood. I remembered to say *"enehapewe,"* which brought forth great gusts of laughter. The two braves left with the can of sausages, while the others continued to rock on their haunches. Tavares was certain that the message had penetrated. From now on it was not just *"eba."* There was also *"nomehan,"* barter.

As we ate, the shadows of the mountains and trees blended into a common gray mass. The fires cast soft orange pools of light against the *chabona* wall. The hard cobalt of the tropical sky melted into softer tints of blue, blending off here and there into grays and pinks. An elegaic mood settled over the village. The dogs snuffled in the gentle gloom, and a baby cried somewhere. We knew then that the women and children had returned from their hiding place in the jungle. We were now truly at home with the Waica.

thirteen

LIFE WITH THE WAICA

~~~~~~

"Now that we're here, what?" was the first thing out of Arnie's mouth in the morning.

"You mean you have to ask?" I replied.

"I ask you a question and you answer me with a question. All I want to know is what do we do next?"

"Okay, I'll tell you. We learn all we can about these Indians—their language, their habits, their religion, how they eat, how they fight, how they play, how they bring up their kids . . ."

"What do we get out of all this?"

"What did you expect to get?"

"Well, can't we make this expedition pay for itself somehow?"

"How much have you got invested in it?"

"Not much, I guess, but . . ."

"Then what are you worried about? Jerry's not complaining. Anyhow, we might get something out of it."

"How?"

"We'll trade for some of the things they use. Maybe the museums will want some of it. Maybe they have drugs and minerals that are worth money. The films might bring something."

"How about gold?"

Jerry got interested. "Yeah, how about gold?"

"All I can say is, I'll recognize it if I see it."

While this conversation was going on, the rest of the Kohoro-shanitari village was gradually coming to life. Children were laughing and babies were squalling; there was a murmur of morning voices, and the household birds were scolding the world through the bars of their flimsy cages.

Tavares had lots of company around the breakfast fire. In addition to his son and Junior and Padre John's four Indians, there were several boys from the village, a dirty, happy gang of naked urchins. There was no mistaking that they were hanging around for food. They looked sickly and underfed. Their eyes were scaly and their stomachs were distended. But they were as playful and lively as any kids anywhere in the world.

Their parents were enjoying a leisurely breakfast. The men were in their hammocks eating plantains. The women squatted on the ground, tending the fires and suckling their infants. The babies were held by straps slung across their mothers' bodies like the bullet belts of Mexican soldiers.

The women contrasted strangely with the men in appearance. Their skin color was paler, and there was a definite greenish tinge to their eyes. The strange quirk intrigued me.

We got a closer look at the women when we wandered around the interior of the *chabona*. They came out to look at us, and immediately elected Jerry their favorite. He was wearing walk shorts, and the hair on his legs glowed a lovely shade of golden red in the sunlight. They ran their hands over it, saying, *"Wari-shana! Wakawaka!"* They also pulled greedily at his beard as if they intended to pluck him like a chicken.

Eugenio explained that *"Warishana"* meant beautiful, which was easy to guess. *"Wakawaka"* meant red, which was the reason for all the excitement, for red was their favorite color. They couldn't believe that a man so beautiful existed. All red, skin and hair, from head to toe!

"Boy, Red," Arnie chided, "are you going to make out!"

Jerry told him to shut up.

We paid our respects to the chief. Eugenio advised us to address him as *"Pareome."* That was his title. The *pareome* was seated before his hut, surrounded by several women, all of whom were his wives. They gave Jerry the same treatment as the other women. The chief, surly as he was, did not seem to mind. I thought to myself that the Waica men were pretty sure of their women. Back home a wife who made a fuss like that over another man would get a dirty look, at the very least.

Not that they had anything to be jealous about. Although we could see all of the women that there was to see—they wore only a thin cotton waistband—there wasn't much worth looking at. There were very few that had what an American would call a youthful shape. They seemed to go straight from puberty to sagging middle age, with almost no transition. Out of some two hundred females, there weren't more than a half dozen that were really attractive. And these few, in spite of their lovely oval faces and delicate, full-breasted bodies, were rendered repulsive by their frightening teeth, which were filed to points like a piranha's, and the putrescent animal fat pomade with which they kept their hair in place.

Eugenio had brought along a gift he believed would appease the young warrior chief, a machete. It was my place to make the presentation. I waited until I had his attention; then I demonstrated the use of the implement on a piece of wood, hacking it clean through. Then I handed it to him, handle first. I said, *"Shorema,"* hoping that he understood that this was a gift of friendship. I pointed to him and said, *"Pareome";* then I pointed to myself and repeated the word. I wanted him to know that he wasn't dealing with a mere deputy.

The chief seemed properly impressed. He hefted the machete with an instinctive comprehension of its power. Eugenio had chosen the gift wisely. With the machete, he was another notch deadlier than the other warriors of the village. And that was unquestionably the only way to stay on top in a primitive society like the Kohoroshanitari.

I was still wondering about the women, their strangely colored eyes, but I did not know how to broach the question. I asked Tavares. He shrugged, not quite understanding what I was curious about. He asked some questions of the chief, who pointed toward the mountains and gave the Old Man a long story, filled with grunts and wails and roars. He even got up and demonstrated something that looked like a fight or an attack of some kind. Every few seconds he pointed to the mountains in the north.

This was the story: The Kohoroshanitari originally came from the north—somewhere near the Sierra Parima or perhaps beyond, in Venezuela. In the old days they called themselves the Masiribueteri. Then the savage invaders came and killed many warriors and took many women, and the village moved and took its new name. The chief's father told him how it all happened. He was a boy himself at the time.

The Kohoroshanitari still lived in fear of the mysterious men who came out of the mountains. They kept the land around the *chabona* cleared to prevent a surprise attack, and they kept many dogs in the village to warn of the killers that came in the night. They armed themselves with bows and poisoned arrows and lances, and axes with three-pointed bone heads that could tear the eyes out of a man's face. With all this, and the strength of numbers, they dared to remain in the shadow of the mountains of death. The weaker villages had long ago moved to the south and the southeast.

I got more than I bargained for. Even though I knew as little as before about the green-eyed women, I had learned the history of the Kohoroshanitari group, or as much, probably, as anybody knew.

I had Tavares ask the chief what the Venezuelans looked like. He drew a blank. The *pareome* just looked at him. Either he refused to conjure up the fearful image of his enemy's face, or he had never seen one. If the invaders were as ferocious as he led us to believe, it was possible that none of the Kohoroshanitari had come close enough to see one and lived to tell about it.

I made up my mind right there that we would try to get a look at the enemies of the Waica. We tried to find out where the passage through the mountains was, but the chief shrugged. He didn't know. What was more, he was becoming impatient. He wanted to talk about himself, not the enemy.

We gave him the opportunity. He showed us his possessions—a handsome webbed hammock made of cotton; beautiful baskets patterned in many colors, the handiwork of his wives; a collection of weapons and other implements.

While we were ooh-ing and aah-ing, the chief spat out a gob of something that was tucked inside his lower lip. I noticed they all seemed to keep something there. He took a pouch off the wall, and got a pinch of something to replace what he had just got rid of.

He allowed us to look at the stuff in the pouch. It was nothing but shredded leaves. There must have been something in it, like nicotine, to make the sucking enjoyable.

That gave me a bright idea. I took out a cigarette and lit it. That alone was well received, but when I puffed on it and produced smoke, that brought down the *chabona*. I soon had the chief puffing contentedly on a butt. He inhaled from his very first drag and never coughed once. That's what sleeping over a wood fire will do for you.

We had a lot more to show the chief than he had to show us, but Tavares cautioned us not to overdo it. The chief might feel that we were trying to embarrass him. We made certain that he went away happy by giving him a hat. He had to be shown what it was for, but once it was on his head it was there to stay.

When the chief left, we visited several of the families under the *chabona* wall. I showed my admiration for the bows and arrows stored under the eaves. The men, flattered, put on a demonstration of their use. They showed great strength in bending the giant bows, which were shaped like long, tapered broomsticks. The arrows were remarkably straight. They were cut from single lengths of reed. The thicker end was hollowed out to receive the tip, a bamboo sliver that looked like a dart. The tips had to be kept separately in a quiver because of the poison coating. To the slim end of the shaft were affixed two large sections of feather, gracefully trimmed to stabilize the arrow in its flight and cause it to rotate.

We watched the little archers with their great weapons. They seemed to shoot at random. After a while there were many warriors gathered in the clearing, shooting arrows straight up into the air and jeopardizing the lives of everyone, including them-

selves. The shafts soared out of sight in the dazzling sunlight, then fell point downward into the hard-packed earth of the clearing.

"What is this, some kind of Russian roulette?" Arnie asked.

We got under the protection of the wall and watched the suicidal display, hardly believing our eyes. During a lull in the barrage I ducked out and tapped one of the braves on the arm. I wanted to use his bow. While I was trying to get him to understand what I wanted, another warrior stepped up and offered me his weapon. It was my friend Kamboe.

Drawing the arrow back took just about all the strength in my arms. The bow was considerably more rigid than any I had ever used before. The arrow had good distance, but it was a little light and had a tendency to sail. After a while I got the hang of it. Kamboe seemed as pleased as I. I decided to trade for the weapon. I pointed to it and said, *"Nomehan,"* barter.

Kamboe nodded. *"Eba sebara."*

Tavares told me that Kamboe wanted a knife. He had probably seen the machete I had given the chief. Tavares voted against the idea. Apparently Kamboe was an ambitious warrior. He wanted to compete with the chief. I asked Tavares what I should offer him instead. He suggested a smaller knife.

I showed Kamboe a hunting knife with an eight-inch blade. He didn't reach for it at first, but after I showed him how it stripped the bark off a limb he decided he wanted it. There were several others watching the transaction, so I decided to get up a game of "territory," the good old American diversion that gives the land to the man who handles the knife best.

The warriors, who could hurl a lance with deadly accuracy, had little trouble mastering the two-foot toss of the knife, but they couldn't understand the point of the game, and quickly lost interest. I suppose they did not grasp the concept of real-estate ownership.

But they did understand the knife. All eyes followed it as Kamboe tucked it under his cotton waistbelt. The blade lay flat against his thigh in a way that made walking a hazard. The Kohoroshanitari seemed to like living dangerously.

While I had the men together, I offered to trade for other handcrafted items—bamboo quivers, bone earrings, baskets, and the like. I showed them what they could get in return—fishhooks, pocket knives ("See? Open, close."), matches ("Look. Make fire. *Kiewaka*."), candles, combs, and rubber balls. That was plenty for a start.

They let me know when something was pretty by exclaiming, "*Shorema! Shorema!*" When something startled them, like the matches bursting into flame or the balls bouncing higher than their heads, they howled, "Owoo! Owoo!"

They brought me things from their shelter without so much as consulting their wives. In some families the wives were not even at home. They were out gathering firewood and fruit, with their babies strapped to their sides. Yet the men showed great deference to their spouses in most matters, and did the heavy work on the plantations: I guess the household possessions were just not important enough to argue about.

While all this was going on I lost track of my two friends, who were prowling about the village on their own. When they showed up for lunch I asked them what they had been up to.

"Jerry's been making out."

"Why don't you shut up?"

"Are the women still picking on you?"

"Yeah. I have to wear long pants from now on or I'll have hairless legs. By the way, put this down in your journal: The word for beard is *haweke*."

"How do you know?" Arnie challenged him. "They never saw a beard before. Maybe *haweke* means hair."

"No, they only say *haweke* when they pull my beard. When they pull the hair on my legs or head they say *pawahanah*."

I added both words to my journal.

Arnie brought up a new subject. "Did you see my mascot? I have a kid following me around. I had to chase him away before someone came after me for kidnapping."

"What does he want from you?"

"Nothing, as far as I can tell. He thinks everything I say is the greatest. He offered me a live grasshopper. When I told him I

didn't want it, he ate it himself. I swear I thought I saw it kicking in his stomach. Don't they feed the kids around here?"

"Sure," Jerry said. "Every one of the women seems to have a baby at her breast."

"Yes, but the older kids, especially the boys. I see them eating bugs and frogs and anything that doesn't bite them first. What a way to take care of kids."

"Out here that's the best way," I told him. "They're learning to take care of themselves. In a few years they'll have their own families. Look at how young some of these fathers are. They're younger than we are, and they're supporting a household."

Arnie erupted with laughter. "Supporting a ha-ha-house . . ." He thought that was the funniest thing he had ever heard. "A house-ha-ha . . ." He couldn't even get the word out.

Junior and young Tavares looked up from their rice and milk and started to laugh along with Arnie. He had a great knack for reaching kids that way.

"What makes you think it isn't a household?" I asked him.

"A house-*hole* is more like it." He insisted on having his fun.

After lunch we discussed our plans for the remainder of our stay. We would continue to gather information and specimens, photograph the Indians, and record their voices on tape. We would also make some overland trips to see whatever else there was of interest in the area, particularly other Waica groups. I had a special yen to explore the mountains to try to find the passageway of the invaders.

We asked Eugenio about the other groups. He said that there was no telling how many there were because they moved around a lot and kept changing their names. Only a few stayed in one place for very long. Those were the larger ones, which were strong enough to defend their *chabonas* against attack. Once the bigger villages—with populations of two hundred or more—settled down and started farming in earnest, they were reluctant to wander very far from their plantations.

I asked the Old Man what the best way was to find the other groups. He said the Kohoroshanitari might be induced to guide us, unless they were at war with their neighbors. If we had to go alone, the best way was to follow the rivers, for although the Waica hardly swam and had no boats, they had to be near the rivers because of the fish, a staple part of their diet. However, Eugenio did not recommend that we travel from village to village by ourselves.

We wondered if he knew of any villages that he could take us to. He was certain only of two. One was the Shamatari village on the Rio Maiá, which he believed had been contacted before by outsiders. The other was a smaller village at the very headwaters of the Cauaburi, which he had heard about but had never visited. That was the village of the Amarokawebueteri. All the other groups in the area—there could have been a dozen—were either deep in the interior or constantly on the move.

Until we adjusted to jungle life well enough to attempt an overland trip, I hoped to use our time to advantage right in the *chabona* of the Kohoroshanitari, doing a study of this one group in depth.

My guess was that Kamboe would be the best source of information. He was responsive and communicative, and he had a businessman's instincts. I picked him the same way I picked Ruey and most of my contacts in strange places, on the basis of mutual self-interest. I was always wary of favors. I had been shown time and time again, to my regret, that there was no such thing. The padres? They were very helpful, but we were also helping them. The Indians we contacted were all potential converts. These four hundred or so Kohoroshanitari Indians represented quite a haul of heathens. For every person it was self-interest, but you had to know what the person was after.

Arnie asked me why I didn't go right to old *pareome,* the boss.

"Because for my money, old *pareome* will take what he wants when he wants it. He's not going to sit still for any trading. He's too used to having things his way. I'm just going to dole out enough gifts to him so he doesn't cause trouble. I don't think he likes us."

"He's not so dumb after all," Arnie cracked.

That afternoon I looked around the *chabona* for Kamboe. I

found him in his hammock conversing with his son, a bright little five-year-old boy, and a lovely daughter of about eight. The boy's name was Poko-yewe. We called him Pequino for short, mainly because he was short, and that was the Portuguese word for "short." The girl, a delicate jungle flower, was named Ama. Ama busied herself doing the things her mother did. In perhaps as little as five years she, too, would be a mother.

Kamboe's wife was not at home when I first visited, but she was present in everything that belonged to the domestic side of the household. The hammocks, baskets, and other artifacts were of superior workmanship, her workmanship. It was clear that the quick-minded Waica warrior and his wife were well mated.

I started by making friends with the children. Kamboe encouraged them to accept my gifts. He seemed especially indulgent toward the boy. I gave Pequino a balloon, and showed him how to blow it up. He did the same thing with the balloon that I had done with my first balloon. He turned it loose with the neck open and watched it spin itself to exhaustion in the air and come to earth with a flop.

Ama's gift was a comb. I had observed that grooming the hair was the woman's job in the village. I demonstrated the use of the comb on myself, but I did not envy her the job of trying to pass that same comb through a head of matted Waica hair.

Maybe she would use it just to scratch the tops of heads. I noticed that all the people in the village had their hair cut away on the crown of the head to form that characteristic bald spot about four inches across. The reason for this peculiar hair style was one of the real idiosyncrasies of Waica behavior. For the time, however, the reason for it remained a mystery.

Kamboe and I exchanged gifts and information. We quickly established a basic vocabulary between us. Most of it was Waica, but a few Portuguese words and some Americanese crept into it. I started with *shorema* and *nomehan* and the few other words I had learned under Eugenio's tutelage, then moved on to the identifying words for all the objects in Kamboe's home—hammock, *nenkake;* bow and arrow, *chereka;* quiver, *tura;* large basket, *we-ere;* small basket, *shotokahe;* tube, *mokohiro.*

I asked Kamboe what the tube was for. I couldn't get a thing out of him. I put the question in the back of my mind for another time, when perhaps communication between us would be better. But somehow I knew that in asking about the tube I was treading on sacred or dangerous ground.

Kamboe supplied the first physical anthropological statistics for my journal. His basic measurements were as follows: Height, 5 feet 2½ inches; neck, 13½ inches; chest, 36½ inches; foot, 10 inches. Kamboe's height was within the normal Waica range for a full-grown male, and his outsized feet were typical, but he was somewhat slimmer than most of the others. His friend Horoma, for example, was only five feet tall, with other measurements to match, except that his chest was 39 inches around.

Horoma was a typical specimen of Waica manhood—short, muscular, and barrel-chested, but with small wrists and ankles and delicate facial features.

Knowing that the Waica were fearful of having their wives taken by strangers, I decided to forego measuring the women. But as a guess I would say that the typical Kohoroshanitari mother was a little less than 5 feet tall, with glamour measurements of 36-28-36 and rather small feet and hands.

I tried to be as businesslike as possible in my dealings with the tribe. I couldn't allow myself to become a matinee idol like Jerry or a court jester like Arnie. Someone had to be chief or we would all lose their respect. For what is a tribe without a chief, and with whom would the *pareome* deal if we had no leader? I made certain to keep them reminded that we had a leader and that the leader was me. I stood for no nonsense and I did not engage in horseplay with the subjects of the chief. That included Kamboe.

We followed the system that had worked so well on our river voyage; when necessity did not require our being together, we went our separate ways. In that way, as the days passed, we melted into the pattern of village life, each amusing himself or educating himself according to his own bent. Our four Indian helpers kept mostly to themselves.

Jerry learned to use Waica weapons skillfully, and made some shrewd trades for valuable specimens. Arnie pulled together work parties when they were needed. He also liked to get up games among the men and boys. They all played practical jokes on him, and but for his size, they could have made him the sorry victim of their primitive sense of humor. Simple things made them laugh, like a pratfall. That is the basic universal joke, watching the other guy get his lumps. Arnie came very near being the other guy.

Tavares stuck close to home. He watched the two caboclo boys closely, for fear they would take up some of the offensive Waica ways. Now that he was a good Catholic it was proper for him to be offended by some of their practices, but I still wondered about his sleeping over a wood fire on our way up the Cauaburi. That was a Waica custom for sure. Every household in the *chabona* had at least one smoldering wood fire that the woman of the house kept going day and night. The family's hammocks were strung almost directly over it. The father's hammock had the place of honor nearest the fire.

Such habits as these did not violate the Christian code of ethics. Tavares' practicing them, therefore, raised no moral questions, although I did wonder whether he retained them from his youth or had picked them up in his travels on the Cauaburi.

Then there were the other customs practiced in the village, the ones that the Padre Johns and Padre Antônios would discourage when they brought their religion to the Kohoroshanitari.

Performing the sex act in public was one. This was sure to be high on the missionaries' list. On countless occasions I saw husband and wife enjoying coitus in a hammock while their neighbors on either side went about their business and the children played nearby on the ground. And homosexuality. Once or twice we saw adult males enjoying each other. This happened when the wife of one of them was menstruating, and apparently at no other time. The practice made a primitive kind of sense, but I could not get used to the sight.

Probably the first practice the missionaries would attack was nudity. In this we had given them a good start. The chief was already wearing cotton shorts. Many of his subjects wore individual items of apparel, such as a hat, a shirt, or a single sock, and one young man had mosquito netting wound around his head like a turban.

They didn't understand clothes. They had no shame of their nakedness. To them, anything not a part of the body was decoration, like their feathered armbands and colorful belts. Once they put something on, they never took it off, rain or shine, and during our stay it was mostly rain. We saw them come in out of a downpour with wet clothes clinging to their bodies and not bother to remove them; the rain didn't annoy the Indian, so why should the dripping garment? One boy ran around wearing a sock until it rotted off.

Arnie sang:

> "Diddle diddle dumpling, my son Uhú
> Went to sleep with his stocking, peeyew!
> He had just one sock instead of two,
> Diddle diddle dumpling, my son Uhú."

Everyone loved the guitar, as poorly as we played it, and little Uhú with the one sock was one proud Waica to have the bearded giant sing about him.

For singing was a serious thing with the Waica. Their songs were like ancient sagas of heroic conflicts between man and man and between man and beast. Once we heard an old warrior chanting a legend about a battle between a Waica brave and a jaguar. He sang to a monotonous rhythm that worked like self-hypnosis; he was swallowed up in the fantasy. We could hear the growl of the animal issue from the man's throat. His voice grew husky with the strain of battle. It was a weird performance full of primitive sounds and endless repetition.

There was no special occasion for his singing. The old fighter just made up his mind to emote, and he did. When we heard him begin we scurried to get the tape recorder, and returned in time to capture several minutes of the remarkable song for posterity.

Was there a religious significance to the chant? There was no way to know, for, strangely, there was no religious leader and there were no specialized religious functions in the daily life of the Waica. Was the jaguar a god? Only if by definition a god is something that fills men with dread, like snakes and man-eating fish. One of the priests told me that the Waica worshiped the sun; but if God is a god of fear, then it was the darkness that the Waica worshiped, for the Kohoroshanitari hated to leave the village at night. And when it was imperative to venture into the darkness, they held a smoldering stick before them, waving it back and forth to keep the tip glowing.

I don't think these fears were a matter of faith but a matter of knowledge, the knowledge of what could be waiting in the darkness of the night—a boa constrictor, a fer-de-lance, a bushmaster, a poisonous spider, or the jaguar himself.

The great South American cat was undisputed ruler of the jungle. His scream, like the anguished cry of a woman in labor, froze the blood of every living creature for miles. There was no protection but flight, and few creatures could elude the speedy killer on land or in the trees or even in water. We heard the jaguar scream several times in the night. Suzy arched her back and spat in terror at the darkness. If we had her eyes and ears we would have known just where the jaguar prowled. He could have been right in the middle of the village. But we did exactly as we did when we encountered the nocturnal gunman in Manaus. We minded our own business, and so did the local populace. In the darkness the animal reigns.

fourteen

THE POWER OF "ABANA"

The day-to-day monotony of life with the Waica was broken one afternoon when the men left the village and headed into the jungles to the south. We grabbed our cameras and followed to see what was up. The warriors moved so swiftly that we almost lost them. Luckily they were following a path, which enabled us to keep from getting lost even when they were out of sight.

We followed the trail for a few miles and found ourselves at a plantation. We watched the Indians gather pods of the urucú plant and extract the waxy red seeds. With these they painted designs all over their bodies—zigzags, squiggles, crosshatches, and other vaguely geometric patterns. Kamboe was there, and so was the chief.

Kamboe smiled sheepishly at me as if I had caught him in the middle of a forbidden act. He made no sign of welcome. I gathered that this was a ceremony during which the braves wanted privacy. I think Kamboe was afraid that I intended to break into the ritual and embarrass him.

We stood back and took pictures of the activity. When the warriors were finished decorating themselves, they left in the direction of the village. Again we panted along behind.

There was no reason for us to take special note of the fact that the braves had weapons with them in the jungle. They never left the village unarmed. But they kept their lances with them within the *chabona* wall, and that was unusual.

There was a stir of activity throughout the village as each man returned to his shelter and came out again carrying his lance and two other objects. One was a small pouch made of leaves. The other was a *mokohiro,* the tube Kamboe had refused to discuss.

I knew something big was about to happen. I told the others, "Keep your cameras handy and stay close to those Indians!"

Again the warriors left the village, but this time they gathered in the clearing outside the wall. I noticed that the women and children hung back silently. Tavares shook his head fearfully and took his two charges by the hand.

Out in the clearing the warriors began to chant and follow each other about waving their lances. Then they opened the pouches and took out pinches of snuff, and disposed of it in the most amazing way:

They put the snuff into the tube, placed one end into the nostril of a fellow brave, and blew into the other end to force the snuff up his nose.

Instead of sneezing, the warriors just danced harder and brandished their lances more menacingly.

"Something's wrong!" I exclaimed.

"Yeah," Jerry said. "Those guys are on dope."

We watched the Kohoroshanitari warriors work themselves into a frenzy. Their eyes were glazed and their features were distorted. I hardly recognized Kamboe. He looked like a demon.

"That's your buddy out there, isn't it?"

"Yes, but he never told me he used the stuff."

"You should be more careful about the friends you make in the jungle."

"I'll ask next time."

Our humor was something akin to whistling through the graveyard. There was the ugly possibility that this party was in our honor. We were told that the Waica had been cannibals at one time. I wondered when that was; things change kind of slowly with the Waica. I remembered Kamboe's sheepish grin and thought to myself, If I was going to kill a man for dinner, that's just the way I would look at him.

The dance continued until dark. Then everyone went back within the wall. We retreated to our corner of the *chabona,* and waited.

For a while all was quiet. Then the warriors emerged from the shadows fully armed and slipped out of the village. We did not follow. This was a war party and they were after somebody's neck. That neck might well be severed by a steel blade, I thought, for Kamboe had taken along his hunting knife, my gift of friendship.

We arose early the next morning and looked for the members of the war party, but their hammocks were empty. There was nothing to do but wait.

The day passed in the usual way. The women nursed their babies, spun thread out of cotton, and went out to gather firewood. The gangs of boys played at war with little spears and hunted frogs and lizards to eat. It rained heavily in the afternoon and we lay in our hammocks, smoking, talking, waiting.

The sun was starting to set when the warriors returned. Their bodies were streaked where rain and perspiration had made the red dye run. Fatigue showed in their faces. There was a stranger with them. He limped along with the broken shaft of an arrow protruding from his thigh. Our men had brought back a prize of victory.

"There's your friend. Go say hello," Arnie said, pointing out Kamboe in the group.

"Don't think I won't. I'm going to try to get the story."

"Think he's too tired?"

"Never too tired to brag."

I found Kamboe in his hammock. His wife was preparing a meal for him. First I brought up the subject of the tube. This time he wanted to talk. He pointed to his nose, *"Koshepa."* That much I knew, but what was in that pouch?

"Abana."

I showed that I did not understand. Kamboe demonstrated the

act of sniffing the tube, then placed his hands on his chest and said, *"Kamboe patapata,"* Kamboe is big.

So that was the power of *abana.* It gave the warriors courage to fight. I wanted to know what had happened during the time the warriors were away from the village.

How do you ask a half-drugged savage a complicated question like that? I drew a circle in the earth and pointed to it, saying, *"Chabona."* Then I drew the figure of a man within the circle and said, "Kamboe." I indicated the departure of Kamboe by drawing a line out through the village gate and into the jungle.

Kamboe took it from there. He continued the line for a foot or so, then suddenly sprang from the hammock and landed in a crouch. *"Ha!"* Kamboe was ready to attack. He drew a large circle, another *chabona,* with many small circles within it. I took those to mean people or groups of people. Kamboe spread his hands low to the ground and hissed. He was stalking. For a moment he waited, as still as a rock. He raised his outstretched right hand gradually until it pointed to the horizon. *"Parepounshemoto,"* the sun. It was a dawn attack.

The warrior raised his body, and wailed, *"Eeee-ooo."* He took the hunting knife and slashed the picture of the enemy *chabona* into oblivion. Kamboe stood panting over the torn earth and boasted, *"Nohewanepo rereie,"* the enemy runs. *"Nohewanepo noma,"* the enemy is dead. *"Kamboe patapata."* It was then that I noticed clotted blood on the blade of the knife near the hilt.

Kamboe was exultant, but I wasn't very proud of myself. There was no denying that I shared responsibility for the death of at least one Waica. There was no telling how many enemy warriors Kamboe had skewered in their hammocks, to say nothing of the chief, the leader of Kohoroshanitari warriors, who had an eighteen-inch machete in his arsenal.

Kamboe looked over his shoulder and pointed, *"Eih? Eih?"* It was more a grunt than a word. Something was bothering him. I looked at his back. There was a long gash under his shoulder blade, and the whole right side of his back was covered with dried blood. The wound was on its way to healing, but the pain had only begun.

That was more of the power of *abana*. It had rendered Kamboe immune to pain. Now that the effects were wearing off, Kamboe was mortal again. He felt pain; he was capable of fear. He was *"patapata"* no more.

I felt a revulsion toward Kamboe. What a degraded way to face your enemy—to build up your courage with narcotics and then stab him to death in his sleep. They fought like animals, these Waica, no ritual, no code, no honor.

Well, Fred, what did you expect? I asked myself. This isn't Victory Field. I remembered the teen-age wars, the rumbles in the sports stadium that became a battlefield by night. I recalled one of those nights.

We had our own kind of *abana*—cigarettes, beer, and cheap perfume. We wore black leather jackets that shone in the moonlight as we waited with our girls on the handball court. One of the girls had a beer bottle with her. She splintered it against the handball court wall and gripped the jagged remainder of the neck. I remembered her face in the cold moonlight. Her lips were stained with tobacco and her features were distorted with fear and hate.

A figure walked out of the shadows of the grandstand and I went out to meet him in the infield of the cinder running track. I walked fast, straight at him. He started to sidle a bit when we were ten feet apart. I knew he was scared. It was over fast. He didn't want to fight. I could tell. He just put up his hands and hoped.

I went back to where the Cousins waited. The girl smashed the rest of the bottle against the wall and screamed curses at the gang across the field, her tortured nerves unwinding like steel springs.

Then, like Kamboe, we went home to brag.

There were similarities, and one basic difference: We played it for looks; Kamboe played it for keeps.

fifteen

MOUNT ONERI

We had a long way to go before we could call our study of the Kohoroshanitari complete, but staleness was setting in among the members of my expedition. I could almost smell that sweet lotus in the wet breeze, and I made up my mind to shake things up a bit.

I decided to tackle the toughest job first—Mount Oneri. The peak was the tallest in the area, and dominated the landscape to the west of the Rio Maturacá. It was part of the range that stretched to the north above the headwaters of the Maturacá, then ran eastward, parallel with the Rio Ariabo, a creek that joined with the Maturacá not far from the Kohoroshanitari village.

After watching that mountain rise out of the mist every morning, I longed to climb it and stand where probably no man had ever stood before. And from there we could begin our search for the passageway used by the Venezuelan Indians.

I told Arnie, Jerry, and Tavares of my plan. As usual, Tavares accepted it passively. Arnie and Jerry were full of questions. They wanted to know how we would go—we had a river to cross—what we would take along, who would go with us, how long we planned to be away, and so on.

I couldn't answer most of the questions, but the Indians could.

In fact, I wanted some of them along with us, for several reasons. First, they would know the shortest route to take. Second, they would know of any dangers to avoid. Third, they would show us a few of their tricks about living off the jungle. Fourth, if we left the village by ourselves, the Kohoroshanitari might think we were going for good and start splitting up our possessions. Not that the Waica stole, as Eugenio would be so quick to remind me, but they did have a chief who ruled on all matters of ownership, from wives on down, and he might rule us right out of our equipment. Once that was done, there would be no appeal.

Tavares and I paid the chief a visit and gave him an idea of our plan. He seemed a bit agitated. The question written all over his face was, "Why would anyone want to go into the mountains? There are so many nicer places to visit in the other direction." He reminded me of the priest in Uaupés who deterred us from continuing toward Colombia. He also had offered an alternative, a trip back to Manaus.

I wasn't going to be deterred again. We sweetened the chief's disposition with some gifts, and soon we had some of his men assigned to our project. To my disappointment, Kamboe was not among them, but I decided not to ask for him. The allocation of work was the chief's business.

We went back to our shelter to pack, and I noticed Eugenio looking glum. He wouldn't say anything, but I realized that he didn't relish the thought of climbing the mountain. He considered himself a riverman. I let him out of the trip without injuring his pride. I told him that, on second thought, he could do us more good in the village caring for our equipment and specimens than coming along to Mount Oneri. Of course, that went for the boys, too.

The overland expedition began early the next morning in a heavy downpour. We were loaded with equipment—cameras, foodstuffs, machetes, a medical kit, dry clothes, guns, flashlights, and other things that we considered necessities. Our four Kohoroshanitari guides took only their bows and arrows. The four Indians who had come with us up the river decided at the last minute to remain behind.

I made it clear to the guides that I wanted them to lead us to Mount Oneri; all I had to do was point. They understood, and immediately headed off in a different direction. Jerry was annoyed. He wanted to stop them, but they were loping along like greyhounds. We had all we could do to keep them in sight.

After a while I decided it was no good that way. We were wearing ourselves out under the weight of our packs, while the Indians ran ahead like their lives depended upon getting somewhere. I shouted after them, *"Wai-ha!"* Wait! Drat Eugenio, why wasn't he here to keep those savages in check!

When we turned the next bend we found our guides standing around, looking back at us with vacant expressions, a dumb and naked quartet. I let them know I was angry. I scowled at them and barked orders that I knew they couldn't possibly understand. When they were thoroughly confused, I took the pack off my shoulder and handed it to the nearest Indian. *"Yohepo!"* Carry! He took it meekly. The others accepted Arnie's and Jerry's packs.

"That evens it up a little," Jerry said with satisfaction.

With the Indians loaded down and us traveling light, we managed to keep up with them, but just barely, for the Waica were marvels on land. They floated, glided, flew—everything but walk. Their movement was too graceful and swift to be called walking. I couldn't take my eyes off them as they moved through pools of light and shadow under the brooding trees. They would disappear in the darkness for a fleeting instant, then materialize in a ray of sunlight and disappear again, blooming and melting, again and again, hypnotically, on and on, endlessly, tirelessly, effortlessly through the jungle.

I remember them as I saw them then, creatures in their element. There was nothing between their feet and the ground, nothing between their skin and the air, nothing between their head and the rain, a continuum of nature that had existed for a thousand Waica generations wheeling back endlessly in time, but destined to end abruptly with this generation. I feasted upon them with my eyes and my soul. The next visitor's eyes might not see what I was seeing. The next soul might not care.

We were passing through an eerie twilight world. There were

giant plants with roots standing twelve feet out of the ground like enormous spiders. There were trees leaning under the weight of parasite vines, and patches of matted undergrowth, like walls thrown up in our path, through which we had to cut.

The air was alive with smells, constantly changing with variations in plant life. There were smells that could root you to the spot—minty smells, sweet smells, intoxicating perfumes. There were others that would make you run to escape—bitter, rancid, fetid. And all from the saps and leaves and blossoms that lined our way.

The silent green cavern suddenly opened up and we emerged into the hissing gray world of an Amazonian rainstorm. We found ourselves on the bank of a river, at the foot of a slender vine bridge.

Tough woodlike vines were bound together to form the walkway, and two more strands were hung above the walkway to act as retainers. At intervals, there were loops of vine running from one retainer under the walkway to the other, so that the entire bridge would sway or sag together under the weight of a person.

"Are we supposed to cross on that thing?" Arnie asked.

"Why not? It looks like it's been used before," I said.

"But not by me. I'm twice as heavy as these guys."

"Well, what do you want to do, turn back or keep going?"

"How deep do you think the river is?"

"What's the difference? You can swim, and you're only wearing sneakers."

"That's true. Okay, I'll try it."

According to my information, we were at the Rio Ariabo. The river flowed eastward, down from the plateau. We could see it divide at an island to the west, and beyond the island it combined with the southward-flowing Maturacá.

I had two of the Indians cross first; then we crossed, with the other two Indians following. The guides ran across with quick little steps, like surefooted monkeys. Arnie, Jerry, and I inched across with both hands on the retainers. The bridge sagged almost into the river under our weight.

Our path swung to the west and then to the south in an arc

that paralleled the curve of the Ariabo as it met the Maturacá. The jungle closed in on us again; it became dark and the rain came through gaps in the leafy roof and descended on shafts of sunlight: "And God divided the light from the darkness." In the great natural cathedral of the jungle I felt as if I were witnessing the Creation.

When the rain stopped, we called a halt for lunch. The Indians shared our food. They washed it down with fresh water from the vines. They selected a certain variety that was thick and bristly, and broke it open. The water gushed out as if from a garden hose. The Indians held the severed vines over their mouths and let the water run in, overflow, and run down their chests.

I hacked open one of the vines with my machete and took a drink. The water was fresh and cool. This, then, was how the Waica satisfied their most basic need when they were on the march. The vines must have come in especially handy in the dry season, when many of the little creeks disappeared and the water level dropped on the rivers.

I wanted to see how the Indians got their solid food. I asked them for *hata,* fruit. They studied the branches above us and picked out a tree swarming with squirrel monkeys. They pointed and informed each other, *"Gua-she,"* monkey. One of them elected himself fruit gatherer. He ran right up the slanting tree trunk, like a monkey himself, while the little chatterboxes scattered in all directions, their tails flailing the air.

Our treetop harvester returned with a load of berries cradled in one arm. We thanked him and passed the dessert around. Jerry decided to return the favor. He took out his .38 revolver, aimed carefully, and fired a shot. The braves blinked and sprang backward. A monkey fell at our feet. They studied it carefully and murmured, *"Noma. Noma."* Dead. Now they had seen the magic of the fire tube.

They left the monkey where it fell. I had no way of knowing whether it was because they felt it was Jerry's monkey, were afraid of the magic that had killed it, or were simply too full to think about food. As for saving it for later, we knew they would never bother. The Kohoroshanitari hardly stored food even in their homes, except for plantains.

It was a hot, sticky afternoon as we continued along in a southwesterly direction. The Maturacá was two or three miles to our left, and Mount Oneri was about a mile to our right. Every time we came to a break in the jungle we looked up at the peak towering over us. We continued along the base, hoping to come to a less precipitous slope, or, with very good luck, to a path through the mountain.

We were now traveling through the soggiest terrain I had ever seen. We crossed creek after creek, swamp after swamp. Where the ground was not rocky it was spongy and black like humus. One of the wider creeks must have been the Maturacá itself, where it trailed off into the high ground, but it seemed that all the rivulets together were one vast drainage system that fed the Cauaburi and its tributaries. The Indians seemed to seek out the stream beds as they traveled, since that offered the solidest footing. The water didn't bother them, as long as they didn't have to immerse their entire bodies.

But the water gave us problems. Our sneakers were soaked and our socks were bunched up inside and chafing our skin. I felt as if I was walking on burs.

Finally we came to open ground at the foot of the mountain where the slope was more gradual. There, by the side of a creek, we set up our base camp.

There is no simpler dwelling than a minimum base camp. There are four vertical supporting posts, several crosspieces lashed to the supports, and a tarpaulin or leaves over the top to provide shelter. We used a tarpaulin. Working fast with our machetes, we had the whole thing put up in a half hour. Then we moved our gear under the shelter and hung up our hammocks.

The Indians had a different system. They had not taken their woven hammocks with them, so they had to make new ones. They sliced strips of bark from a tree with razor-sharp slivers of bone. They tied the strips together at each end, and strung them up with vines.

Their next job was to get the fires going. They used a round, tapered stick of wood, which they kept in their quivers with their bone blades and arrow tips. They forced the end of the stick against another piece of wood on the ground, and piled shredded bark against it. Then they twirled the stick between the palms of their hands until smoke began to curl out of the bark. They continued to twirl and blow until the bark sprang into flame. They shielded the precious fire with one hand while they added twigs with the other. The fires were, of course, right under the hammocks.

The Waica method was quite similar to that of many North American Indians, except that the more advanced tribes of North America used their bowstring as a mechanical device to provide faster and easier rotation of the stick. It seemed like a minor advance, but one that the Waica might never achieve by themselves.

With the shelter and hammocks up and the fires going, I decided to give Mount Oneri a try.

I hardly knew where to begin. Whichever way I looked, the mountain rose sharply and was covered with trees like a green carpet. We scouted around the base looking for a path, a creek bed, a crevice, anything that would indicate a passageway to the other side. But no luck.

An hour of fruitless searching sapped the last of our energy and interest. We returned to our camp for food and rest. Our bodies were stiff and aching from the march. My leg muscles were sore from the unnatural way I had to walk over the uneven terrain. Arnie, sitting on a rock with his head hanging down, looked like a big shaggy lump. Jerry looked even worse. His eyes were glassy, and every once in a while a tremor ran through his body. I figured that with the exposure and fatigue, his cold was getting worse.

We built a big fire to dry our things and to get something hot cooking. The place was suddenly chilly, the sun having disappeared behind the crest of Mount Oneri, and we huddled to keep warm. In the end we wrapped ourselves in whatever we had and climbed into our hammocks. Amazingly, the naked Indians in their unsheltered hammocks did not seem cold or uncomfortable. Their only worry seemed to be that the fires would go out. They chatted animatedly before they went to sleep. I think being so far from the village and so close to Mount Oneri made them nervous. If it wasn't for the orders of their *pareome,* they quite likely would have deserted us halfway to our destination.

The mosquitoes were incredibly thick around the hammocks. Each of us hung suspended in a cloud of tiny whining specks in the tropical twilight. We dozed fitfully through a night of torment.

When I awoke I didn't know where I was. I was enveloped in a limbo of noxious whiteness. It was the mist rolling off the mountain. That malevolent rock poured every kind of evil upon us. First darkness, then insects, and now a pestilence. We had progressed from the Creation to Exodus.

I could hear Jerry groaning and chattering in his hammock. I got up to wake him so we could build a fire. When I touched his head to rouse him, it felt as if there already was a fire going, in his skull. Jerry had a raging fever.

I looked closely and saw that he was wide awake, but all he was doing was chattering and staring straight ahead. I shouted to Arnie to help me.

"What's up?" he asked through his yawn.

"Something's wrong with Jerry."

In an instant Arnie was at my side. "What do you mean? What's wrong?"

"It's a fever. Get me the medical kit." I turned to Jerry. "Did you take your malaria pill yesterday?"

He shook his head.

"Oh, my God!"

I tried not to panic, but I suddenly realized that all that stood between Jerry and a marshy grave was my half-baked medical knowledge and the contents of my medical kit.

I gave him Alarin tablets, and tried to take his temperature. Arnie held his jaw steady so the thermometer wouldn't fall out.

"How much has he got?" I asked him.

"Christ! A hundred and five!"

"We've got to get him back. I can't do much for him here."

We rigged a stretcher out of the tarpaulin and two branches. We gave one Indian the front end and another the rear, and started them back along the path. We knew they could handle the unwieldy load much better than we could in the thick jungle. We took over carrying part of the gear.

I walked alongside Jerry, mopping his head and praying that the sound of his chattering teeth would not stop. I didn't look ahead or to either side until we came to the river. Oh that those waters could have parted! We had to trust the Indians to take him across just as he was, all bundled up in the stretcher. Arnie crossed first and I stayed in back, so that if Jerry fell into the water, one of us would be no farther away than half the width of the river.

They made it across without a slip, and we raced along the path toward the village as the sun rose straight over our heads and the ground steamed under our feet. We plunged into the tree-walled tunnel, our eyes straining to see Jerry's face. Our party covered the clearing near the village at a gallop and I directed the stretcher bearers right to our corner of the *chabona*, where we were met by a startled Tavares.

"*Febre! Malária!*" I shouted. It was hardly necessary. He had seen it many times before. He showed a genuine concern for Jerry, the one gringo whom he had singled out on his island to befriend. The Old Man hovered over him, the firstborn of our expedition, like a shield against the angel of death. We did what we could for him, as much as was within our feeble power. Mostly, we watched, prayed, and waited.

One of the Indian men ambled over to see what the trouble was, as aimless as a chicken in a barnyard. He saw Jerry's shivering body under the blanket, and began to prod him all over with his fingers.

Arnie became angry. "Get him the hell away. What does he think he's doing?"

"I think he thinks he's curing him, the poor idiot." I coaxed the Indian away, thanking him profusely. I refrained from giving him a gift of gratitude, because that surely would have encouraged all the others to come over and give Jerry the paw treatment.

"Eugenio, you keep them away. Please," Arnie begged.

Eugenio understood.

We forced some hot broth down Jerry's throat. He didn't cooperate or resist; he simply didn't know what was happening. We took his temperature several times during the afternoon. It hovered between 104 and 105. Then, in the early evening, it held at 104 for three readings. We began to feel hopeful.

"Take it again," Arnie urged.

"We just took it five minutes ago. Let him rest a while."

"Take it anyway. I have a feeling."

I yielded. We read the thermometer. 103. Hallelujah!

I looked up at the red evening sun hovering over the misty peak of Oneri like a witch over a cauldron. Tavares handed me a cup of hot soup. It was the first food I had touched since the sun had last set on that pillar of evil.

Arnie asked, "Are we going back again?"

"Not even if it was solid gold."

sixteen

THE SHAMATARI

~~~~~~

That night we soaked up sleep as a sponge soaks up water. In the twilight of consciousness I could feel the painful, ecstatic rejuvenation of my bones and muscles. My body purged itself of fatigue and drew new life from the night air.

In the morning I thought that the journey to Mount Oneri and Jerry's fever were nightmares. When my head cleared I remembered that the nightmares were reality, and I shuddered. When Jerry awoke he knew where he was but he didn't know how he had got there. He was gaunt and weak, but his fever was down and he was on his way to recovery.

Arnie and I made the rounds of the village and dropped in on the chief—"Never show you are ill." We ran into unexpected trouble with the *pareome*. His braves had told him about the .38 revolver. Now he knew it was a fire tube, just like his shotgun that couldn't make magic. He desired the pistol with a lust that showed on his face.

"*Eba,*" he demanded.

I shook my head, "No!"

He insisted, "*Eba! Eba!*"

I looked him straight in the eye and refused again.

He began to shout and wave his hands. Arnie thought I might

be pushing him too hard. The chief was surrounded by his cronies. He couldn't back down in front of them.

"We take a bigger risk by giving it to him. I don't trust him," I told Arnie.

The chief consulted with his cabinet, but he did most of the talking. He gave them a long story, and they agreed with whatever it was he said. Finally he turned to me.

"*Nomehan.*"

Arnie said, "He's backing down. Now he wants to trade for it."

"That's worse than wanting it outright. I know what's on his mind. As soon as he gets the gun he can kill us with it and take back whatever he traded. He's afraid to fool with us now, because he doesn't know what the gun can do."

"*Nomehan!*"

"No *nomehan, Pareome,*" I said, shaking my head.

"*Nomehan! Eba!*"

"No," I shouted.

I turned to Arnie and said, "Watch this. Just do what I do." I looked straight into the chief's eyes for a few seconds, then turned on my heel and marched away. Arnie did the same. The chief kept talking at our backs and we kept walking. And that was the end of it. It was the same trick that I had used on the gun-wielding drunk outside the Veronica in Manaus. I ignored him and he lost his composure. I found that many people reacted the same way; if you acted as if they didn't exist, they started believing it themselves.

Arnie was worried. "Don't you think he'll be out to get us now?"

"Not while we have the guns. I feel surer of him now than I did before. I know how he thinks, now. The guns are the strongest magic. As long as we have guns and he doesn't, he won't fool with us. The way to treat him now is real cool. Be polite and do what you want. If we don't push him he won't push us."

I checked in on Kamboe. I found him whittling on a piece of bamboo with the knife. He was showing Pequino how to use it. The boy was like his father, bright and curious. I thought it

would be fun to show Kamboe another aspect of modern technology—the boat.

I invited him to come with me to the *"pa-k-o,"* river. The confidential way in which I beckoned to him made it clear that I had something interesting in mind. He got right out of his hammock and came with me. Pequino followed. A number of other men tagged along. They knew that when Kamboe and the white *pareome* got together, something exciting was sure to happen.

The two dugouts were lying bottoms up on the riverbank, with the paddles underneath. Arnie and I turned one over and started dragging it to the water. The Indians jumped to our assistance. When we got one end into the water I climbed in and pointed to the dugout, telling Kamboe to *"o-bra-o,"* stand, on this spot. I got out; Kamboe got in and so did four others. They all stood there bunched together in one end of the dugout, waiting for their next instructions.

The load of Indians could have stood the boat up on its end in the water, so Arnie and I got into the other end. I instructed them to *"ro-o,"* sit. They lowered themselves gingerly. Arnie and I tried to pole the boat into the water with the paddles, but it wouldn't budge under all that weight. I called to the other Indians, who were watching with rapt attention to *"yo-he-po,"* lift. They lifted our end; we gave one shove with the paddles and slid into the water.

The Indians kept moving around and rocking the boat. Arnie and I were so busy keeping it steady that we couldn't settle down to paddling, to say nothing of giving instructions. I shouted *"ro-o"* several times before they all got down and stayed put. We showed them the use of the paddle in propelling the boat, making it stop and making it turn. They picked it up in no time at all.

The dugouts became a favorite toy with the Indians after that. We stayed with them at the river, making certain they did nothing foolish. The boats were, after all, our only means of getting back.

By spending time at the river we got a chance to see how the Kohoroshanitari fished. They used the bow and arrow, just as when they hunted on land. They crouched close to the water and kept the bow drawn and the arrow almost touching the surface. When a fish rose to the top they let go and impaled it; then they waded in after it.

It was a crude way to fish, and with the river high and the fish staying close to the bottom, a very unproductive way, too.

Away from the *chabona*, the Indians never sat with their buttocks directly on the ground. They took large leaves from any nearby tree and placed them under themselves like mats. It struck me that after several days with the Indian group this was the first time I had noticed it. The reason was that the Indians seldom sat down when they were away from the *chabona*. They were at home on their feet, like true land animals.

Jerry got a little stronger each day, but it looked like a while before he could go on another march. We asked him how he felt about staying in the village alone while Arnie and I did some exploring. He said it didn't make that much difference.

"Eugenio takes good care of me, and I don't see much of you guys all day anyway."

So we organized another overland journey, this time to the village of the Shamatari. We could have gone by dugout down the Maturacá to the Cauaburi and then up the Rio Maiá, but the Indians were not sufficiently experienced to be trusted in boats, and two men paddling would not be enough, especially on the return trip.

Instead we plotted our course through the bush to the southeast, which would take us to the Cauaburi near the point where it joined with the Maturacá. From there we would continue in the same general direction toward the Maiá until we came to the Shamatari village, which we knew was somewhere along the banks of the Maiá.

Tavares told us a little about the Shamatari group. From what he said they seemed very much like the Kohoroshanitari. One difference, however, was that they were supposed to have been contacted by outsiders some six months earlier. It was said to have been a German expedition. Other than that Tavares knew nothing about them, as he had not gone in with the explorers. I

wondered whether being the second white men to meet the Shamatari was an advantage or a disadvantage.

The Old Man told us another interesting thing. "Shamatari" was a new name that the Indians had taken when they moved to their new home, just like the Kohoroshanitari. But there was a difference. The Shamatari were originally two groups—the Wauanateri and the Hereweteri—which joined forces for the same reason that they moved south, out of fear of the Venezuelan Indians.

We greased the *pareome*'s palm and let him know that we still were his *shorema*. He assigned four guides to us. We split up most of the gear among them and held onto the guns, cameras, and machetes ourselves.

The terrain was considerably easier to negotiate than the swampy ground at the foot of Oneri. This was thick jungle, but with a network of paths. We passed the Kohoroshanitari plantations and saw some of the men in the fields doing the community farming.

The guides, or bearers, showed the same impatience at our slow pace as the others. They kept increasing their speed until we barely managed to keep up. After a while they began to pull away, and I shouted, "*Wai-ha!*" They kept going. "*Wai-ha!*" They were almost out of sight. "This will stop them."

"What are you doing with that gun?"

I shot six rounds into the air over their heads. Instead of stopping they bolted. We lost them completely.

"You scared them."

"I meant to. They know what the pistol is."

"What are we going to do now?"

"Keep going."

We did, and about a half hour later we found them by the side of the path, sitting on leaves and looking glum. After that they walked at our speed.

They knew we wanted to go to the Shamatari village, so we left it to them to figure out a way to get us across the Cauaburi. Sure enough, we came out of the jungle at a vine bridge. It was constructed like the bridge on the Ariabo, which is to say it was just as flimsy. And like the other bridge, it crossed the river not far from a fork. In this case the fork was the confluence of the Cauaburi and the Maturacá.

From there our march continued in a southeasterly direction through dense jungle. The paths became more obscure as we went beyond the perimeter of Kohoroshanitari-controlled territory. We were literally in no man's land.

The going got to be very slow. Most of the time we had to cut away foliage and vines at every step. There were few creeks that we could use for walkways, although there were many small bogs that forced us to detour. Even the Indians, topheavy with gear, used the path we cut for them. The light that filtered through the green canopy was gray and bleak. There was a steady shower hitting the leafy covering and sprinkles here and there where the leaves parted. The rest was gloom and silence.

But silence is in the ears of the listener. The jungle that yielded no sound to me spoke to the Waica in a million voices. The lead bearer stopped at one point and motioned to the others. They whispered among themselves and peered into the darkness. I strained to listen and finally picked up a faint rustling sound. The Indians not only could hear it but could also interpret it. Whatever was producing that infinitesimal disturbance was something the Indians did not want to meet. They took us on a wide arc to avoid the encounter.

Their eyes were equally sharp. Many times they froze like a stopped frame in a motion picture. It was always because of a snake, lying camouflaged like a fallen vine. The Waica's keen eyes picked them out every time. We never stumbled across one by surprise while the guides were with us.

To the Waica, the jungle was filled with signposts telling them where they were and who else was in the vicinity. A bent blade of grass was a traffic light; a hiss was a policeman's whistle.

We ate cold food right out of the can for lunch and continued until the light began to fade. The sun was descending to the left of Oneri, which gave us a rough measure of how far we had traveled. The Indians helped with our overnight shelter and then put up their bark hammocks. I saved them some work by starting their night fires with my lighter, to their genuine appreciation.

We cooked a hearty supper on the open fire. The Indians squatted on their leaves and shared it with us. Then they joined us for a smoke. This was a cigarette we had walked many rugged miles for, and it gave us indescribable satisfaction. A little thing like a cigarette can mean so much at a time like that. It filled my head with memories and my body with peace. The Indians took out their shredded leaves, rolled them up, and tucked them under their lips. That was their peace.

The tobacco smoke mingled with the smoke of the wood fire, and we slept.

Arnie and I felt exceptionally fit the next morning. No staleness or stiffness. We were rested and ready to go. We were adjusting to conditions in the bush, an adjustment we had no opportunity to make on the first overland trip.

The guides brought berries for breakfast. We put it on the menu with the cereal, condensed milk, hardtack, and coffee, and all of us pitched into a good meal. The Indians carried pouches of berries and other foods that would keep. Those probably were their emergency rations.

We picked up where we left off the evening before, hacking, walking, wading, and making slow, wet progress toward the Shamatari village. At noon we stopped for a sit-down lunch. I tried to get an idea of how much farther we had to travel, but our communications were not up to it. One thing the Waica were notably weak on was time. Day and night and the seasons were their only units of measure. I asked, "How many *ma-ha-ro?*" That was the best I could do. They nodded agreement; yes, it was day. I tried it the other way. How many *ma-ha-ro?* How many *mi-te-te?*" They insisted, *"Ma-ha-ro?"* It is day. They must have thought I had lost my mind and couldn't tell night from day. Arnie had a good laugh. He hadn't mastered the language either, but he had a knack of getting his message across that transcended language. Not that it was any help at that moment.

We continued moving southeast, around ponds, across creeks, through bogs and dense foliage. Then we came to a barely discernible path. The guides became agitated, but we followed the markings until we came to a well-beaten path that permitted us to put our machetes away and walk upright in single file.

We built our shelter and sat down to a lonely meal. Jerry, Tavares, the four bearers, and the two boys were back with the Kohoroshanitari; Arnie and I were camped out with our guides somewhere on a jungle trail; ahead lay the Shamatari village and a lot of unanswered questions. This wasn't exactly the way I had planned it.

I was awakened the next morning by rainwater running down my hammock rope and into my shirt collar. The cigarettes were wet and we had forgotten to put dry wood in the shelter. We ate a cold breakfast and moved out into a mysterious world of mist, gloom, and rain.

We kept to the same path, which joined with other paths and became wider as we went. It gradually swung due east, and I realized that we were traveling parallel with the Rio Maiá.

Then the jungle opened up to a great clearing, and before us was the *chabona* of the Shamatari. It was almost identical to the village from which we had come.

There was movement around the entrance; we had been spotted. Well, now our questions would be answered.

Our reception was less formal than the previous one. The entire village came out to meet us—men, women, children, and dogs. We knew immediately that Eugenio's information was correct. Outsiders had been here. There were machetes and other implements lying around, and some of the Shamatari wore the ragged remains of garments.

We knew someone had visited the Shamatari; now we would find out what kind of impression they made.

"*Eba! Eba!*"

That's what I thought. We spread the gifts around, but we had to use restraint. We weren't carrying much in the way of gift items, and there were hundreds of Shamatari. The village looked even larger than that of the Kohoroshanitari, and there were additional huts outside the *chabona*.

I asked for the *pareome*. He came out smiling with his hand extended.

"*Shorema*."

"*Shorema*."

"*Eba*."

I gave him an assortment—fishhooks, a knife, a mirror, and some other gimcracks. Then I looked at him, and he knew I was done handing things out. He turned and walked away.

I told Arnie: "We'd better take care of our business and head back. These Indians know only one thing, *eba*, and we don't have much to give them."

"Boy, somebody sure spoiled them," Arnie agreed.

The ripple that our sudden appearance caused died away in a matter of moments. The Indians treated us in a way that was almost too familiar. I suspected the hand of Padre John in this. That stop at the mouth of the Maiá! He could have paid the Shamatari a visit from there and let them know we might be around. He had "business" in the area, all right, and I believed we were an important part of it. It was typical of his behavior, and that of the other missionaries, to look after you without telling you about it.

We were shown to a hut where we put up our hammocks. Village life went on as usual, and we looked around. In general, there was not much to differentiate the Shamatari from the Kohoroshanitari.

But the women were different. They were dressed, if that is the word, like the women of the Kohoroshanitari—cotton belt, earrings and, in some instances, skin decorations painted in red—but they had an entirely different social status. We saw them carrying heavy loads of plantains into the village, something that the women of the other group never had to do. They did most of the hard labor and were more subservient. What's more, there were plenty of them. The village was rich in women, the commodity that many of the other villages lacked, the prize for which one village raided another.

We learned that braves of other villages came to trade with the Shamatari for wives. They didn't kidnap them. They would not risk an attack on so powerful a group, for even if they escaped, the Shamatari could probably wipe them out in retaliation.

We asked about the two groups that had joined to form the Shamatari group, but were given a reproachful brush-off. They were Shamatari now, lords of the upper Maiá, possessors of many women; they didn't want to be reminded of their past.

Their attitude toward us was suspicious and unfriendly. Familiarity, it appeared, had bred contempt. We felt safe but unwelcome. I didn't envy Padre John his task of converting those five hundred arrogant savages. All they seemed to know was *"eba."*

Arnie and I traded for sundry items. There wasn't much that we hadn't already traded for with the Kohoroshanitari. The only friendliness we experienced was with the children. As usual, Arnie was the Pied Piper.

Upon awakening on our second morning, Arnie said, "What do you say we get out of here?"

"I'm with you," I said, and we packed our things. We made one goodwill stop at the chief's hut with a gift to keep him peaceful while we were still within the boundaries of his empire. Our departure was as uneventful as our arrival.

We started back along the same path we had used only two days before. It couldn't have changed very much, but it looked astonishingly different going the other way. The compass told us we were headed in the right direction, but we still welcomed the presence of the guides.

seventeen

THE FUNERAL

Jerry was considerably improved when we returned, but worried.

"Ama's sick. I think she's going to die."

"What's wrong with her? She looked fine six days ago."

"It started like a cold. She sneezed and had a running nose. Poor Ama. They gave her their medical treatment. They pawed her all over. And when that didn't work they dipped her in the river. We didn't dare interfere."

"Where is she now?"

"In her hammock. Think you can do anything for her?"

"I don't know. Let's have a look."

It was pneumonia, and she was sinking rapidly. I had treated Indians for cuts, yaws, infections, and other minor ailments, but this was something I couldn't touch. Ama was already in the last stages.

Kamboe looked up at me hopefully. I put my hand on his shoulder and shook my head. He understood, as much as a loving parent can understand when he is watching his child's life drain away before his eyes.

Helpless, powerless, impotent. That is what we all are. Ama was too weak to plead for comfort. A great sigh shook her body as the wind shakes a leaf. Then she was still.

A great wail went up in the village. Ama's death moved the

Indians profoundly, perhaps because she was a female and young. Perhaps because she was Ama. Some people say the good die young. Saying that is a way of preparing for the worst, but the Waica were without homilies or philosophies. They were not prepared. They cried the cry of the helpless.

Father John, where are you now, when your flock needs you? Irmã Alice, you ministering angel of Tapurucuará, where were your protecting wings when the shadow touched Ama?

We went sadly back to our corner of the *chabona,* thankful now that our home was away from the rest of the village. The mourning was pitiful.

"How's your cold?" I asked Jerry.

"Just about gone."

"Were you around Ama much?"

"You mean before she got sick?"

"Yes."

"No, not much. Maybe once or twice."

It wasn't my intention to point a guilty finger at Jerry, but only to find out what had happened. I was satisfied that I had the answer. Chalk another one up to civilization. They were starting to go, the Waica, one by one. By the machete, by the knife, by the virus. What next, the gun? Not if I could help it.

They were piling firewood in the middle of the *chabona.* Ama's body, wrapped in her hammock, was placed on the pyre, and the fire was lighted. The family kept it going constantly for two days. We instinctively avoided the smoke. The smell of burning hair, flesh, and bone was too disturbing a reminder of the dead little girl.

When the embers of the fire were cold, I saw several Indians poking around in the ashes and removing the calcined bones. My brain reeled. They still weren't done with her!

In horrified fascination I saw them pound the bones to powder, then mix it with a pudding that must have been made of plantain. The mixture was rolled in plantain leaves and, while we watched, Kamboe was offered the grisly preparation.

He accepted the first portion, his wife the second, and Pequino the third. From there the remains were passed around to the other members of the village, perhaps in the order of some vague genealogy. My hair stood up on the back of my neck at the thought that I might be asked to partake of the funeral feast.

I backed away so I wouldn't be noticed, but the offer was never made, thank God. Thank the Lord and thank the Waica god that decreed the ritual as a way of returning the soul of the dead one to its family.

When the remains were gone the ritual of mourning ended. Ama was once again a part of the cycle of her family's generations. The village of the Kohoroshanitari went about its business, and the memory of Ama slipped quietly away like the feet of a small girl walking into the shadows of the jungle.

eighteen

VILLAGE OF THE DOOMED

~~~~~~~~~~~~~~~~~~~~~~~~~~~~~~~~~~~~~

We began thinking about our next overland journey. This was to be the most ambitious of all. It would take us all the way to the sources of the Cauaburi at the base of the Sierra Imeri range, and to the village of the Amarokawebueteri, one of the permanent Waica settlements Eugenio had told us about.

I was especially interested in the village because it lay in the direction of the Rio Marauiá. If we reached it from the Cauaburi, then again from the Marauiá in the east, I would be able to construct a complete map of the perimeter of the area bounded by the Cauaburi, the Sierra Imeri, the Marauiá, and the Rio Negro.

I was also curious to see how well the village had withstood the attacks of the Venezuelan invaders, as it lay in the shadow of the border mountains. The mighty Kohoroshanitari and Shamatari groups had fled, but the Amarokawebueteri, numbering only one hundred and fifty, had stood firm.

Meanwhile, we were increasing our knowledge of Waica civilization through our daily contacts with the Kohoroshanitari. We had observed their work and play, shared their joy and sorrow; we had watched them go off to war, walked with them through the jungle, fished and hunted with them, traded with them, argued with them, competed with them, learned something of their language and a fragment of their history, eaten their food,

recorded their voices, photographed them, obtained their artifacts, and recorded some of their customs.

I had not been able to learn the source of *abana,* although I
acquired some from Kamboe after much bargaining, and I
watched the slow manufacture of the poison used on the arrowheads. The warriors would pack shreds of what looked like a root
into a funnel made of leaves, then let water seep through it and
drip into a gourd. The black fluid that collected in the gourd
was the poison. The process was so simple that had I known
which root to use I could have made some myself.

To get a good photographic record of village life we had to
develop our own method of shooting motion pictures. A camera
in plain view would always upset a natural situation. Some
Indians would become curious, walk right up to the camera, and
look it in the "eye." Others would become frightened at the
whirring noise and back away.

We overcame this problem by shooting most of our footage
through a hole in a blind made of mosquito netting. When it
wasn't practical to set up the netting, we used Arnie to hold the
Indians' attention with his madcap histrionics.

The result was dozens of reels of excellent footage showing life
among the Waica before our visit wrought its many changes.

There were still a thousand things that I wanted to know but
that I knew I could never hope to learn in my short stay. However, two things interested me most: birth and marriage. We
didn't stand much chance of celebrating a new addition to the
Kohoroshanitari, since none of the women were in advanced
pregnancy. But marriage. I wondered if there was a possibility of
attending a Waica wedding.

I asked Jerry, "While we were gone did you see anything that
looked like a wedding ceremony?"

"No, but I saw a new couple set up housekeeping in the
chabona. Maybe there isn't any ceremony, or maybe they're not
really married."

We paid the newlyweds a visit. I didn't recognize their faces.
That was not remarkable, since there were some four hundred
faces in the village. But I got the impression that they did not

know us either. They were as shy and curious as the other Indians had been when we first set foot inside the *chabona*.

Tavares and the boys were with us, so conversation picked up after a while and I learned that the warrior and his wife had been in the jungle since before our arrival. They had been alone. I wanted to see where they stayed, so we organized an excursion with the Waica groom as guide.

He led us to a place a few hours from the village where there was a small lean-to, the honeymoon cottage. It was obviously a temporary dwelling that had been built for a specific purpose and then abandoned. There was nothing of special note, except heaps of ashes that indicated unusually big fires.

We talked to the Indian and had Tavares make further inquiries. The brave was a little reticent, perhaps because he thought we had designs on his bride. Arnie's comment was, "Tell him not to flatter himself."

Little by little we pieced together the story of Waica courtship and marriage:

When a young man reaches maturity, some time during his early or middle teens, he chooses one of the village belles of about eleven, twelve, or thirteen. He announces his intentions to the girl's father, and they settle on a price that the suitor must pay to his future father-in-law. The payment is always in meat— a certain number of tapirs, a certain number of capybaras, and so forth.

The young brave then sets out into the jungle to accumulate the dowry. He builds a lean-to that will become his home for several weeks, and every day he goes out to hunt game. Each night he dries the meat over a fire and chars it with hot ashes to preserve it.

When he is ready to make the exchange, he decorates his body with dyes from jungle plants. He and the father perform a simple trade, after which the bride returns with her groom to the lean-to in the jungle. They hang their hammocks there and honeymoon for about a month, then return to the village to set up permanent housekeeping near their parents in the communal *chabona*.

They go on to have their own children, seldom more than two.

while the husband hunts and works on the plantation and the wife devotes herself to domestic duties. There is no romantic love as we know it, but a certain kind of good fellowship, and an occasional violent argument.

The matter of family arguments was an interesting one, and the study of it solved a riddle that had been plaguing me—the bald spot on top of the head.

When a man and a wife had a spat, each took a wooden club and beat the other over the head. But strangely, it was not a free-swinging battle royal, like the family fight we had witnessed in the caboclo settlement, but almost a ritual. The two antagonists took turns hitting each other—there may have been a prescribed number of blows—until one of them collapsed or ran away.

Arguments between men sometimes took the same form, but more often than not the arguments between men were over important matters that had to be settled by the chief, such as personal-property disputes. The chief might get involved in family matters if there was something serious enough, such as infidelity. In such cases, the woman would not resist the advances of another man, simply because she had been taught from birth to submit, but she would nevertheless be judged guilty and treated harshly by the entire village. Which only proved that the double standard is not the sole property of our civilization.

As for the circle of exposed skin on the crown of the head, it was cleaned and tended after the fight so as to prevent infection. This could not have been accomplished had the spot been covered with hair. So, after all, there was a method to the Waica's mad haircut.

To complete the story of marriage, there were two other marital situations. One was when a woman was captured from another village. She would become the property of the chief, who would either keep her as his own wife or assign her to some deserving bachelor.

The other situation was most interesting. It was a sort of practice marriage for the male, who would live for a short time with an older woman, usually a widow, to familiarize himself with his role as a Waica husband. His training completed, he would then go on to seek a permanent mate. The temporary wives were beyond the childbearing age, so there were no problems arising in the way of offspring.

We saw a lot of merit in this arrangement. The implications of such a custom in our society were something to think about, especially in the light of Kinsey's findings concerning peak periods of sexual activity.

Hanging around the village made Jerry impatient. We were one up on him in overland trips; one and a half if we disallowed his unconscious return from Mount Oneri. We yielded to his urging and to my curiosity and prepared ourselves for the voyage up the Cauaburi.

For a voyage it would be. Although we were to begin by cutting eastward overland to get to the river, we would continue on the major part of our journey by boat. This meant portaging the boat and all our supplies through miles of jungle. That was an expedition in itself.

The chief allowed two of his men to go with us. As usual, we started out not knowing whether they were meant to go all the way or not. We took our chances. This time, however, Eugenio and the boys came along. He was, after all, our river pilot.

There were all Indians and no chiefs on this journey; everyone carried his allotted share. We took turns, three at a time, carrying the dugout, while the others carried the rest of the gear. Suzy tagged along at the end of a rope. As portages went, this one was ambitious and colorful.

Like all our journeys, the trip started out in high hopes and heavy rain. The endless rainy season had become a condition of our lives. We were always wringing things out and hanging things up to dry. We alternated between trying to keep dry and saying to heck with it and getting soaked.

We covered less than ten miles the first day. The Kohoroshani-tari pathways played out sooner to the east than they had to the southeast, probably because in that direction lay the ominous southern wall of the Sierra Parima. The dugout was a terrible burden. I kept hoping the effort would be worth it when we started the river journey. I had every reason to believe that it would, since our guide was the Old Man of the Cauaburi himself.

Our camp that night was on a higher elevation than the Kohoroshanitari village, and the night was therefore colder. We bundled up in our hammocks under the shelter and shivered the night away at the foot of the towering Sierra Parima.

In the morning we put the heavy dugout back on our shoulders and pointed its inverted prow into a sea of mist. We hacked and staggered toward the Cauaburi all morning, the Indians showing their usual boredom at the slow pace.

At midday our dirty, sweating expedition found itself on the bank of the Rio Cauaburi. It was narrow but, thank heaven, navigable.

We had hot food and fresh fruit on the rocky ground by the side of the river, which was really no more than an *igarapé*, or creek. Then we lowered the boat into the water, loaded it up, and pushed off upstream to the northeast.

There is no question that traveling by dugout was better than climbing over the vine-matted boulders that lined the banks, but propelling the boat was no easy chore. There were fallen trees all over the place, the toll of weeks of rain and flooding. Branches and roots stuck out of the water like the arms of skeletons, warning us of dead logs jammed against rocks beneath the surface. When we couldn't cut our way through, we had to portage.

We were seeing a slightly different kind of country—rocky, scraggly, and cold. But there was no shortage of life in the trees. This area was not so heavily hunted as the country to the west and south. There were squirrel monkeys as thick as moths, as well as other varieties of simian. There were white herons and smaller birds with pink plumage. Ocelots showed themselves several times. They hissed defiance from high branches, and Suzy watched us bring down a few of her wild cousins with rifle bullets.

The ocelots were a gift to our guides. They skinned them in a crude fashion, stripping off the largest portion of skin with the help of a bamboo sliver, and leaving the rest to rot with the body. They didn't eat the meat.

We camped out that night about five miles from where we entered the river. That, plus the twelve to fifteen miles we had traveled overland, was all the distance we had covered in two whole days.

We traveled a little over thirty miles in the next three days, nearly half of it on the third, because the small trees that grew on the high ground were never big enough to force a portage.

Into the Cauaburi from the mountains flowed dozens of tiny rivulets and one fair-sized creek, which we passed on our first full day of paddling. A tingle went through me at the thought that the creek could be one of the passages used by the Venezuelan Indians. The fact that the Brazilian Waica had no boats was no reason to assume that the Venezuelans had none either.

We didn't follow up on the hunch. Our destination was the village of the Amarokawebueteri.

At the end of the three days the Cauaburi became so narrow and shallow as to be impassable by boat. We camped out that night and continued overland the next morning along the base of the Sierra Imeri, leaving the dugout behind. We picked up a path that ran parallel to the Cauaburi, or what was left of it. We seemed to be headed right for the southernmost promontory of the mountain range. It was at the foot of the promontory that we came upon the village of the Amarokawebueteri.

The village was much smaller than either of the other two we had visited, and the land around it was not so thoroughly cleared. There were several openings in the *chabona* wall, and we entered through one of them to find the place entirely deserted.

Jerry said, "Here we go again" and we did.

The scene was a budget remake of the drama that had unfolded at the Kohoroshanitari *chabona*. For some reason we were not so nervous as the first time. Familiarity does breed contempt. We could have been picked off with poison arrows by these Indians just as easily as by the more numerous Kohoroshanitari, but we didn't worry about it.

The only good sign was no sign—no bloody cotton, no animal skeleton, none of the standard death signs that we had seen or heard about.

There were the smoldering fires, the hammocks and plantains hanging from the crossbars, the hard-packed earth floor, and the stink. And silence.

We waited, and after a while the Amarokawebueteri made their appearance. We shouted *"shorema"* to them as soon as their heads popped up. They approached warily, all men and all armed, but we went through the preliminaries in jig time, the *"eba,"* the courtesies to the chief, and all the rest.

There were only about thirty warriors on the reception committee. Figuring that there were fewer women than men—this was a frequently raided village—and a handful of children, we estimated the total population at about sixty. The *chabona* was built to hold many more, and Tavares had earlier estimated the strength of the group at one hundred and fifty.

It was the attacks, coming from all directions, that had decimated the Amarokawebueteri. They were being hit by the Kohoroshanitari and the Shamatari from the west and southwest, the Venezuelan Indians from the north, and the Rio Marauiá groups from the east and southeast. The only good news in all those disaster reports was that we were within raiding distance of the Marauiá. That meant we were also within marching distance of it, and could reasonably expect to reach the same village on the eastern leg of the expedition.

We could see the importance of wise leadership in the survival of Waica groups. The Kohoroshanitari had moved south to lessen the danger of attack. The Shamatari had done the same thing and also had worked out a union of two villages, something normally repugnant to those hostile groups. But the Amarokawebueteri stayed where they were like sitting ducks. The suicidal tendency of the Waica, demonstrated individually by the Kohoroshanitari with their random target practice, reached community proportions with the Amarokawebueteri.

Not that they did not adapt in their own way to the threat of attack. We noticed that they had cut many escape hatches into the base of the *chabona* wall, so that when a war party stormed through the gates they could scurry through the holes like rats.

If the village was not entirely wiped out, it eventually would have to become nomadic. The more primitive nomadic groups were said to have no more than a few dozen members each. The Amarokawebueteri had almost reached that point.

So, while other groups were climbing the ladder toward civilization, the Amarokawebueteri were sliding backward. The course of progress is always two steps forward and one step back.

I gave the village a scholarly once-over—some photographs, some notes, and a rough map. That was all; we needed sleep. The Indians retired when we did, but there was no sign of the women and children. They kept the few they had left well hidden in the jungle. Perhaps there were some warriors with them. I wondered at the strange mentality of these people that made them cling to this desolate spot in the wilderness at the expense of safety and peace of mind.

We put up our own night watch, lest we get caught in one of the raids. The Kohoroshanitari knew us, but under the influence of *abana* they would probably not differentiate between our sleeping bodies and those of the Indians in the next hammocks. I enjoyed a grim chuckle at the thought of Kamboe slitting my throat with the knife I had given him. As for the Venezuelans and the Waicas of the Marauiá, we had no reason to feel safe with them, either by day or by night.

It was our good fortune that we chose a peaceful night. We decided not to push our luck; our next night of sleep would be on the Cauaburi. So in the morning we bade our reluctant hosts farewell, without having met their families.

Our journey downstream felt like a Sunday drive in the country. The current pushed us along as fast as we cared to go; we used the paddles only to steer. And we took advantage of the openings we had cut through river debris on our way up. Suzy sat on the prow and blinked into the wet wind. We made it back to the Kohoroshanitari village in three days, just a trifle more than half the time it took us to go the other way.

Compared with the moribund Amarokawebueteri village, the old Kohoroshanitari homestead looked like a thriving metropolis.

nineteen

KAMBOE IN TRANSITION

~~~~~~~~~~~~~~~~~~~~~~~~~~~~~~~~~~~~~~~

I paid a visit to Kamboe to see how he was getting along after the tragic loss of Ama. I found him eating his evening meal with his wife and son, who was now more precious to him than ever.

His home had undergone a change. Many of the objects we had given to other Indians had found their way to Kamboe's abode. He was truly a businessman. Through *"nomehan"* he managed to acquire irreplaceable tools, garments, and toys in exchange for food or implements that he could produce himself. He had an edge over the others in intelligence and industry.

I got the impression that everything he did now was for the boy. Most striking was the little dugout he had carved. In showing him how to use the knife, he had shown him the way to the outside world. If Pequino had his father's makings, the next step would be a full-sized dugout, and he would be in it, down the Maturacá and down the Cauaburi to the twentieth century.

The name of Ama did not come up. My sympathy was in my manner, if Kamboe cared to look for it. However, I had the feeling that our relationship had reached a leveling-off point. Somehow I was certain that true friendship was not possible. The gulf between us was too great.

Still, I had an investment in Kamboe—my time, my wrist-watch, and my conscience, among other things. In return I wanted one more favor, the opportunity to see a lone Waica in the jungle, not guiding white men, not burdened with gear, but the free, swift Indian pursuing game in the natural habitat of both hunter and hunted—the jungle.

Although the Kohoroshanitari seldom hunted alone, I persuaded Kamboe to do so. There was a bribe involved; that was the common denominator of our friendship. He took his bow, some arrows, a quiver full of poison arrowheads, and a small pouch of food. He surprised me by also taking with him a cloth pouch, one of our gifts. It was filled with his most prized possessions, an assortment of objects we had given or traded to him.

I took along my .38 revolver, some ammunition, a tin of sardines, and a pocketful of hardtack.

I jogged behind Kamboe, keeping up with little difficulty; I was now a hardened overland traveler, and somehow Kamboe was not flying along as I had expected. The vision I sought was exorcized by the watch on his wrist, which now and then picked up a ray of sunlight and reflected it in splinters against the gray foliage. The pouch emitted a clank now and then to remind me that the long arm of Long Island City, or wherever it was that they made steel spoons, was reaching all the way into this virgin jungle to mock my dream with an obscene gesture.

In the area where we hunted game was remarkably scarce. We passed up the monkeys and small birds for larger animals, but there were none to be seen. Once we came across the half-eaten remains of a small animal about the size of a rabbit. An ocelot or jaguar must have been there minutes before.

Kamboe adjusted the cloth pouch several times, I believe to keep it from making noise. It was possible that the metallic sounds were warning off the animals. After a while he gave up and let it swing as it would.

When we stopped for lunch, Kamboe produced his knife from the quiver and cut himself a large leaf to sit on. I saw him admire the clean cut made by the blade in the meaty stem. He loved his knife.

The lunch consisted mainly of the food I had brought along. Kamboe was fascinated by the way the key rolled back the face of the can to reveal the little fish swimming in olive oil. He reached out his hand in a way that almost said, "Don't mind if I do." We shared the sardines and hardtack.

He struggled with his thoughts as he ate. I could see him forming words with his lips. He licked his fingers, and noticed the watch. He listened for the tick, and studied the sweep second hand, the strange little antenna that raced relentlessly around the face of that tireless timepiece. I wondered if he associated the movement with the winding that he performed every morning faithfully.

I watched him squatting there in the middle of nowhere, his weapons carelessly laid aside, his mind struggling with strange new thoughts—the ticking of the watch, the wonderful containers filled with food that grew somewhere in the white man's jungle. He wheezed a little. I wondered if he was coming down with a cold.

My experiment was a failure. Instead of capturing the body-mind of the Waica functioning at the peak of its powers, I had isolated one Indian at the troubled moment of transition. He was not yet a man of my world, but he was already something less than master of his own.

The body-mind no longer operated as a unit. Kamboe was a slightly tired Indian whose body was burdened with unnecessary trivia and whose mind was distracted by many things—the objects in his pouch, the fire tube the white *pareome* might give him, the steel pot he hoped to acquire from his neighbor, the mirror he had hidden safely in the *chabona*. (Was it safe, or was there perhaps another brown face peering into it at that very moment?)

Kamboe had learned greed and trickery and suspicion. He had learned to kill the white man's way, with steel. He had learned to hope, and therefore to regret.

He had learned all this during our short visit. And there were greater forces still to be unleashed against the Waica—whiskey, religion, and a greed more devouring than the lust of a man for a woman—gold fever. For all around us, in the creek beds and in the ground under our feet, was yellow sand that I recognized as a type rich in gold ore.

We headed back along a different path. Kamboe was scanning the trees carefully, his bow drawn. A Waica brave does not return from the hunt empty handed.

There was still plenty of hunter left in Kamboe. Having given up hope of bagging something big, he went after monkeys and birds. He killed a small turkey and two monkeys and, tying their legs together, slung them over his shoulder with a satisfied smile.

His step seemed lighter and swifter. He was no longer troubling himself with the worries of another world. For a moment he was once again the head of a Waica family returning home with fresh meat. So at the last instant I did catch a glimpse of what I had been seeking, the man-animal at home in nature. But I knew that the end was in sight.

A portrait of Kamboe remained etched in my mind—not the confused, troubled Kamboe I left behind, but the free Indio that lived in a timeless, changeless world before the coming of the bearded strangers. This is the portrait:

In the sleeping heart of the Brazilian jungle, five hundred miles and a thousand generations from Manaus, the morning sun awakens Kamboe. A white radiance illuminates the cool mist around him and turns the smoke of the breakfast fires into rose-tinted columns. Before his eyes are opened to the light, Kamboe's ears detect the hushed roar of the waterfall far to the north in the Sierra Parima, where the invaders come through secret mountain passes. Nearby, on the Rio Maturacá, macaws, toucans, and parakeets scream across the water and monkeys chatter among the leaves.

Familiar smells hang in the air—the wood fire that burns constantly near Kamboe's hammock, the sleeping bodies of his wife, son, and daughter, and those of his neighbors on either side in the long communal lean-to; plantains and sweet potatoes roasting, the musty smell of dogs and their dung.

Kamboe opens his eyes wide and welcomes the first dizzy impact of bright, indefinite images. White mountain peaks reel across the hard blue sky and collide silently with olive-gray treetops. Soon the landscape settles into place—the hard-packed earth floor of the village, the shadowy interior of the lean-to on the other side of the clearing, the lacy foliage surrounding the village like a drawn curtain, jagged peaks poking up from behind the trees, and a flawless blue sky covering the world like a crystal dome.

Kamboe spits out the roll of shredded leaves that he has kept tucked inside his lower lip all night and replaces it from the pouch that hangs over his head. He reclines again and allows the juices to seep into the corners of his mouth. While satisfying his first appetite he waits for the eye of his belly to focus on the foods that are made known to it—the plantains and sweet potatoes, the monkey, ocelot, and piranha meat cooking over open fires. The juice of the leaves puts his belly to sleep, and Kamboe forgets about food for a while.

For Kamboe is a Waica Indian, a body-mind that lives in an infinite present. His history is the accumulation of practical skills and a vague tribal memory of having originated somewhere beyond the Parima. His future is this morning's meal, this afternoon's hunt, and tomorrow's raid on another village, when he will inhale snuff through his nose and transform his body-mind into a gleeful dancing spirit.

In a place of many rivers Kamboe avoids the water, but on land he is a creature in his own element. His compact body, less than five and one-half feet tall and unencumbered by clothing, passes among the trees and vines like a spirit, and glides over sharp rocks, deep mud, and tangled grass with impartial ease. His brown body, materializing suddenly in a pool of sunlight and vanishing again into the shadows, seems to be an evanescent condition of the jungle itself rather than a separate corporeal entity. Climbing a tree, Kamboe takes on the quality of a weightless object in liquid, rising along the vertical trunk with no apparent effort. He is a being in complete harmony with his environment and an integral part of it.

But the body-mind is also a man, with fears, loves, absurd beliefs, and an idea of beauty.

Kamboe fears his chief, the jaguar, the darkness of night, and the enemies from the mountains. He loves his children, the ecstasy of *abana*, the pleasure of uniting his body with another, the excitement of hunting, indolence, laughter, and a full belly.

Kamboe believes that the soul of a dead relative is restored to the family when they eat his charred bones, that sickness can be shaken out of a body or washed away in the river.

Kamboe sees beauty in his body when it is decorated with colored stripes for the dance of *abana*. He sees beauty in his wife when her teeth are filed to points like the teeth of the piranha. The patterns in his straw baskets, the fur of the ocelot and the jaguar, the flutelike song of the parakeet, and his own storytelling singsong—these are beautiful to Kamboe.

Guided by these thoughts and ideas, Kamboe passes the days in his brief span of life, a life that represents a single cycle in the changeless ebb and flow of Waica civilization. Twenty-two years old and already past the midpoint of his life, Kamboe can count his years by making circles in the sand. But he draws his pictograph with no number in mind—there might be ten or fifteen or thirty circles—and leaves it to be erased by the rain and wind.

For Kamboe does not consider posterity. He is concerned only with now, this bright, acrid, teeming morning of now.

And now is the time to eat. (What shall breakfast be? Plantains? Agouti meat?) Now is the time to listen to the parakeet with his ears and the rippling skin of his back. Now is the time to learn of many things near and far by tasting the air with his nostrils. Now is the time to stroke his thighs and remind them of consummate pleasures. Now is the time to flex his chest muscles and revel in their great relaxed power. Now is the time to bathe in the palpable warmth of the morning sun. Now is the time to live fully in the many dimensions of the present known only to the body-mind of Kamboe.

But the eternal Now had ended. With my steel knife, my gun, my ambitions, and my restless curiosity I had helped it end.

twenty

RETURN TO TAPURUCUARÁ

It was time to leave. With no more gifts to distribute, our popularity was waning fast. The Kohoroshanitari became more restless and less cooperative.

We packed our things. Among them were the following ethnological specimens from the three Waica groups we had reached:

Nineteen bows, 61 arrows, 207 poison arrow tips, 17 bamboo quivers, 5 armbands, 2 cotton hammocks, 3 *abana* tubes, 1 canteen of *abana* snuff, ¾ pound raw poison, 15 rodent incisor chisels, 1 large basket, 6 assorted small baskets, 7 belts, 6 arm decorations made of parrot feathers, 18 pairs of bone earrings.

We kept our weapons handy while we packed. The mood of the Kohoroshanitari was changing so rapidly that we didn't know what to expect. It was difficult to press bearers into service to carry our packs down to the river. We finally got the help of a couple of men and loaded the boats as quickly as we could.

When we bade farewell to the chief we gave him all that remained of our gifts, to keep or distribute as he saw fit. Then we got out. The last we saw of the Kohoroshanitari were a few braves fishing listlessly from the riverbank.

The fast current carried our two dugouts swiftly away from the landing. When we were well on our way, with nothing around us but water, sky, and trees, a feeling of elation welled up inside us.

The Cauaburi expedition was a success. We had conquered the river and visited three Waica groups, two of which had never before been seen by an outsider. We had mastered the rivers and the jungle, and were on our triumphant way home with a substantial haul of specimens, photographs, and information.

We laughed and talked a lot. The boys jumped around and chattered. Even Tavares smiled.

Just for a lark we detoured into the Rio Maiá, but lost interest when we reached the first rapids. That was one thing we had had enough of on the Cauaburi. The entire trip back took only two days, portages and all. We made a stop at the caboclo landing where we had left Padre John, and dropped off the four Indians. We looked for Padre John, but the missionary was off somewhere by himself.

We dropped Tavares and son off at their island. Eugenio was back where he started, but the younger Tavares was well on his way to becoming his father's successor as the Old Man of the Cauaburi. He had traveled the entire length of the river.

All our opened foodstuffs were added to the Tavares larder, and I gave Eugenio the one gift that showed I held him in higher esteem than the Indians—a gun. Those things and a small amount of money, in cruzeiros, were his payment for seeing us through the trip. I hoped he was as satisfied as we were. To the end he remained taciturn.

And then on the broad current of the Rio Negro we returned to Tapurucuará and Santa Izabel, to civilization and comfort. All four of us, Junior included, let out a spontaneous cheer when the steeple of the church came into view.

Brother Tom and Padre Antônio were there to greet us. They asked many detailed questions about the Waica villages. Padre Antônio's cross-examination was exhaustive; our information would probably provide him with the groundwork for the conversion of additional Waica villages. The condition of the Amarokawebueteri interested him most, since they represented a potential new nomadic group. His converts on the upper Marauiá were the members of such groups whom he had induced to settle around the mission. They fitted in well with his strategy of setting up a permanent base of operations and letting the Indians come to him. That was the key to his success. The permanently settled groups offered more resistance to conversion, perhaps because they were too set in their own way of life.

At our first dinner at Santa Izabel we were joined by another American, about our own age. His name was Dean Reed, and he was a professional folk singer and guitarist. We hit it off together, and I had my answer ready when the request came.

"Can I tag along with you guys?"

"Sure, if you don't mind sharing the work and expenses."

Of course he didn't. I had never met a prospective explorer who wasn't willing to share the work, until the time came to do it. Armand and Guilio made the solemn pledge and had broken it.

Still, Dean seemed like one of us from the very beginning. I acted as if I had to consider the question deeply; then I told him, "I guess we really do need another guitar player. You're in."

Dean was a sort of wandering troubador. He loved to sing, he loved to hear other people sing—all kinds of people. He was in Brazil on a nightclub tour, and had taken a vacation to visit some out-of-the-way places.

Once he became an official member of the party, he declared himself in competition with Arnie. He vowed that by the time we returned from the Marauiá his beard would be longer than Arnie's, in spite of Arnie's head start. The beard-growing contest became a permanent addition to our collection of running jokes.

We replenished our food, ammunition, and gift supplies at the store in Tapurucuará, and restocked the medical kit at the Santa Caza.

Our bodies cried for attention, too. We were underweight and covered with infections. The grime that had worked its way into our skins for an entire month came off a little at a time under hot showers. Fatigue had accumulated like poison in the marrow of our bones. We slept long nights, dozed every day before lunch, and napped in the afternoons to free our bodies of its numbing grip.

Life had continued in its natural course during the month we were gone. The newly settled Indians were behaving a little better; the cattle were fewer; and a pall continued to hang between the Catholic mission and the mission of the Seventh-day Adventists like the Berlin Wall.

We entertained the children again, this time with the professional help of Dean. The natural folk style with which he spun out his musical tales of joy and sadness went straight to the hearts of his young listeners. His language of song was as universal as Arnie's language of laughter.

We spent nearly a week at Santa Izabel, experiencing the entire cycle of physical and mental change, from near total exhaustion to impatience to get started again.

Dean added his few belongings to the common property of the expedition, and one day we packed to leave for our second trip into the interior.

twenty-one

THE RIO MARAVÍA

~~~~~~

It was, as always, a dawn departure. We loaded our gear into three boats. One was the padre's launch, which had a cabin with a small stove and a few other conveniences. The second was a motor-driven dugout. The third was an ordinary open dugout used mainly to carry drums of fuel.

The little Indian whom we had nicknamed Junior showed up at the boats, ready to join us for another adventure. I told him we weren't taking him along.

He stood there on the muddy shore looking forlorn, and Jerry interceded with me on his behalf.

"What have you got against the kid? Give him a break; let him come along."

I cut him short. "Look. I said he's not coming and that's it. Stop worrying about him; he'll get over it."

With all the problems of getting started, I was in no mood for explanations, but the explanation was simple. Junior knew the Waica language pretty well, certainly better than we did. I noticed several times on the Cauaburi trip that he listened in to our conversations, then told the Indians what we were talking about. That was giving him the benefit of the doubt. More likely he was distorting and embellishing what we said in true caboclo fashion. We could do without a troublemaker like that on this trip, and we did.

In addition to the four Americans, there was Padre Antônio, his personal assistant, a motorista named Babette who worked for the padre, Babette's helper, two dogs belonging to the padre, and Suzy.

We were not more than an hour out of Tapurucuará when the motor of the dugout broke down. Babette tinkered with it, but it refused to start, so we lashed the three boats together and continued under the power of a single engine.

With our speed cut down considerably, it took us another two hours to reach the mouth of the swift Marauiá. There was no mistaking the river. Its water was a cloudy white, in contrast with the opaque black of the Rio Negro into which it flowed.

For a while the river was nothing but a series of confusing turns; then it straightened out and we headed due north. We continued like that for the rest of the day, doing nothing but watching the walls of vegetation slide by. There was very little animal life except macaws, but there were countless numbers of those.

We pulled into a deserted landing at about five o'clock, with just enough time to set up our camp before dark. The site had been cleared by Padre Antônio on his first trip up the Marauiá more than a year earlier. The little lean-tos were still standing, but they were covered with vegetation and the palm leaves with which they were thatched were brown and withered. The ceilings were crawling with every kind of bug imaginable.

We got the fires going and washed ourselves in a makeshift bamboo shower. Then darkness set in, and we ate our supper to the accompaniment of a million chirping crickets. The mosquitoes and piums were also out in force. There didn't seem to be a day shift and night shift as at Jerusalem.

Dean made the evening more bearable by singing some of our favorite folk ballads, but eventually we had to confront the problem of sleep. Even with the protection of netting, I spent the first two hours of the night swatting mosquitoes. Then I got up and took a walk before trying it again.

I had almost dropped off when there was a new disturbance. There were wild pigs snorting around nearby. The padre's dogs heard them and started barking. Again I got out of my hammock, as did Jerry, and the two of us went looking for the pigs with flashlights and Winchesters. We never found them.

The next thing I knew it was five o'clock in the morning, the sun was rising, and all my bones ached. One night on the Marauiá had undone all the good of a week at Santa Izabel.

Over coffee and hardtack Padre Antônio told us that the first rapids were right around the bend. He promised us that the rapids on the Cauaburi were nothing compared with those on the Marauiá. To make matters even more difficult, we were nearing the end of the rainy season, and the water level was dropping. That meant more rocks, more detours, more portages.

The mist and the water were almost the same chalky color. For the first hour I had the sensation that we were sailing on a cloud. Then the mist lifted and I saw the rapids kicking up foam ahead of us from one side of the river to the other.

The padre being the expert on this river—the Old Man of the Marauiá so to speak—he directed the crossing of the rapids. We pulled the smallest dugout through, the one with the drums. One man stood on the bank with a towrope while the rest of us got out and pushed. We made it through without incident, then went back and got the larger dugout. It was the padre's launch that gave us trouble. Because of the heavy load, the launch drew too much water to make it over the rocks. We had to put all our equipment and supplies on shore and then drag her through with sheer force. Then we had to reload our cargo, carefully, so as to maintain an even distribution of weight.

With that done, the boys decided that they needed a little recreation. They swam out to the middle of the river where the breakneck current snatched them up and dragged them toward the center of the rapids. This was part of the game. The other part was to break out of the current and race for shore.

They competed in several of these daredevil races, which the caboclos found hugely entertaining. Then they decided to do it one last time, and that was the one they regretted.

I saw Jerry make it to midstream, then turn around to race back. All of a sudden he was struggling. He had got too close to the falls. He shouted for help, and then disappeared into the foam. The last thing I caught sight of was his hand sticking up before he went over the twenty-foot drop.

For more than a minute we saw nothing; then Jerry's head bobbed up a few hundred feet below the falls. After tumbling over all those rocks he was sure to be bleeding. If he remained in the water much longer, every piranha on the lower Marauiá would assemble to finish him off.

Arnie ran along the bank until he caught up with the floating figure, then leaped in after him. The caboclos got one of the dugouts into the water and went after the two of them.

When we got him on dry land, Jerry was only half conscious and moaning with pain. Though he was covered with cuts and bruises, the only important injury was a broken toe. He was lucky at that.

The boys held him down while I straightened out the toe and put a splint on it. For a while it looked as if we would have to set up a camp so that Jerry could remain behind to mend, but in a couple of hours he was able to hop around, and the only pain he felt was from the bruises.

With the delay, it looked as if we wouldn't make the second set of rapids before dark. Babette opened the throttle all the way, and we made no more stops that afternoon.

At the foot of the rapids we came to a caboclo family stationed there to perform the same service for travelers as the caboclo family on the Cauaburi. They also were porters in the service of the church. The family included the father, the mother, and four husky sons.

We estimated that there was enough daylight left to get one of the boats over, so we tied up the two larger boats below the rapids and started hauling the smallest one over, while Jerry and the caboclos got our camp started. Jerry had cut away a piece of his right sneaker to give his bandaged toe freedom. Every time he stubbed it against something, he shouted and danced a jig on his other foot.

The first boat went over more easily than we expected. The mossy covering on the rocks helped it slide along. The whole job took only half an hour. This encouraged us to try the second

boat. That one was bulkier and it took us about twice as long.

By the time we had the two dugouts secured above the rapids it was almost dark, but with two boats taken care of it seemed a pity to leave the last for the next day. Padre Antônio encouraged us to get the job completed, reminding us that there were several sets of rapids to go.

With everybody pitching in we brought all our cargo ashore. Then we started the big job of hauling the padre's boat over the rocks. By that time it was dark and we had to use flashlights to see what we were doing. We stumbled over small rocks, slipped on the moss, and strained every muscle in our bodies, but we completed our work before anybody took a single bite of food.

Rather than go through another sleepless night in the hammock, I laid the hammock out on the rocks like a mattress. Just as at Jerusalem, the insects were not thick near the fast-flowing water. In the middle of the night I awoke to find that the others had done the same thing.

About an hour before dawn the rain came down and sent us scurrying for shelter in the cabin of Padre Antônio's boat. Everything was so wet we couldn't even get the stove started. For breakfast we had to settle for water and cold rice. We got started without delay in order to make up time lost the day before.

Padre Antônio took our minds off the discomforts of the expedition by telling us stories of the Marauiá. He had experienced several narrow escapes on the fearful rapids, the worst of which were yet to come. He told us about the Indians that had settled down around his mission, and about the villages deep in the interior that he hoped eventually to reach and convert—the Xamatauteri, the Mokarinxiobeteri, the Pukimabueteri—names that made a strange kind of music.

The river became wider and sluggish. We were now in typical piranha water, certain death for anyone who fell out of the boat. We also saw giant caymans. They floated along on the current like logs, their snouts barely breaking the surface. Others were gathered along the banks.

Animal life in general was more plentiful. Macaws flew in

great flocks over our heads. Now and then a toucan would dart across the river, followed by its mate. Most abundant were the Brazilian parakeets, not like the blue-and-green birds that are kept as household pets in the United States, but birds brilliantly plumed in red, yellow, blue, and other colors, like miniature parrots.

We tried to stretch out in the boat, but it was impossible. Lying crosswise, some part of one's body was sure to hang over the side, a real danger when piranha are about. I remembered a guide on the Essequibo River losing a finger that way. He reached into the water for a paddle that had fallen out of the boat, and the next instant a large fish—a piranha or something like it—snapped a finger clean off below the first joint.

Traveling hour after hour in the boat made us seek some kind of diversion. I took out the dictionary and practiced my Portuguese. Arnie and Jerry played cards, and Dean stretched out in the sun so that he would have a good tan when he returned to civilization. He lay on his back with his eyes closed, preening his beard with his fingers.

We spent thirteen hours in the boat that day, as cramped and uncomfortable as we had ever been. Toward late afternoon we found ourselves in a part of the river where the current was fast and very changeable. It was then that we realized how important Babette was to the expedition. With one small engine pulling three boats against a fast river, he managed to seek out the invisible thread of slack water and walk it like a tightrope. Under the hands of an ordinary pilot that engine could never have done the job.

When we stopped to make camp the rain started. We had to shave the bark off branches to make dry firewood. Padre Antônio put together a temporary shelter, and we huddled in it to eat. We hung mosquito netting over our hammocks, but the mosquitoes were as thick inside the netting as out. Since lying in the hammock was no more comfortable than walking around, I did a little of each. I thought of starting a fire to drive the bugs off, but the others were in their hammocks and I didn't want to disturb them. Finally I climbed into the boat and went to sleep on the floor.

That morning it was freezing cold, the first cold morning we had experienced on the Marauiá. We were getting into high country. Ahead of us in the distance we could see the majestic Sierra Imeri.

We were all groggy from lack of sleep when we pushed off. Padre Antônio said that the next rapids were three hours ahead. I was so worn and tired I didn't see how I could be of much help.

The caboclos and Padre Antônio had managed to sleep a little better than we, and Dean Reed was holding his own. Considering the fact that he was a novice, he was doing surprisingly well.

When we came to the rapids I volunteered to man the tow-rope. That was the easiest job. The padre chided me and called me "the director." He got into the river with the others and for the first time he took off his cassock. Jerry sat in one of the boats and jeered at us for having to carry him over the rocks.

We took his teasing without comment because we knew it was a cover-up for the pain of the infections he had all over his body. He never complained, even when he was suffering terribly. He also found a way to do his share of the work: All cooking and domestic duties that did not put a strain on his foot fell to him. No one asked him; he just did it.

We were making good headway along a winding but unobstructed stretch of river when the padre suddenly told us to pull in to shore. When we got the boat up against the bank, he jumped out and stood there shaking. It was his malaria. He told us to continue without him, that he would catch up later.

I refused to budge, but Babette started the motor and we pulled away. We couldn't believe that the padre meant what he said, but about two hours later we came around a bend and saw him waiting for us on the bank.

We were amazed that any man, and a sick one at that, could travel that swiftly through the jungle. The only possible explanation was that the tortuous Marauiá had doubled back upon itself, in which case Padre Antônio would have had to walk only a short distance over a neck of land to pick up the Marauiá several miles upstream.

We never did learn why the attack of malaria prompted a walk through the jungle. Perhaps it was part of the padre's policy of never letting anyone see him ill.

We hit another set of rapids in the afternoon. They were small enough to negotiate by boat, and we rode straight through between plumes of spray. The riverbanks looked unusually high. Padre Antônio told us that the slackening of the rain in the mountains was causing the river to drop. That meant that the rapids up ahead would be all the worse, and the return trip downstream would be a rocky nightmare.

We stopped that night at an abandoned camp used by Indian rubber tappers. This was the deepest penetration of commercial activity that we had seen. After a dinner of sausages and rice I climbed into my hammock. As I was settling down, the cords broke and I landed in the mud. I was too tired to restring it, so I went back to the boat for another fitful night on the wooden floor.

Upon awakening in the morning, I discovered that Suzy was missing. Her rope was either chewed through or had broken at a frayed spot. I thought that her wild instincts were coming to the surface as she matured—she was now about nine months old—and she had run off into the jungle after food or a mate.

I made everyone search, but after an hour we gave up and decided we would have to leave without her. Dean suggested that we give it one more try. He went back and found Suzy looking down at us from the branch of a tree just a few feet away from camp. She had probably been there the whole time, enjoying the fun.

After Padre Antônio held mass in one of the rotted huts, we got into the boats and shoved off again. The morning was the coldest yet. We had to wear our Army jackets until the sun broke through the mist about noon. Because of the change in temperature, we all had colds and sore throats. I made the most of the sunshine by stripping down to the waist and stretching out on a bench. I slept that way for the remainder of that day's journey. We pulled into shore at six o'clock, the latest we had ever been on the river.

My hammock was torn in so many places that it let mosquitoes in by the hundreds, and there were more of them around us the higher we got into mountain country. Arnie was awake for the same reason. We wound up sleeping on the rocks with mosquito netting over us.

In the morning the padre was gone with his man and one of the boats. We couldn't imagine what had happened. We asked Babette, but he would give us no answer. He waited for us to tell him whether to go on or to wait. I couldn't guess what reason the padre had for going ahead, but I knew for certain he had no reason to turn back, so I told Babette to start the engine and head up the river.

We traveled through the first half of the day without any sign of Padre Antônio. At lunch we conjectured as to what might have happened to him.

Then, about two in the afternoon, we spotted his boat in a cove by the side of the river. As we approached we saw Padre Antônio standing there with a big grin on his face. He was with an Indian family from his mission. They were from the Xamatauteri tribe. They were completely naked and had the same physical structure and features as their cousins on the Cauaburi.

The padre said that he had been waiting with the Indians to help us through the next rapids, which, owing to the drop in water level, were now extremely dangerous. That was all the explanation we got. The amazing missionary did not tell us how he had managed to guide the boat in the dark of night or how he had arranged to have the Indians waiting for him exactly where he wanted them.

We continued up to the rapids, maneuvering the boats in and out of rocky channels through the strongest current of the entire trip. The rapids were about a mile long. In a few places we had to get out and push. We always had someone on shore holding fast with a rope. The angle was bad for pulling, but it was a good safety measure.

Once past the rapids it was only five more miles to the mission. Along the river the undergrowth was a little thinner, and here and there we saw an Indian peering from behind a bush at the strange visitors. Padre Antônio was the only other white man they had ever seen.

Finally we came to a clearing, and there stood the little mission in the middle of the jungle that had been Padre Antônio's home for the past year.

twenty-two

PADRE ANTÔNIO'S MISSION

The main structure of the mission outpost was two stories high. It was built of crudely trimmed logs tied together with vines and covered with palm leaves. The first floor served as chapel, school, workshop, and clinic. The second floor was Padre Antônio's private quarters. No one went up there but the padre himself, and when he was at home he kept the ladder pulled up after him.

Nearby was the beginning of a newer, more permanent building. It showed the evidence of many helping hands. Skilled hands at that. The padre was teaching his converts carpentry, a basic craft for people first learning to live in houses.

Not far away were three encampments inhabited by nomadic Waica groups that had settled down around the mission. They formed a loosely knit community of partly assimilated Indians. Scattered among the nomads were expatriates from the larger villages, such as the Xamatauteri family we had met on the Marauiá.

The Indians were in all stages of transition. Some were completely naked, spoke only Waica, and lived in makeshift huts. They lived mainly on food that the padre gave them, plus whatever else they could find in the jungle. At the other extreme were Indians who wore clothes, knew how to use tools, lived in enclosed one-family dwellings, spoke a few words of Portuguese, and raised vegetables in little patches in the jungle.

The padre treated them all according to a strict code of rules. Everyone attended mass, whether they liked it or not. Most of them didn't; they talked and giggled and fidgeted. They hung around only because they knew there would be a handout of some kind after the service. I am certain this did not escape the perceptive eyes of the padre. I believe he felt that if he could first inculcate the habit of churchgoing, the understanding would come later.

He also forced into their lives by sheer willpower the concept of work. Once he taught them enough about farming and carpentry to be able to call upon them for help, he insisted that they perform tasks in exchange for the things he gave them. He tempered this rule with an understanding of the limitations and needs of each Indian.

One of the most important things that happened to the Indians as the result of the padre's presence was the creation of new needs. Once a Waica learned how to use a machete, he never wanted to be without one. Once he wore clothes, he was uncomfortable naked. The same held true for tools, metal pots, and various kinds of food. That was the way the Waica became addicted to civilization.

With new needs came new kinds of immorality. In their tribal state, the Waica seldom committed robbery because in the jungle one Indian seldom lacked what another one had. But now that there was an imbalance of wealth, the Indians learned to covet and to steal. They learned theft at the same time that the padre was teaching them, "Thou shalt not covet. Thou shalt not steal." That was part of the confusion civilization had thrust upon them.

It was similar to the confusion that stemmed from getting things for nothing at first, then later having to work for them. Only the padre's determination could have made such a seemingly faulty system work.

His policy of letting the Indians come to him made good sense, however. The nomadic groups were small, and the constant prey of hunger and attack. They welcomed the opportunity to settle down safely in a place where there was a dependable source of food. The area surrounding the mission was well hunted out, but the missionary was able to satisfy most of their needs, and taught them how to satisfy the others by their own efforts.

I had little doubt that the padre would be able to convert the larger groups once he was well enough established. For the present, however, he was content to enlarge his mission and bide his time.

The first thing we did when we arrived was look around for some kind of shelter. There was none, so we hung our hammocks under the trees and stored our supplies in the mission. We caught up on our sleep and made plans to look over the surrounding area during our short stay.

We took a short trip by dugout up a tributary that ran eastward out of the Marauiá just north of the mission. We shot a large tapir, which we brought back for the padre.

For a time we considered making a more ambitious expedition toward the east, the direction of the Demeni and the Araçá, but once again we were warned away. Those rivers were closed off for a good reason, the padre told us. The uprising we heard about had not yet settled down. He warned us that if we tried to reach those Indians, we were almost certain to be attacked. If we managed to escape, we still would have to answer to the government for entering a prohibited area.

He saw no harm in our exploring the area to the west. The Indians there, never having been in contact with white men before, were less likely to be hostile. That was my opinion, too, and since the west was the direction in which we originally planned to travel, I allowed myself to be persuaded.

We visited the encampments around the mission. The conditions were abject. There is something about a shoddy imitation of a house that makes it more pitiful than an ordinary Indian dwelling that pretends to be nothing more.

We witnessed several incidents of violence. Out of sight of the padre the Indians had no moral restraint. And with no *pareome* to settle disputes, a disagreement could quickly develop into a bloody battle. With stealing had come violence. The butchery was all the worse for the availability of machetes. These were no head-knocking rituals.

So that was the beginning of "civilization" on the Marauiá, established as the furthest link in a chain that was held together by river missions, airplanes, boats, and the courage of men like Padre Antônio.

I conjectured as to the possible fate of the converted Indians had the padre not entered their lives. It could have been better; it could have been worse.

With good luck, good leadership, and lots of time the nomadic groups might have banded together to form stronger groups like the Shamatari; they might have learned farming, like all the well-settled villages; and they might have been able to escape or fight off their attackers.

The other possibility, which was more likely, was that disease, starvation, and enemy attacks would wipe them out in a generation or so. I had to remind myself of that every time I became too critical of the missionaries.

The one thing those Indians did have going for them was a superior human being in the Salesian missionary who had been assigned to their area. If any converted Indians stood a chance in our world, Padre Antônio's stood the best chance of all.

I also had reason to be thankful to him. He gave me the opportunity to see exactly how the church accomplished the job of turning a Waica into a caboclo.

twenty-three

STALEMATE

One thing that troubled me was our physical condition. Somehow, instead of hardening us to jungle life, the Cauaburi expedition seemed to have weakened us. We all had colds and sore throats, and fatigue clung to our limbs like a sloth. In varying degrees we had developed a condition that caused every scratch and insect bite to fester. Jerry was hardest hit of all. The wounds he received going over the falls formed a pink glaze instead of scabbing, and each cut was ringed with red. His fever returned once, and he had to wrap himself in a blanket and wait it out.

But the worst was that leaden weariness. It made us want to lie down in our hammocks and never get up. Everything we did required great effort. We spent four days in all at Padre Antônio's mission after our trip up the Marauiá, but we couldn't shake the sluggishness in our bones.

As long as waiting served no purpose, I decided to get started into the interior as soon as possible. I enlisted Padre Antônio's help in hiring bearers. Many of the Indians around the mission were willing to come along for a few fishhooks and their keep. We wound up with thirteen Indians, including one young boy who decided to tag along with his father.

I could tell immediately that many of our "guides" and "bearers" would be totally useless. Some looked unfit to do much carrying, while others looked too interested in our belongings to be trusted. However, the wages being what they were, I let everyone come along who wanted to.

I asked Babette to join the party, but he declined. He was a riverman, like Tavares, and also had a special allegiance to the padre that I had to respect.

Arnie and Jerry were grimly determined to stick with the expedition as planned. In spite of their ebbing vitality, I let them make their own decision. They had learned enough about the jungle to know what was in store.

However, I did question Dean, who was full of confidence in spite of, or because of, his inexperience. I asked him if he thought he could keep up with us in the bush. He was prepared for my question; out came the newspaper clippings. Shades of the adventurers!

"Look at this," he said. "I outwalked a mule on a fifty-mile hike in Colorado. Think I can't keep up with *you?*"

"That was on flat ground," I said dubiously, wondering whether this expedition was no more to Dean than just another opportunity for publicity.

"Don't worry about me," he insisted. "I can take care of myself."

We sorted out our supplies for the overland journey. We scrutinized our cargo much more selectively than at Tapuru-cuará, because we knew we might wind up carrying it ourselves. The more we looked at our load, the bigger it seemed to get, but cutting it down became a touchy issue. While no one wanted to leave his own things behind, each of us found plenty that was expendable in what the others were carrying.

Arnie couldn't see why Dean needed his guitar. Dean couldn't understand why I needed so many cameras. Jerry couldn't imagine what we needed all the trade goods for. In the end we took along just about everything we started with.

The padre helped us plan the course of our journey. On our map, the two nameless tributaries that joined to become the Marauiá formed a Y a few miles to the northwest of the mission. As we looked at the map, our position was below and to the right

of the point where the streams joined. The tributary that flowed in from the west, forming the left fork, came from the direction of the Sierra Imeri and the Amarokawebueteri village, our eventual destination. The water was too low to permit the use of dugouts, but the padre suggested that we follow the stream bed on foot, which would probably take us directly to the village.

I decided that as long as we were going to walk anyway, I would rather plan an overland journey that would take in as many villages as possible. We would make our first destination the village of the powerful Xamatauteri group, situated on the other side of the Marauiá about a day's journey to the south. We would then swing back up to the north and northwest and work our way village by village toward the Amarokawebueteri.

The others went along with the idea enthusiastically. Having finally reached the vicinity of several untouched groups, they agreed it would be a shame to return without having seen them.

With that settled, the padre advised us to start by crossing the two narrow streams, which would get us to the other side of the Marauiá without encountering all the logistical problems that the big river would present. We would first cross the eastern tributary by dugout a little below the spot where we shot the tapir, then cut left through a narrow strip of jungle and cross the other tributary, the one that pointed toward the Amarokawebueteri, by means of a vine bridge.

I made a mental note that for the third time we were to use a vine bridge, and for the third time the bridge was located just upstream from a fork of some kind. I wondered what this pattern meant, but the explanation eluded me. I wrote it off to coincidence or a quirk of the peculiar Waica mentality.

One of our problems was that beyond the Xamatauteri village there was little known about the location of the other groups. The Mokarinxiobeteri and the Pukimabueteri were in there somewhere; that was certain. But there were others whose names were not even known. In addition, there were any number of nomadic groups that we might run into by accident. The padre asked that we direct them to the mission if we did meet any.

We received our blessings one bleak morning and set out on tired feet for the final portion of our expedition, thirteen Indians, an ocelot, and four explorers. Because of the rivers, we started out wearing sneakers rather than boots. Jerry had finally taped up the hole in his sneaker. He said he would rather squash his broken toe than stub it.

The first crossing was routine. We left the boats turned bottoms up on the far shore. There was little chance of them being washed away, as the stream was getting lower every day.

The vine bridge was a novelty to Dean. He insisted that I take motion pictures of him crossing. The whirring camera brought out the ham in him. He got so absorbed in putting on a show that he nearly fell into the river.

Then the long walk began. We traveled single file. A guide led the way, with me close behind. The other explorers were scattered among the bearers. As usual, either Arnie or Jerry brought up the rear, rifle in hand, keeping as much of the column in view as possible.

We moved along at a good clip, the slope of the land favoring us. The Indians had no trouble picking out the paths, so there was very little cutting to be done. Our only hindrance was Jerry's bad foot. We had lunch at high noon, and all of us except Jerry changed from sneakers to boots. The rocky ground was turning the soles of our feet black and blue.

There were no other stops until late in the afternoon, when the paths began to broaden out and we knew we were in the neighborhood of the Xamatauteri village. As was our custom, we camped out in the jungle in order to rest up overnight and be fresh when we met our hosts in the morning.

Arnie had been complaining about his legs all day long. When he finally got a chance to remove his pants we discovered that his thighs were covered with great sores. He had a flourishing case of yaws.

Arnie was alarmed. So far he had escaped the bad luck that plagued Jerry. He wondered whether he was in for a siege of illnesses. I told him he was coming down with an acute case of hypochondria. Dean said he knew the cure for that—shave off his beard. That quieted Arnie down. The one thing that was forbidden was self-pity.

We didn't dwell very long on Arnie's illnesses, real or im-

agined, because there were too many other things to worry about
—securing the equipment, putting up hammocks, and preparing
a meal for our entourage.

The guide and I had tried to hunt game for the evening meal
during the day's march, but the noise of the bearers behind us
scared everything off the trail. The only wildlife we saw were
monkeys and birds, and monkey meat was still something I tried
to avoid. By evening, all we had to show for our efforts were a
half-dozen birds, and there were seventeen hungry mouths to
feed. That meant that on our very first night we would have to
dig deep into our own food supply.

Living off the jungle had become almost a lost art to the
mission Indians. There was something depressing about the way
they lined up for food at suppertime. All they contributed to the
meal was the firewood and their appetites.

I watched the Indians make camp for the night. They put up
the same kind of bark hammocks as the Waica of the Cauaburi,
but they went about it like a family out on a Sunday picnic. I
had thought that being in the vicinity of the Xamatauteri would
make them a little wary, but the whole idea of the jungle seemed
to have changed for them. They had less fear of the night, less
fear of human strangers, less fear of the unknown.

Part of the change could be attributed to the teachings of
Padre Antônio, whose God dwelt in a faraway place called
heaven, and not in the bodies of slithering creatures that
haunted the dark. Our guns probably also bolstered their courage. They knew what a bullet could do, having seen the padre
use firearms, and they could see for themselves that we were well
armed.

One thing that civilization had not changed was the Waica's
playful nature. They made our camp a place filled with noisy
fun. Dean added the music, having taken over that department
since joining the expedition. He sang our favorite song, "Sherry,"
and a whole repertoire of folk ballads that had the Indians
entranced.

When the long evening ended we set up our guard and turned
in for the night. I had the kind of dreams I have when I am very

tired—mixed-up dreams, filled with familiar people in strange settings and strange people in familiar settings. I saw Denise, the Manaus nightclub dancer, swaying in the jungle, and Kamboe on an ocean liner. I saw naked, faceless Indians sprawled out in the living room of my home. When the dog barked, the Indians got up and danced. Then they marched out the front door in single file, and the dog wept. I wept with the dog.

The next morning we checked everything out for the short march to the Xamatauteri village. The most important things to remember were to keep the guns out of sight and all valuables carefully packed. The weather was favorable, the path was clear, and we moved out at a brisk pace. Jerry was managing nicely on his bad foot, so we didn't have to hold back for his sake.

When we started the morning's march, Dean was near me at the head of the column. A little while later I looked back and saw that he had fallen back about three places. After an hour he was with Arnie, bringing up the rear. Finally, he dropped out altogether. I signaled the guide to stop; then I called back to Arnie,

"What happened to Dean?"

"He doesn't like our company. He's used to walking with jackasses."

I knew then that Dean was not very far away. Arnie's remark was obviously meant for his ears.

"Okay, let him catch up, and tell him we won't wait for him again."

Dean rejoined us, and stuck with us the rest of the way in grim silence. But that didn't reduce the chatter of the Indians. They made enough noise to let the Xamatauteri know well in advance that we were coming. It was just as well, I felt. There was no point in surprising them.

The Xamatauteri *chabona* sat long and low in the middle of a vast clearing, just like the dwelling of the Kohoroshanitari. The construction was the same as the other *chabonas,* except that in addition to the communal lean-to there were many separate dwellings—round thatched huts that looked like individual family units.

We crossed the clearing unchallenged and entered the village.

Inside the wall the Indians were waiting for us, curious and excited, but friendly. The reception was a social event rather than a military operation, and there were plenty of women about.

As usual, the women went straight for Jerry. He was uneasy, but he tried hard not to show it. The Xamatauteri men were less forward. They stood around waiting for something to happen. With one eye on Jerry, I paid my respects to the chief.

The *pareome* was older than the leaders of the big Cauaburi groups. He seemed mature and affable. He accepted our gifts graciously. The others waited for theirs, but this time I dealt only with the chief; there were hundreds of Indians and a limited number of gifts. I let the chief worry about the *eba,* and took care of the *nomehan* myself.

The first things we traded for were comestibles, mainly large birds and plantains. I was trying to keep our packaged food intact.

We settled down in the big *chabona* just as we had done once before. The smells, sights, and sounds were the same. We felt at home. Only after a couple of days did we perceive certain characteristics that differentiated this group from the others.

Once again, the main difference had to do with the status of the women. Like the Shamatari wives, women were considered the property of their husbands, but there were so many women in the village that the chief accepted suitors from outside. The one proviso was that the married couple remain among the Xamatauteri.

In this way the wise old chief stole the cream of Waica manhood from the other villages to the north. The braves of those villages seemed only too eager to make the move, as the Xamatauteri were a strong and prosperous nation.

The Xamatauteri also performed a ritual that we had not seen before, the harvest dance called the *hama.*

We got advance notice of a *hama* celebration one afternoon when we saw a number of wives decorating their husbands' bodies from head to toe with *urucú.* We hung around to see what would happen. After a while the sound of drumbeats began to issue from one of the huts.

The dance began when several families showed up at the house. The visiting families entered in pairs. One partner went to the left and the other to the right. They moved sideways around the interior of the hut with their backs to the wall, humming and making hand motions to the rhythm of the drum. When they met at the opposite end of the room, the next couple entered. When all the guests were seated, a meal of harvest foods was served.

The drum intrigued me, since it was completely different from the hollow log drums we had seen in the Cauaburi area. It looked something like a bongo, a hollow wooden cylinder covered at one end with a parchment-like skin. I studied it, wondering what kind of animal the skin had come from. When it struck me that it might have come from a human being, my own skin began to crawl.

The Xamatauteri was the only village where we were ever alone with women. Once, when we were bathing in a creek, we found ourselves being watched by several giggling females. We could tell by their gestures that they were interested in the parts of us that were usually covered. They had never before seen men who wore pants, and apparently that had piqued their curiosity.

Aside from the obvious differences between us and the Indian men, we must have seemed strange, appearing in the nude as we did without the waistbelt loop used by Waica men to support their genitals. When we came out of the water, the women ran off into the woods laughing. We started to follow, and the laughter turned into titillated shrieks. At this point we stopped the sport, lest a jealous Xamatauteri husband come along and take our joke seriously.

Arnie didn't miss the opportunity to kid Jerry. In a mockingly confidential tone he told him, "Just between us, kid, it's you that they really wanted."

We spent a few days with the Xamatauteri, and when we reached the end of their allotted portion of *eba,* their attitude suddenly changed. In the States it would be described as, "What have you done for me lately?"

We felt like staying longer, since none of us were physically up to par. Jerry was still suffering with his cold and skin infections.

Arnie's yaws were clearing up with the help of medication, but now he had dysentery. Dean had experienced a violent reaction to insect bites, and the strange food was getting him down. I was suffering from a number of minor maladies, which were taking their toll in subtle ways. For one thing, I found myself getting very short-tempered. That is a bad state of mind for the leader of an expedition.

Our guides said they did not know the way to the next village, so we asked the chief for help. He gave us one guide, who was to go only part of the way. We thanked the chief and got out while we were still on good terms. We wanted to preserve a little good-will in case we had to stop at the same village on our way back.

Now we were headed toward the mountains, and the incline was against us. There were still intermittent rains. They were less frequent than during the previous month, but when they came they came just as hard.

The trip to the Mokarinxiobeteri village took one-and-a-half days. At the end of the first day, when we stopped to set up camp for the night, the guide pointed northwest, the direction in which we were to continue, and disappeared back down the path.

"He didn't have to point the way," I remarked. "All we have to do is pick out the roughest ground to walk on and we know we're going right."

Appreciative sounds from the others told me that they were starting to feel the strain, too.

The Mokarinxiobeteri were a smaller group than the Xamatauteri, and a lot more suspicious. They had hidden all their women in anticipation of our arrival. The fact that we came from the direction of the enemy village might have helped make us suspect.

Small in number though they were, we were playing a danger-ous game entering the Mokarinxiobeteri village in our present condition. We were violating the dictum "Never show them you are ill." We were in a bad way—too sick to hide the fact and too tired to care.

The men of the village gathered in the middle of the *chabona* when we entered. There wasn't much of a reception. Although they weren't openly hostile, we got the feeling that we weren't welcome. It was more a case of them fearing us than hating us; the Mokarinxiobeteri were frequently invaded. They probably had never come across strangers who turned out to be anything but enemies.

Still, we wound up spending a few days in the village. We needed rest and food. By that time I shared Jerry's attitude: If they don't like us, let them make us get out. Once again we fell back upon our strongest support, the gun.

We never once saw a woman during our stay at the village. At some point the Indians were certain to get fed up with their women being away. Then they would have to kill us, or chase us out of the village, or trust us and bring the women back. That made the odds two to one in favor of us having trouble. In a vague way I understood that fatigue was weakening my judgment. On all previous occasions I had been careful to avoid situations like this. But conditions had changed and so had I.

Arnie ate more Enterovioform tablets than food. I wanted him sound again for the march to the next village. We couldn't handle a stretcher case. In two days the diarrhea stopped and he began to hold his food, but by then he was thin and weak, a shadow of his former strapping self.

Poor Arnie. In addition to his physical suffering he had to bear the jibes of the rest of us. A man with the runs is like someone doing a pratfall. He is an object of humor. Some of our remarks were a little on the vicious side. The stress of the journey brought out the worst in us.

Trading had dwindled to the purchase of food. We couldn't carry anything bulky, and we didn't have much left to offer. I figured that on the way back we might get rid of some equipment we no longer needed in exchange for some specimens. In the meantime, the cameras did my collecting for me.

When we asked the Mokarinxiobeteri chief for guides, he wanted something in payment. We gave him a machete and some dime-store trinkets, and he put one of his braves at our disposal. We drove just as hard a bargain as the chief. As long as we were paying for the guide, we let them do some carrying.

Having a large company of bearers gave me a certain feeling of importance, but there are two sides to every coin. Having a lot of help also meant that we were outnumbered, and strength of numbers can breed rebellion. I was always on the lookout for that kind of trouble, because if it did crop up we would either nip it in the bud or not at all. I saw the signs of it brewing on that part of the march, and I was ready for it.

When it came time to put up our camp for the night, two bearers refused to help. I gave them a good tongue-lashing, but they didn't respond. I was about to go a step further when, surprisingly, their fellow tribesmen came to my aid. They advised me to let the two recalcitrants do without supper. That sounded like a fair punishment, and I went along with their advice.

The stratagem worked. The two Indians missed their supper, but the next morning they pitched right into the work of the camp. In return I allowed them to fill up at the breakfast table.

The second day of walking to the Pukimabueteri village was worse than mountain climbing. We were going uphill, but not at enough of an angle to permit the use of hands. In addition, the vines were matted and tangled around rocks. We had to lift our feet high to keep from tripping.

Our guide turned back within a few miles of the village. We went on alone to meet the Pukimabueteri, who also had moved their women into the jungle. I was beginning to feel like a leper. I went through the motions of offering my friendship to the chief, but I was angry. I had no right to be; I was a stranger in a country where strangers were seldom seen, but a certain belligerence was rising in me. I was tired of being unwelcome. I decided to face the issue directly, and I asked the chief where the women were. I got no answer, only an angry stare.

In spite of that, we had no trouble gaining entry to the village. It was working out the way Padre Antônio said it would. The groups that had never seen or heard of white men were the least hostile. That was the difference between the Cauaburi and the Marauiá.

The practice of hiding the women was really no reflection of the Indians' attitude toward us. It was simply an extension of their attitude toward all strangers. If another Waica came nosing around their village, the chances were that he was after a bride.

We needed a good rest, so we established a comfortable spot for ourselves in the *chabona* and made ourselves at home. The tribesmen didn't know what to make of us, but they gave us no trouble.

When we were feeling a little more like ourselves, we started to get back into the swing of trading, playing games, and learning. Dean was our official troubador. He entertained the Pukimabueteri and eased the atmosphere a little. The Indians were willing to be wooed.

The village was in high country, cold and sparse as equatorial places go, and almost in the shadow of the Sierra Imeri. Every morning I told myself that the moment my legs were up to it, I would head for those mountains and pay my promised second visit to the Amarokawebueteri.

The moment finally arrived, and we set out for our final destination, with no guides and nothing to direct us but the compass and the familiar peaks of the Imeri range. I felt that those were all we needed. Wherever we hit the base of the mountains, we would follow it to the west and eventually come to our destination.

We didn't make it to the foothills the first day, so we camped overnight in the middle of nowhere, and moved out again at about noon on the second day. We were still a couple of miles short of the mountains when we stumbled unexpectedly upon a *chabona*. It looked a lot like the one we were searching for, but it wasn't it.

There was a deathly stillness about the place. We guessed that we were in for another Kohoroshanitari-style reception. This time we had our rifles ready. There were no boats waiting to whisk us away in case of danger. If these Indians were hostile, we would have to stand and fight.

We entered the *chabona* cautiously. There were several openings in the wall and numerous escape hatches behind the hammocks. There wasn't much place to hide, but we saw no one.

At first the sight of smoke did not arouse our suspicion. We were accustomed to seeing fires burning in every village. Then we realized that some of the smoke was coming from a section of the wall that had been burned to the ground. And on closer scrutiny we could see arrows sticking out of the wall. The village had been raided that very morning.

We spread out and looked the place over. Each of us had his gun ready. All signs bore out our first impression. Personal property was scattered everywhere, as if the inhabitants tried to grab whatever they could and flee before the attackers. Yet there were no Indians, living, dead, or wounded.

On the other side of the village we discovered a creek running from west to east. The water was quite low. It was probably the same creek that ran from the the Amarokawebueteri village into the Rio Marauiá near Padre Antônio's mission. We knew then that we were somewhere between the Amarokawebueteri and the mission, assuming that the creek was the one we thought it was.

We weren't quite certain which way to go, and while we were deciding, our position remained very dangerous. The attackers might still be about or the Indians who had fled might return and wreak their vengeance upon us.

We had to decide what to do. If we continued toward the Sierra Imeri we could conceivably contact the Amarokawebueteri group, but if there was a war party in the area, they were likely to be somewhere in that very direction, especially if they were the dreaded Venezuelans.

There was also no guarantee that the Amarokawebueteri were still around. They could have moved or been wiped out. Not that the Indians themselves were my goal. I wanted mainly to fix the geographic location of the village.

However, the decision was no longer mine alone. The others wanted to hold a caucus, and I agreed. We sat down in the shade of the *chabona* wall and talked, while the mission Indians wandered aimlessly around the clearing. I wanted to push on, and so did Arnie and Jerry, but Dean complained that his vacation was already up and he had contractual obligations to meet. That seemed like a strange thing to bring up. I wasn't even aware of what day of the month it was, and here was Dean, planning to entertain at such-and-such a nightclub on such-and-such a date. I really found it hard to believe that he was serious.

Arnie was in a contrary mood. He told Dean, "If it was up to me, we would go right over those mountains into Venezuela."

I didn't know if he meant it, but all at once it sounded like a great idea. Jerry thought so, too. That started a new round of discussion, and while we were talking it began to rain heavily. The Indians came in out of the rain and huddled together. They were in no mood to pick up their packs and start walking again. That, plus our indecision and the soaking downpour, added up to one thing: a stalemate. I suddenly realized that we weren't going anywhere that day.

While the others went on arguing I started to build a fire. Soon they realized that they were hungry, too, and the argument stopped. By the time the meal was ready it was starting to get dark. That meant that for all our discussion we would wind up spending the night in the worst possible place, right in the burned-out village.

The only pleasant thing left to anticipate was a warm supper, but even that was denied us. Just as we were about to eat, we were swarmed over by grasshoppers. We tried to beat them off with our jackets, but there were millions of them. We even tried foolishly to throw up a barrier of flame by pouring lighter fluid along the ground and setting it afire, but the giant insects came flying right through. We had no choice but to cover our food and wait for the attack to subside.

Eventually it did, but the grasshoppers were followed by fireflies. By that time we were too hungry to fuss over a few bugs, so we uncovered our plates and dug in. Our meal was a cold mush of rice and milk sprinkled generously with fireflies. Several times I was about to swallow a mouthful of rice when a light went on in my spoon. I flicked the insect away and continued to eat.

Tired as we were, we had no choice but to stay awake and keep an eye out for attackers. Jerry decided that we had enough pairs of eyes without his. He wanted to sleep. Rather than argue with him I invited him to join us for a cup of coffee before he turned in. The normally suspicious Jerry accepted without hesitation. The cup of coffee I gave him contained five Dexedrine tablets. Jerry stayed awake that night.

By morning there was no longer a decision to be made. We knew we had to turn back and retrace our steps all the way to the mission. We could have given the creek a try, but in our mental and physical condition we were not about to strike out into a new part of the jungle. The exploration part was over. Safety and certainty were now our guideposts.

There were no unusual incidents on our way back, except for one unexpected bit of good luck. We ran into a friendly nomadic group. We found them sitting around a big palm-thatched hut right in the middle of the jungle. I wondered how we had missed them the first time. The hut looked as if it had been there for at least a few days.

We camped out for one night with the nomads. They were completely primitive—very few possessions, apparently no permanent home and probably no farm. We tried to tell them about the mission, but they didn't seem interested.

For all their backwardness, these nomads could out-Waica all the other Waicas we had met. They could climb up a straight tree trunk as fast as a man could walk, and being nomads, I am certain they could outdistance the other Waicas just as easily on land.

We paid our last visit to the Waica in the village of the Xamatauteri. We stayed there two days to refresh ourselves, and it was there that I came closest to getting into a private fight with one of the Indians.

I had offered all that remained of my trading goods to the men of the village in return for parakeets. I broke it down to an exchange of fishing line, two fishhooks, some matches, and a knife in return for one mated pair of birds.

The Indians understood the deal well enough and went off to get the parakeets. In most instances they brought them to me in cages of closely woven vines. I was well along in the trading when I noticed that one of the cages held only one parakeet and a handful of feathers.

I called to the Indian who had short-changed me and asked for my goods back. He became indignant and refused. I really don't think he was cheating me, but had misunderstood what I wanted. However, I kept insisting, and held my hand out for the goods. The Indian was adamant.

Arnie and Jerry warned me that I might start something I couldn't finish, but I was past the stage where I would listen to advice. Finally the Indian yielded. He threw the fishhooks and other things on the ground and stalked off without even taking his bird. The other Indians gathered around me and patted me on the back. All the world loves a winner.

Arnie, too, almost got into a fight. It was a case of his chickens coming home to roost. For weeks he had tempted fate by indulging in practical jokes with the Indians. He tried it once too often with one of our bearers, who happened to have a machete. The Indian began swinging it menacingly in front of Arnie's face, forcing him to back up. He backed Arnie around in a circle for several minutes, the rest of us looking on and thinking, Well, it finally happened.

But the Indian lost interest after a while, and left a chastened Arnie standing alone in the middle of the clearing.

But the final misfortune was Jerry's. During our last night in the bush his fever returned. By morning he was shaking badly, and we knew we had to get him back to the mission in a hurry.

Arnie volunteered to stay behind and finish breaking camp. Only one Indian was willing to stay with him. All the others wanted to continue with the main party. There was no time to argue. We left Arnie and the Indian behind, and with Jerry once again in a stretcher, we raced back to Padre Antônio's mission.

It was a sorry-looking expedition at that point. We were sick, tired, and scattered about like a retreating army. In the end the jungle had prevailed. For the time being, at least, Nature remained master in that corner of the world, and only creatures born to the wilderness could survive there.

twenty-four

REEMERGING

The smile quickly disappeared from Padre Antônio's face when he saw that Arnie was not with us. Our explanation did not ease his anxiety. For once he seemed really alarmed.

The padre ran into the mission building for his pistol and started back down the trail. He ordered several Indians to go with him, and they obeyed. We sat ourselves down in front of the mission, slightly bemused. Fatigue had dulled our judgment. The thought of Arnie alone with one Indian and a heavy load of equipment in the middle of the jungle did not disturb us in the least.

We were still resting on the ground when the padre returned about two hours later with Arnie and his Indian helper. The padre had met them on the trail.

We rested for the remainder of the day and the padre gave Jerry medication. After supper we returned to our hammocks and fell right to sleep. The next day my fatigue began to wear off, and was replaced by depression.

There was a cold, heavy feeling inside my chest. It felt like a tombstone marking the end of my expedition. Worn and whipped as we were, I was still sad to see it end. The excitement of exploration is not something that can be recalled easily. Once it is gone it is gone. You have to keep going back into the jungle to know the feeling again.

For all the resolutions never to go through the pain of another expedition, I knew that I would continue to seek out new, untouched corners of the natural world, and follow the paths of unshod feet to the dwelling places of primitive men.

Those were my private thoughts. The others had theirs. For Dean I imagined his career would come first, now that this lark was out of his system. Jerry was difficult to figure. The expedition had opened up a new world to him, but I wasn't sure that it was a world he liked. More precisely, I was not sure he liked the kind of person he had to be to survive in that world. Arnie was a complete mystery. He had gone all the way from a full-fledged hellion to a do-gooder in three short months. Back in Manaus he was willing to goof off and leave the work to Jerry. But on the Marauiá he was the first to plunge into the water to save him from the piranha, and on the last day he was the one who volunteered to stay behind and break camp. That is the jungle. It brings out mysterious qualities in men.

We suddenly felt like strangers at the mission. The feeling had come over all of us that we no longer belonged. After two days of rest we decided we were fit, and made quiet haste to return.

The padre assigned us the large boat. Babette came with us to make sure that the launch and its passengers all got back safely.

Seeing the familiar sights along the Marauiá did not give us the same feeling of elation as the return trip on the Cauaburi. Somehow we knew we could never return to the same world again. For even if we did come back, the place and the people would be changed.

We had many portages on the way down. The dry season was upon us, and the river was a wildly plunging rock-ribbed sluice, but there was no excitement in it, just work. The element of anticipation was gone.

With the water almost down to dry-season level, sandbars appeared in many places. And with the sandbars came sand fleas. They were worse than all the piums and mosquitoes combined.

Their bites itched, burned, and bled, all at the same time. They made our last nights on the river a sleepless hell.

As we approached the lower part of the river, we felt as if we were reemerging from some dim past into the twentieth century. Depression gave way to impatience, aimlessness to determination.

At last we found ourselves on the black water of the Rio Negro. We swung left and traveled with the current back toward Tapurucuará.

It was still daylight when the familiar steeple appeared in the distance. Our spirits rose. In fifteen minutes we would be at the mission.

But the jungle decided to have the last word. With hardly any warning, just one gust of warm air, a storm broke loose that turned the whole world dark. We were stunned. Just minutes from safety we found ourselves in the worst danger of the entire expedition. Babette headed the boat for shore with bolts of lightning striking all around us. The thunder rolled in behind the crackling swords of light like booming cannons, and the wind whipped the black water into white foam.

We leaped into the shallow water and dragged the boat ashore, almost whimpering with fear. The raging storm seemed to bear a personal animosity toward us. There was no shelter to be found; we just waited and prayed and hoped, and finally the storm subsided.

When we landed at Tapurucuará it took us a while to regain our composure, but when we did, the conversation quickly turned to travel arrangements, business plans, and remembered obligations. We also regained a sense of measured time—minutes, hours, weeks—which for a while had had very little meaning for us. With jungle dirt still under our fingernails, we were rapidly readjusting to our own world.

The next morning we inquired about transportation. The director told us that there would be an Air Force Catalina in a couple of days. I used those days to separate the things I wanted to keep from those I didn't. I turned my medical supplies over to Irmã Alice in the Santa Caza. My worn clothing and certain implements also became the property of the mission. The good sisters were most appreciative. I felt sorry for them, thinking of how it would affect me if I had to remain at Tapurucuará indefinitely.

I finally cut the luggage down to the point where I was certain the Catalina could handle it. I did not want to risk being turned down as we had been at Uaupés.

At last the iron bird arrived. The clanging metal under our feet, the great impersonal power of the engines that restored our muscles to their puny status in modern civilization—these were the real signals of the end of our visit to the time-locked world of the Waica.

As we took off, the rugged jungle below us became a vast green canopy that covered the home of the Indians, a place where a germ had been planted.

EPILOGUE

The seed we planted in Kamboe's jungle has borne deadly fruit. The Cauaburi and Marauiá rivers are now infested by a tough breed of prospectors—called *garimpeiros*—who have come to wrest the wealth of the jungle with gold pans and diamond sieves. They are armed with shotguns and *cachaça,* which have taken their toll of Indian life and health. Many of the Waica we knew as free savages are now caboclos, dependent upon the capricious generosity of the hard-bitten fortune seekers, and upon their own dubious ability to do business with visitors from the twentieth century.

What remains of the Waica way of life is still under siege by the missionaries. Padre John Badelotti continues to travel the area in search of converts, still using the mission of Santa Izabel as his base of operations. Padre Antônio Goyz has been hospitalized by his malaria. At latest word he is in extremely serious condition. He may well be one of the Salesian missionaries destined to give his life in the same strange land where he gave so many of his years in dedicated service. He is one of Brazil's true explorer-missionaries. The country and the world could use more like him.

The Protestant missionaries are close on the heels of the

Salesians, having recently established themselves at the mouth of the Marauiá.

If any of the Waica we met followed our path down the Rio Negro to Manaus, I would not be able to locate them in the floating city, for the floating city no longer exists. The Brazilian government has relocated all the caboclos to settlements, burned down their huts, and broken up the rafts. The harbor of Manaus is clear, and the Indians who were river dwellers for a time have gone back to the land.

Arnie Dietrich returned with me to Brazil the following year on another expedition. He was undergoing a transition at the time, a continuation of the moral change that began to show itself on the first expedition. The fast-living Arnie of old who recognized no authority higher than himself is today a devout Christian. He has rejected his sinful ways and is dedicated to teaching all other sinners, including myself, the error of theirs. In a recent letter to me he wrote:

"Watch yourself and don't take foolish chances. I can't tell you much about the old crowd because I hardly even see them. As for myself I keep busy with my job and serving God as best I know how."

If Arnie returned to the jungle today, it would undoubtedly be as a missionary.

Jerry Falls had a lot to prove to himself on our expedition and, having done so, returned to what the world considers a normal life. He has a job with very regular hours at John F. Kennedy International Airport in New York. I sometimes wonder if, when he passes the big airport sign on his way to work, he recalls the Indian boys of Tapurucuará shouting "Viva Kennedy" on the Fourth of July, 1962.

These days Jerry thinks about advancement in his job, investing his money wisely, and enjoying the benefits that the American way of life has made available to him. He admits that if a grasshopper landed in his dinner plate he would lose his appetite. If there is any interest in the jungle left in him, he satisfies it by running off the motion-picture reels of our expedition.

But Jerry did not waste his time by coming along on the expedition. He discovered in himself many important qualities— among them courage and loyalty—that a civilized life might never reveal.

My own life has been profoundly changed since the expedition of the Innocent Assassins. I have returned to Brazil every year since that time. The country has become my second home. I have been in the Mato Grosso, the Territory of Rondônia, the State of Pará, and all the regions of the east. I have explored several rivers, including the Aripuanã, the Machado, the Tapajós, the Creporie, and the Jamachim. I have visited several Indian tribes, including the Digut and the Caiapó.

By a strange coincidence, I ran into one of the adventurers on one of my recent visits to Manaus. It was Guilio. He had broken with Armand and this time had a different companion in tow. He claimed he was in Brazil for scientific studies, but whatever his reason for returning it was clear that the jungle had won him over. Perhaps in time he will evolve from an adventurer to an explorer. At least he seems to know now that there is a difference.

Exploring has become a way of life for me, and in order to avoid those long, frustrating interruptions caused by the need to arrange new financing, I have tried to turn my expeditions into profit-making ventures.

I have done photography on assignment; I have collected specimens of drugs, plants, minerals, and animals for commercial and scientific use; I have panned for gold and dredged for diamonds. Meanwhile, I have never lost that compelling interest to seek out the Indian in his natural home. I am sure I shall never outlive my sense of kinship with him. No matter how many expeditions I make, one of my reasons for going into the jungle will always be to meet the Indio.

It is no flight of fancy to say that death is a companion on every expedition. Jerry nearly met his Maker twice, once by disease and once by disaster. In general, my expeditions have been fortunate in avoiding that catastrophe. The single exception was in 1964 when a dugout overturned on the Tapajós, and four bearers were lost. Since that time I have had premonitions on several occasions. Perhaps they are warnings, like Arnie's, to avoid taking foolish chances.

I have been a little less fortunate with disease, that other invisible companion. After surviving all my expeditions with nothing more serious than skin eruptions and loss of weight, I was taken out of the Mato Grosso late in 1965 with a bad fever. After getting several conflicting diagnoses in Brazil, I went to Georgetown, British Guiana (shortly before it became the independent nation of Guyana), where my illness was diagnosed correctly as malaria and I received proper treatment. When I felt well enough, I returned to the jungles where I first began my explorations, and traveled to the headwaters of the Mazaruni River. At that time, just before the rainy season, diamond hunters were working the river with suction dredges. They were a colorful lot, and I was with them long enough to see some small fortunes made. I returned shortly afterward to Brazil to pick up my expedition in the Mato Grosso where I left it when I fell ill.

There are some questions about the expedition of the Innocent Assassins that remain unanswered. One is the nature of that mysterious powder, *abana*. The sample I brought back was tested in two ways. In Manaus, a young Brazilian inhaled it in the prescribed Waica manner and experienced the following effects: His vision became extremely clear, but objects seemed more distant, as if he were looking through the wrong end of a telescope. He had full control of his body, but felt as though he were wearing it like a suit of armor and manipulating it from within. There was no sense of touch. When the man came out of his trance, he had only partial recall of what had happened, and his recollection came to him in segments like motion-picture episodes.

The other test of *abana* was made in a laboratory. Cats were injected with the substance. Each one developed spasms and diarrhea, then died. The experiments were dropped before any useful knowledge was gained.

There is another unanswered question, the fate of Kamboe. Of him I have no knowledge. I can only say that he exists today as he did when I left him, in the shadowy jungle of my memory. If he is alive, I know I exist for him in the same way.

We leave a part of ourselves in very place and person we touch, and take something permanent with us when we leave. Time and distance cannot break these ties.

GLOSSARY OF WAICA WORDS

Language spoken by the Waica Indians of the Rio Cauaburi and Rio Marauiá areas. The groups include the Kohoroshanitari, Xamatauteri, Mokarinxiobeteri, Wauanateri, Hereweteri, and Shamatari. Certain words in this glossary, such as "canoe" and "paddle," are used only by the Cauaburi groups that have come into contact with artifacts of Western civilization and have either developed a terminology for these objects or have learned to apply existing Waica words to them.

AFTERNOON: mu we ate
AGOUTI: she hewa
ALIVE: te me te me
ARMLETS: pa he sike
ARMS: po ko ki
BABY STRAP: pey wa huko
BAD: wa re t wer
BASKET, LARGE: we er e
BASKET, SMALL: sho to ka he
BEARD: ha we ke
BEAUTIFUL: wa ri sha na
BIRD: ste w she ha a
BLACK: en sh en she
BLUE: on shu ho o
BONE EARRING: e me se
BOW AND ARROW: cher eka
BOY: e he ro

CANOE: a ra k se
CARRY: ye he po
CAT, OCELOT: era hen ha
CHIEF: pa re ome
CHILD: hiro cabe
CLEAN: ou ma a
CORD: do rap e tap
COTTON SPINNER: she mo ra ra ma
DAY: ma ha ro
DEAD: no ma
DIRT: sha me sha me
DOG: he e ma
EARS: ni me kaki
EAT: e yi e
ENEMY: no he wan e po
EYEBROW: ey wa o ma shik
EYES: ma mo roshi
FIGHT: she yo o
FINGERS: e me he shok
FIRE: ki e wa ka
FISH: ma ro ha
FOOD: coma ura a
FRIEND: sho re ma
FRUIT: ha ta
GET: tai e
GIRL: swe e her ru
GIVE ME: e ba
GOOD: wa ri sha ma
GRAB: who ai
GRASSHOPPER: se h se kema
GREAT: pat a pat a
GREEN: lea le a
HAIR: pa wa ha nah
HAMMOCK: nen kake
HAVE: ta po o
HEAR: wa ke rel
HOUSE: cha bona
JAGUAR: er ra
KNIFE: se ba ra
LEG: ma tak k
LOVE: no ke man
MACAW: ki ya rara
MAN: yan o na me
MONKEY: gua she

MOON: pa re po
MORNING: ha ri ka
MOUNTAIN: pa e ma ka
MOUTH: ka hah
NAME: w ha
NARCOTIC: a ba na
NIGHT: mi te te
NOSE: ko sha pa
NOW: ke ha
PADDLE: shu he ma wa
POISON: ma mo ko rima
POISON ARROWHEADS: era na mo ma mo
QUIVER: tu ra
RAIN: ma sh
RAPIDS: po ra
RED: wa ka wa ka
RIVER: pa k o
ROCK: ma ku ma
RUN: re re ie
SEE: ma mo
SHARPENER: toma nakie
SIT: ro o
SKY: he to me se
SLEEP: me yo
SMELL: re e sha e
SMOKE: ki e wa k she
SNAKE: o ro
STAND: o bra o
STOMACH: ma kas se
SUN: pa re po un she moto
TALK: wa ye w
TAPIR: e sh ma
TASTE: wa mo to te he ta we
TEETH: na ke
THANK YOU: e ne ha pe we
TRADE: no me han
TRAIL: pi ki yo
TREE: he te a he
TRIBE: ya he p wan ha
TOBACCO: pa e
TONGUE: a ka
TOUCH: ho pa ha
TUBE: moko hiro
WAIST BELT: pey wa pey shoke

WAIT:	wai ha
WALK:	wo we
WATER:	sho ki
WHITE:	aw se aw se
WOMAN:	su wey
WOOD:	o re he
YELLOW:	ha no ha na

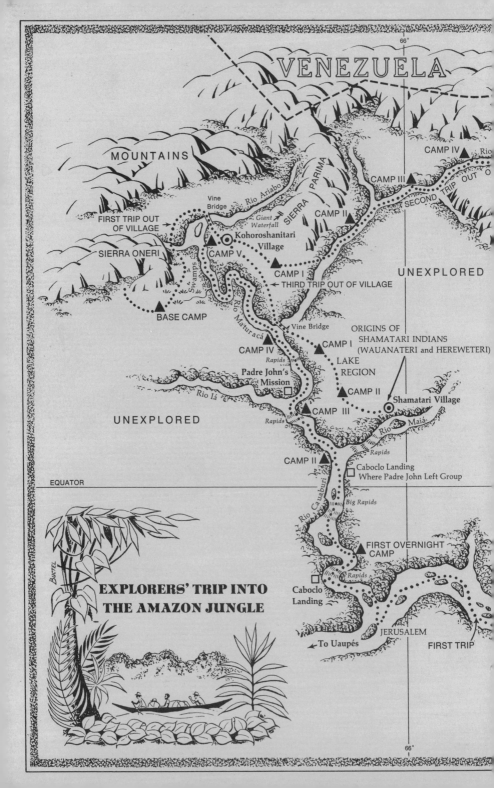